D1587196

Yoga and Buddhism in the life of a contemporary person

Editorial series THE DIRECT PATH
Volume 1

CANOPUS

Květoslav Minařík

Yoga and Buddhism
in the life
of a contemporary person

Collection of short texts

CANOPUS
Prague 2010

Květoslav Minařík
Yoga and Buddhism in the life of a contemporary person

Editorial series The Direct Path
Volume 1

Published in Prague, 2010 by Canopus, o. s.
Synkovská 14, 160 00 Praha 6 The Czech Republic
www.canopus.cz/english
english@canopus.cz

Translation Danica Klempová
English Language Editor Dawn Birbeck
Book Cover design Richard Bergant
Typesetting prepared by Canopus
280 Pages
Printed in the Czech Republic by Těšínské papírny, s. r. o.

ISBN 978-80-85202-40-3

Contents

Foreword to the English translation

The work of a great Czech mystic Květoslav Minařík (1908 – 1974) has been, until now, unknown to English-speaking readers. In this book, we present several of his short writings, which Květoslav Minařík had, in the year 1973, before his death, chosen for translation. He could not publish them in his own country. During most of his life, Czechoslovakia was a prey of totalitarian regimes: 1939 – 1945 of Nazi Germany, 1948 – 1989 of Communist Soviet Union. For those who have lived and grown up in democracy, it is impossible to imagine the oppression, to which free thinking of any kind was exposed. The turbulent destinies of Czechoslovakia at that time were reflected not only in the content of his books, but, first and foremost, in his personal destiny and the destiny of his work.

Květoslav Minařík is an extraordinary figure among the authors of spiritual writings. His writings are founded solely on his own experience gained on his path to perfection. They are not based on the knowledge from Buddhist or Christian literature. Only after he had already enunciated his first book, he encountered the Mahayana Buddhism of a Tibetan school and concluded that his own knowledge corresponded to it. In his autobiography, he characterises himself in this way:

I am the one, who has obtained initiation into Mahayana, which I have, afterwards, transferred to Europe in order to pass it, as a fruit of favourable karma, to people who are at the end of the dark night of ignorance.

Květoslav Minařík's work is based on the psychology and the way of thinking of a contemporary person. He perfects their being as a whole in a way that he harmoniously develops, at the same time, its physical, inner as well as mental component. He leads the one who seeks to independently discover the laws of the spiritual life and cautiously choose the means on their path of spiritual development.

From the time when he attained enlightenment, Květoslav Minařík lived mostly in a totalitarian regime, where it was dangerous even to keep spiritual literature other than Christian. Therefore, he could not publicly establish a spiritual school. He led his disciples individually and had to meet them secretly. He reacted to their development also individually in dozens of short writings, and by a gradually growing number of book manuscripts. Out of them, he managed to, during his life, publish the first (The Direct Path, 1939) and second (The Inner meaning of the New Testament, 1945) out of the intended book series and from among the short texts gradually four (On Yoga in general, 1968 – 1969). However, he completed the intended main book series and entitled it "The Direct Path". Besides the two already mentioned, it is composed of these books: The Path to perfection, The Light of geniuses, A Discussion of gods, The Salvation, A Small mystic encyclopaedia, autobiography Kechara and four books, in which he has commented on the writings of other authors, who wrote on Tibetan Buddhism (W. Y. Evans-Wentz, H. P. Blawacki). Detailed comments explain these writings to the contemporary reader.

In spite of all the oppression, Květoslav Minařík was writing his texts with a hope that someday they would, after all, serve people who seek on the path to perfection. He prepared them for publication and also trained his disciples who were supposed to fulfil this task. Since the fall of Communism in Czechoslovakia (1989), all books of the above-mentioned main book series were published in the Czech language. Moreover, several collections of short writings, all short commentaries (on Nyanatiloka, A. David-Neel, Patanjali and Lao-Tzu) and three collections of selected correspondence were also published.

The short writings in this book are ordered in a certain way; however, the book is not meant for a systematic reading. We are publishing it as the first one, because the author himself was of an opinion that, in these short writings, the reader can find more simply formulated answers to the problems which they encounter in their life – in the external world as well as in themselves. This is also true in case of those, who were not interested in yoga or Buddhism before.

From his entrustment, we are trying to realise that from which he was prevented, and we are fulfilling his wish for his teaching to also be made available to readers in English.

We wish the readers of this first book to find in it clues which will help them to solve questions and problems on their path to perfect themselves.

Prague, June 2010   Zora Šubrtová

Introductory note

This translation adopted some specific approaches.

Double versus single quotation marks: Double quotation marks were preserved in all places where they were originally used by the author. Single quotation marks were used in places where their use was required by the English language, however, they do not occur there in the original.

"Singular they" grammatical form was used in the text to preserve the gender-neutrality employed by the author within the limits of the Czech language.

The term "sensory desire". In many other writings, the reader can find a term "sensual desire". However, due to sexual connotation in modern English, the translator avoided both terms "sensual" and "sensuous", and chose a more neutral term "sensory" to express that it is "relating to the senses" in general.

For the purpose of clarity, the word "nature" was used with a capital "N", where it means "all the things in the world which exist naturally and were not created by people"*. In its other meanings, lower case was used.

---

* Cambridge Advanced Learner's Dictionary 3rd Edition, Cambridge University Press, Cambridge, UK, 2008.

On Yoga in general

1. Yoga

Yoga is generally understood either as a spiritual effort, or as a certain kind of physical exercise. In both cases, people are searching within it for something that will help them to solve the fundamental problems of life, but, at the same time, they are usually unaware what these problems in fact are. However, even though they aren't able to clearly define these problems, they are still directing all of their life's efforts towards being able to live happily. The desire for a happy life is oftentimes covered by a seeming desire for knowledge. Usually, people are not interested in the true knowledge, i.e. in an analytical knowledge of the qualities of the world and all its processes, which determine our emotional experience. They want to know how to achieve a happy sensory life.

Those, who are prompted by their desire to live happily or to obtain knowledge to seek by the means of yoga, often use inappropriate yogic means. Almost always, they let themselves be lured into the last one of the three parts of yogic training – into concentration, regardless of its levels. Yet the first part of yogic training is the moral self-training, which in fact solves the problem of an unhappy emotional life in its full extent. Concentration either doesn't solve it at all, or does so only in some more or less abstract outline of this problem.

You can concentrate with a clear and pure mind, as well as with a dull, furious and biased mind, and the results then look accordingly.

The problem of a happy or unhappy life is an emotional problem. Because, from the point of view of yoga, this problem has to be resolved as the first, **yama** is prescribed as the first step towards the yogic training. Yama means the discipline of emotion. By the help of it, happiness is literally "produced". An angry, obstinate, bothersome, limited person who is interested in many things would like to leave all this aside and simply sit in some yogic position and concentrate until they are happy. However, in the same way it is impossible to fly with a horse carriage and to ride through the town on an aeroplane, it isn't possible to arrive at feelings of happiness by concentration in a yogic position. In the same way, it is neither possible, by means of a simple moral discipline, to attain to the differentiation prescribed by yoga for the consciousness to rid itself of the last remains of ignorance.

Therefore, it is necessary to start with yama. Let's say immediately: in order not to describe stereotypical commandments of morality, how they are described by yama, let us begin simply in another way, without any slightest divergence from these commandments.

Yama prescribes that a person shall not hurt, lie, steal, live a non-chaste life, etc. What does it mean? A person should live in such a way that their mind will not narrow down, darken with malice, be aroused by hatred, ill will, etc. and will not sink into the world of sexual lust. However, to achieve that, it isn't enough that a person holds on to the prescribed moral commandments, which anyway, they immediately forget, even when they want to keep to them. Despite all of the commandments, they get angry, do not wish well, and are desirous and biased etc. Therefore they have to leave the comedy or theory of prescribed morality. For, if they want to be happy, they must implement the moral commandments through the development of a peaceful mind, happy mood, trustfulness and optimism. If they behave like this, they will not provoke anyone either by actions, or by their inner states – and their happiness will be developing. The more they hold on to these states of mind, the more they also eradicate the possible opposite mood states and when they do reach the very end of this moral purification, their happiness will be complete.

Happiness, as well as failure, are thus a matter of inner and mental states. However, while a person is corrupted by pessimism, an unkind mind and bad moods, as well as suspiciousness, the feeling of happiness does not want to appear. To those who constantly strive for good emotional as well as mental states, only time will bring the desirable result, i.e. happiness. When this happens, a person will attain success in the most important part of the yogic discipline, in yama.

The second step is **niyama**. It is concerned with physical, as well as inner, hygiene. A person should be particular about their personal appearance, attentive in contact with people, to not appear extravagant, should educate themselves, train themselves in conscious thinking (as opposed to reflexive thinking), follow the social etiquette as well as the religious one (or, alternatively, lay morality), keep restraint in judgments, i.e. not to react to any behaviour or events spontaneously, occupy their mind by reading of religious books and seek the company of those engaged in noble actions and teachings.

Those who constantly strictly adhere to the commandments of yama and niyama, will achieve a transformation of the qualities of the natural emotional states. They will qualitatively advance in the order of creation, rise above the sphere of beings who are suffering and unhappy into the sphere of beings living harmoniously. Then they will even cross the boundary of the physically limited beings and reach the sphere of the supersensory existence. By that, they will prove for themselves, that they can and have to solve the problem of an unhappy life only by putting the transformation, or change of thought and feeling, into practice. They will realise that, by the constant moral purification and hygiene understood in the sense of niyama, they are raising themselves among gods, into the sphere of pure and blissful experiencing, to the place where their intuition itself suggests to them an idea of the highest happiness.

As a rule, most of those interested in yoga aren't longing for anything higher and if they take up further instructions of the yogic system anyway, they hurt themselves. As, they are mixing up disparate things and this has the same consequences as an excessive consumption of disharmoniously combined foods. However, if it turns out that a harmonious and blissful life doesn't attract a person at all, but they only desire to know, only then is a person sufficiently mature for a gradual realisation of the further instructions of the yogic teaching. Then yoga develops in the following way.

Niyama is followed by **asana**. However, asanas also belong to hygiene. Although the system of asanas as yogic exercises is also supposed to vitalise the body, still, they are supposed to culminate in the achievement of physical non-excitability or, in other words, in the elimination of nervousness. A yogi, who is, as a result of yama and niyama, happy, lively and optimistic, must, by means of asanas, stabilise themselves, in order to prevent the successes in yama and niyama making them again worldly. This means that, by means of the positions, they must attain serenity, i.e. absence of cravings and (presence of) equanimity. Only then should they supplement their exercise by pranayama.

Pranayama begins with rhythmical breathing. To this rhythmical breathing, observation of the rhythm of breathing is added. In this way, a person takes hold of prana, the physical content of breath or breathing. Thus, the rhythmical breathing achieves its purpose, that is – the rhythm and observation of breathing creates a harmony between a human and the nature. A feeling of freshness will appear, a negative aspect of which – the regrasping of the world – has to be suppressed by asanas. Then a person is ready for further steps of the yogic training. These are only significant for those who need knowledge to accomplish their happiness. Through this knowledge, the questions of the place of an individual in the world and its destiny are clarified, and the problems of relationships of individuals to the world are solved, which cause absence of inner freedom or (the existence of) differentiating moments.

When a person is potentially happy and their bliss is only disturbed by a desire for knowledge, they can enter the path of the discipline of mind. This is because in such a case the mind is well prepared for it as the person doesn't desire sensory pleasures. Under these circumstances, the mind is supposed to be gradually fastened on one object and stabilised. This fastening and gradual stabilisation is called **pratyahara.**

A yogi should eliminate the distraction of mind by constantly reminding themselves of their own body. Sitting in a position, they are supposed to dwell with their mind on their body, on its base, on the sitting part, whilst avoiding the trunk. However, until the mind is used to dwelling on one object, an entirely concrete object, it wanders again and again and becomes restless. Keeping the mind from this wandering is actually pratyahara. It can be characterized by tension, which originates in the struggle for the mind's stabilisation. This tension then manifests itself by various mystical effects and accompanying phenomena, which have to be refused altogether, for otherwise the mind would not stabilise.

When the mind stabilises, it passes to another phase, into concentration, which is called dharana. **Dharana** can be characterized as a state of mind, which no longer hinders the inner freeing coming to the fore. When this relaxation is connected with an awareness of emptiness, limitless space and emotional relaxation, it is dharana. When this concentration of mind becomes prolonged and the awareness of emptiness, limitless space and relaxation does no longer disintegrate or disappear, it is the second level of concentration, **dhyana** and when this state becomes continuous and self-sustained (i.e. without the efforts to concentrate), it is the third level of concentration, **samadhi**.

Samadhi thus means realisation of the state of mind, which arose in concentration: that is awareness of emptiness, limitless space and inner relaxation. When these qualities develop in such a way that they become the dominant states for consciousness, when they control the whole psyche of a person and present to them the emptiness of the universe as a living reality, as the absolute, which, although it isn't the direct originator of creation, is still in contact with it, then the person has reached the **nirvikalpasamadhi**. This state crushes the phenomena of the universe into nothingness and by this the mind is redeemed from the samsaric state, from the state of being a slave to the nature. The mind can then realise the state of absolute and, by this, eliminate every predisposition of an individual to be entangled – in the form of a self-aware unit – into overwhelming impulses. At death this kind of person extinguishes themselves without the desire to continue to live or to be.

By this, a tragedy of the ceasing of the conscious being is erased.

What has been said here about yoga until now, is, however, only a general description. If the highest goal of yogic education is not to be lost from view, it is necessary to start with the yogic education in the following way:

One has to start with yama. In the western understanding of the social education it means such a way of behaviour, in which an individual stands in the way of their fellows as little as possible and, as far as it is possible, he or she does not emotionally touch them at all; he or she shall take their opinion as a criterion of his or her correct or incorrect social behaviour. This is the external part of yama, which they have to complement by a direct self-restraint in the expressions of personal inclinations, especially taste. This applies to all actions by which a person caters for their whims. Then there are direct restrictions which are related to sex, for, a person shouldn't serve it "unlawfully". For example, it is not allowed for a man to invest a lot of efforts to win a woman, because this very energy must be used for more serious efforts. The question of a partner has to be left up to the guru to decide to prevent possible mixing of disparate qualities of humankind. In addition to that, a joyful and optimistic mood is required, and the kind of behaviour which prevents a person from having to struggle with inclinations which he or she attacks and removes by yogic efforts.

Then there is niyama. It means purification of the body by water as well as by a pure mind. A person is supposed to have high standards of cleanliness and should not neglect their personal appearance.

In the same way they have regard for their exterior, when they, so-called, 'fall in love', they should have regard for it with respect to their ideal, which can be God as well as an all-embracing, i.e. spiritual, intellectual and mental perfection. A requirement to dress and behave in a way which doesn't raise aversion in others, or as a person who belongs to a higher social class, is associated with this.

Because these commandments may be exhausting for a person and even lead them to distraction or nervousness, it is allowed to complement this effort with concentration. However, in this case, concentration is understood by meaning that a person is supposed to find a time in which their privacy will not be disturbed and in this relative solitude they should sit in one of the yogic positions and force the mind, as well as the whole inner being, into calmness.

When they eliminate all impressions of the everyday life, they should rest for a while in this pleasant mental and inner state, in order to be able to develop a better ability of observation of their own being. The inner equilibrium, disturbed by the efforts for moral and social self-training, should be renewed by enclosing oneself in one's own peace and by a mental effort to directly destroy these influences.

However, to the usual yogis – gurus – it is usually unknown what their disciple is supposed to do when they attain the so-called realisation, i.e. when they fully anchor in the states which they desired, not only on the level of awareness, but also in the subconsciousness. This is a result of the above described preparatory yogic self-discipline and a possible enlightenment, which is an accomplishment of the self-discipline in the so-called 'direct yoga'. Therefore, these lines follow:

Enlightenment and a perfect self-knowledge raise a person to the level of a sage, whilst the preparatory yogic self-discipline rises them to the level of a *totally* happy person. That is, however, one thing. Another is the fact that a yogi who attained perfection cannot be *absolutely* happy, because this depends on a continuous influence of the environment in which they are living, on their being.

Therefore they still have to break the shell of the subtle selfishness and begin to base their perfection and happiness on the actions of virtue which belong to their level and their perfected state. These actions are described by an esoteric teaching, known in the exoteric conception as Mahayana, as well as magic. Also in *Buddhism*, we can encounter teachings on these actions, even though they are incorporated in another level. We can define them as follows:

Recognising myself in everything, I want to be happy in a supersensory sense. Recognising myself in everything, I want to have knowledge. Recognising myself in everything, I want only goodness to be performed. Recognising myself in everything, I want goodness to be absolutely powerful in the face of evil. Recognising myself in everything, I want to be (as the humankind) led only by God and never by his opposite. Recognising myself in everything, I want only the goodness to win.

These few formulae are perhaps sufficient. Magic is contained in them in the words "I want", Buddhism then in the words "recognising myself in everything". This is modified, because, as I sense, this "recognising myself in everything" is related to breathing in and breathing out. Finally, mahayana is in the system of this whole work.

He or she, who, after the accomplishment of the personal perfection, will further work in this way, will overcome the hostile influence of the environment by the path of virtue. Their perfection will then be high, wide, deep and unsurpassable. They will not be able to complain about anything anymore and will be exempt even from the destiny of some sages, as for example, Jesus, even though they, for example, continue to adhere to the very path of Jesus. But this last stage of yoga cannot be realised early. It may not be realised in this human body at all. However, time is no object, because here a person is no longer walking the path of people, but the path of Brahmas.

An opposite of this path is the path of hinayana; it is a path of an absolute renunciation. However, here renunciation means also the loss of interest in attaining the personal perfection. But, abandonment of the idea of personal perfection must not lead to the abandonment of the path of renunciation. For, a person here, so to say, "hits the target" directly. Besides that I can add to it: what kind of sense does a personal or spiritual perfection have for the one who has renounced everything and absolutely? Thus: values have no meaning on this path. Therefore, a person usually doesn't want to walk this path and decides on the previous one, which, on its high levels, becomes the path of Brahmas. This path has its rules and these are described by all that was said above.

2. Yogic practice

Yoga is a two-stage discipline. Its first stage is a preparatory yogic moral self-training, which is, firstly, supposed to turn the student of yoga into a happy and socially flawlessly behaved person. Only then is it possible to start with yoga as a system leading to the knowledge of forces moving the human being, as well as the human society as a whole, the forces controlling their whole life.

After fulfilling the moral prerequisites, which I describe elsewhere, the actual yogic practice is based on concentration of mind. This concentration is its main tool. However, concentration is a psychological problem. A person, who has never attempted to direct his or her mind and focus it in a disciplined fashion, cannot successfully concentrate it. If they at tempt it, the mental indiscipline ambushes them and causes that their mind, instead of adhering to the chosen aid for concentration, on the contrary stiffens, and their consciousness narrows down. This is no longer the path to the development of the sense of obtaining knowledge, but it is a way for the mind to get stuck, a way to developing a fixed idea and, by that also, towards delusions, sometimes perhaps innocent, at other times in the form of a pathological fixed idea.

This difficulty is avoided in yoga by mental training. The mental training begins with a systematic exclusion of impressions originating in the daily life and continues with a gradual relaxation of the mind for so long until the mind finally becomes able to stay focused on one object.

Thus, those who want to be yogis must, after they have completed the tasks required by the preparatory yogic self-discipline, exclude impressions, which they have gathered in their daily life, until they pacify and calm the mind down and, by that, make it capable of the so-called extensive concentration, i.e. able to concentrate on the chosen object, in a similar way to a person who views with fondness something which they like. Thanks to that, the mind calms down even more and gradually, it becomes able to fasten on the chosen object of concentration with higher and higher intensity, because concentration is supposed to peak in the ability to hold in the mind one single object with the entire willpower, without the concentration turning into staring at this object, or into dullness which no longer allows a person to tell if they are thinking of the chosen object, or whether their stupefied and dulled mind unconsciously wanders from one thing to another.

As far as the object on which the mind is supposed to concentrate is concerned, the psychological reasons do not allow it to be some mental image, or anything abstract. The best object is the yogi's own body – and again taking into account psychological factors – that part of their body which is the most neutral: ideally feet and legs. The yogi is thus supposed to focus only on their feet and legs. The feet and legs are supposed to be, to a yogi, both a part of his or her person, as well as an outer object – that which they can feel, as well as that which they can think of as on object totally separate to their person. This way, their own feet and legs can serve them as an object for the training in concentration, until they reach such a level of concentration that their mind will no longer feel capable of movement without the order of the yogi's will.

Then the yogi changes their concentration into the so-called 'analytical concentration'. The mind is able to become analytical, if it is controlled and set to a total standstill. However, for that, both, its perfect focusing as well as its relaxation which prevents its spontaneous and unrestrained focusing, are necessary. For such a mind, the yogi's being is no longer a fortress built from inner petrifications, but an entire scale of states and processes which give meaning to the personal living, because they are interdependent.

A concentration, in whose background there is a perfect self-observation and self-control, leads to the development of the abilities of discernment. With their help, a person learns the meaning of the driving forces of nature, which are always the cause of the arising of circumstances which can be controlled by a person only to a limited extent.

However, knowledge is not only a passive standpoint of the person obtaining knowledge. A yogi, who has attained high levels of the yogic training, may learn from that which they are discerning, what needs to be done in order to break the power of circumstances. Thus an absolute freedom dawns on them, and they know about it, that it will be realised in that moment when they overcome the personal considerations, when they overcome the personality which does not acknowledge the organic interconnectedness of all phenomena of the creation, and which wants to project itself as a phenomenon superior to, and surpassing, everything that exists.

A common person is a being who cannot disentangle themselves from the creation, whether we think of creation in the cosmic dimensions or only as of a human society. Besides that, a human being does not want to disentangle themselves from this society anyway. They constantly have some desires, sometimes completely earthly, at other times superworldly ones, but these desires always form them into someone in the middle of something. This is a factor, or a law, which always limits the person. If the redemption according to the Buddhist conception really exists, it always relates to the realisation of a state of eradication of selfness – every trace of differentiation in the yogi themselves. However, this is an infinitely distant prospect for everyone who is just beginning with yoga. Therefore they have to think in a human way and have only goals which are understandable from the human perspective. They have to make do with a promise that if they control themselves well, observe and concentrate, they will become a knowing person, a person who will understand the meaning of destinies of the human world and later also the path which leads above the level of these destinies.

However, let us return to the concentrating yogi again. Concentration becomes, to a yogi, means of disentangling from the net of innumerable moments of differentiation, i.e. individualisation and differentiation, which are the moments of inner slavery. However, here we are already on the borderline of the possibility to understand states which can be reached by a yogi, because, as soon as these moments of differentiation are overcome, the yogi finds himself or herself in the undifferentiated world, a world not differentiated in the amount of particularities. On the first levels of this world, the yogi's ability of understanding is developed to such an extent, that they understand not only the meaning of coarse 'stiffenings' or inner 'rigidifyings' which determine the process of the differentiated living with all its difficulties, limitations and irresistible drives and pressures of the circumstances, but also the fine 'stiffenings' and 'rigidifyings'. The latter mean that the mind, because it understands and perceives in certain concepts, is already becoming dull and becomes the bridle of a slave – the bearer of this mind. The yogis' plan is to overcome every manifestation of imperfection. Their ideal is freedom, which is being realised only above the state of the differentiated thinking. Over there, where the truths of individuals are no longer valid, the only valid thing is the stream of cognition which is a permanent factor, constantly breaking down the moments of differentiation and in this way protecting the state known as nirvana, redemption from delusions, ill will and hatred.

What do these prospects mean for a modern person? They mean the person's strength, the person's knowledge, their overcoming of every smallness of spirit and development of their abilities to learn and understand. Moreover, later they mean the reaching of a state in which they evidently detect that they have stopped the process of living as a factor creating causes of further and further urgencies of destiny, and, finally, the realisation of such a good state that it is not possible to describe it in words which would be understood.

Up to here, yoga is, for a modern person, a benefit for their life. However, it becomes the very opposite, if, of yoga as a whole, some parts are torn out – some parts evoking images of success in the society or in enjoyments in people who haven't disciplined their cravings beforehand. For, these people are never able to systematically progress in the realisation of the yogic teaching and therefore they start with hope and end with – disappointment.

In a concise summary, yogic practice carried out in this way is thus a systematic method of the gradual absorption of being into an undifferentiated essence of the universe, into the absolute. Concentration of mind is the tool for this method. The analytical concentration can be considered to be a classical concentration. By means of it, it is possible to discern the elements of our being to such an extent that the consciousness is able to identify all qualities of the universe, out of which it is the absolute which is the highest one. By its identification, a prerequisite is created for its realisation. Our 'I' can this way unify with the absolute.

3. Yoga and intellect

There is a lot written about how yoga benefits health. However, in fact it also has a positive influence on the intellect, while this influence of yoga is determined by psychological factors and not by occult or divine ones.

In this sense, I want to talk mainly about myself, but this will perhaps not be of harm if we take into account that, in few words, I want to say a lot.

I already accepted the full inventory of yoga as life directions as an adolescent boy. This was after I realised my inner and physical poverty as well as their consequences for my future life, because I

have been through, in total four years of school education, malnutrition and work exertion of over ninety working hours per week.
During that period, my only friend brought me a paperback about
yoga.

Because I believed that only yoga could help me in my situation,
I devoted myself to it. I carried out breathing practices, as well as
concentrations of mind. However, because I could not follow the
yogic instructions about the place where yoga should be practised,
about the workload and other things, I overstrained my adolescent
organism by incorporating into my schedule two, four, six and later
eight hours of practice daily.

However, these hours of practice didn't include only breathing,
but they also included concentration, particularly out of which I
intellectually obtained a lot. The work-related overstrain caused
permanent damage to my health. However, let this be an uninteresting detail, as I wanted to say something about the intellectual
significance of yoga which is contained in concentration.

The yogic concentration, as I have learned from my practice, must
be based on the extensity of awareness on the one hand, and, on the
other hand, on the intensity of thinking. The extensity of awareness
is more or less given by the interest of a person in everything that
constitutes their environment. The intensity of thinking is, in the
yogic training, based on an effort to focus on an imaginary point
as if it was a concrete thing or object which must be created by
the person who is concentrating by means of the use of their own
thinking.

Thus, when the imaginary point or object is so stable that the
mind no longer tends to wander and the perception of the world
is vivid enough not to allow a dulling immersion, the intellect improves. The psychological conditions for its improvement are simply
in the fact that the thinking is to be not only stable, but also with
a sufficient volume.

And now perhaps just one question is left: why is yoga connected
to mysticism, or, sometimes, the delusory mysticism?

If a person attempts to fulfil the requirement of concentration in the sense that they 'hook' on an imaginary object, and, at the same time, they do not perceive the phenomena of the outer world with sufficient vividness, then their attention presents them with a not entirely conscious or totally unconscious perception of their own inner processes. This appears to a person as a peculiar, or mystical, world. In fact, it is an opposite pole of an extremely strong interest in the outer world, and it adds to the development of inner imbalance.

The degree of intelligence of an individual depends, on the one hand, on the intensify of thinking which follows from the mental stabilisation resting on an imaginary object, and, on the other hand, on the volume of awareness which depends on a vivid perception of the outer world. So far it seems that the education towards a methodical development in both directions is only contained in yoga, and due to this reason, even this aspect of yoga should not be forgotten.

I believe that yoga understood in this way is not idealistic, even in those of its practices which do not relate to the physical positions, and that pedagogy should devote attention to it.

4. Yoga for everyone

We all are, and have to be, interested primarily in a way which yoga can benefit us in an improvement of our inner state. For, the problems of psyche, the soul and its condition are the very thing which nobody is protected against. The rich as well as the poor, the healthy as well as the ill, those competent as well as those incompetent, old as well as young, simply all of those who went wrong in what they expected from life, suffer. Therefore, they hope to escape personal suffering if they obtain riches, power, good health, or if they develop their mental abilities better. Not even those who are able to assume the most awkward positions of the hatha yoga teaching, are spared from that.

Then, what is the point? No matter which good book about yoga we take in our hand we will always find there instruction about "yama" and "niyama" in the fore. It is yoga of its own kind, yoga, by which everyone should begin. "Yama" and "niyama" are simply yoga for everyone; moreover, all people can have even a fantastic success in it.

When the Indian writings on yoga refer to "yama" and "niyama", they tell what a person mustn't do and what they must do. That is because the Indian yoga is understood there as a training system, which doesn't take into account the so-called individuality of a person. On the contrary, a person, who wants to do yoga according to the Indian sources, has to submit to the whole educational system that has a precise plan and a specific target. That target requires a deep depersonalisation, an ability to submit oneself, without allowing a person to slide into slavery, a slavish subordination.

In relation to yoga according to Indian views, we can only sigh that we are Europeans, brought up to awareness that each person decides for themselves what they want or don't want to do; we are people brought up to consider a lack of discipline to be a manifestation of personal freedom, a manifestation of a well developed individuality. Because of this, we cannot successfully do other yoga than the yoga adapted to the European mentality. It cannot be based on "you must" and "you mustn't", but on one's own responsibility on the way to mental and inner recovery: a halt on the way of steep decline, which leads to the deepest demoralisation.

Yoga for everyone therefore, seemingly begins from the end: we will not sit in a position to become happy and to outshine our social environment. We are going to learn how to be happy, in order to be able to sit still and thus create conditions to be able to, of our own will, enter the transcendental world, which however has to be understood in a different way than until now.

Thus, we are supposed to learn to be happy! Is it important at all and does it really belong to yoga? In the esoteric part of the teaching about yoga, we may learn that a horrific danger of the mystical heights can be neutralised by an appropriate level of optimism and joyfulness. Some writer of the so-called occult novels has written that if people laughed more, there would be fewer wars. Through this quote, we are already finding ourselves on our ground, on the earth, in the everyday life, the problems of which we will solve aptly by this "small" yoga, too.

Its principle is very simple. We can feel happy or unhappy without an external reason, only by the power of our own will. The possibility of this is indirectly confirmed, for example by a well known fact that, when someone has some sorrow, they forget about it, if their attention is caught by something else. Based on this very piece of knowledge, a system can be created. By the power of our will, we can turn our attention away from the situations which brought us to suffering, and simply change the whole situation by fastening our attention upon things that evoke good feelings in us.

According to the yogic teaching, emotional experience is the most powerful factor in the life of creatures. It is sustained by a momentum which doesn't only steer the being, it also categorises it. This usual emotional experience can only be counteracted by repeated actions aiming to change its quality. This means to learn to rejoice and feel happy, even without any reason, over and over again, repeating this effort for so long, till joy and happiness become the only inner states which will keep on seizing us, as soon as we stop trying to create such moods.

When we reach that far, we have in fact already changed our inner condition or, in other words, we have moved from the sphere of unhappy people into the one of people constantly being made happy via the effect of spiritual factors. This is already considered as the beginning of the path of a higher type towards the goals of the practical yoga. For, only a happy person, an optimist, obtains from concentration an increasing clarity of the consciousness, an ability of a fine and deep discernment, a possibility of better perception and therefore also better understanding of everything; in short, all that which we may expect from yoga.

Then, it is really sufficient only to concentrate. Only a happy person is able to concentrate in the way yoga instructs, i.e. to think of objects and to observe them without sinking into a mental lethargy and without the clarity of their consciousness been decreased.

Would you like to try it, too? If the answer is yes, then stick to the following principles, which are in fact the whole of yoga in a nutshell:

1. You have to raise yourself from the state of passivity toward reflexive, i.e. automatic, unconscious reactions to the external world by a constant producing of an allsurpassing joyfulness in you.

2. You have to develop and intensify self-control, and you have to do that by a persistent awareness of everything that you do, i.e. that you stand, walk, eat, act in this or that way.

3. You have to attempt concentration in such a way that you think of (concentrate on) a chosen object (your feet and legs), but only in so far as you do not dim your awareness – only in so far as you would return again and again to the normal registering of things of the surrounding world, because only in this way you will ensure the control over vigilance. This type of concentration is called by the Buddhists 'the threshold concentration'.

4. When you will, through this sequence of steps, achieve such a high level of vigilance, that its dimming doesn't occur – not even when you are paying attention only to a single, especially imaginary, i.e. unreal object of concentration, you may change the threshold concentration into the total one. This concentration will help you to transfer the daily consciousness, i.e. the consciousness based on experience into the sphere of inner phenomena, without losing awareness whether you are dreaming or correctly discerning everything that is happening in this sphere. By this you have realised in yourself the state of wisdom.

Explanation for the mystical practice

1. Why to develop joyful mood

We cannot imagine the advancement towards redemption otherwise than that it must be happening through joyful states. People who are not able to rejoice are actually pessimistic and by that, they are closer to the ideas about hell than about heaven. We know about heaven, that it is a place of joy and, on a higher level, even a place of bliss. About redemption we subsequently know, that it is a state beyond celestial states and definitely not to be found beyond some culmination of obstinacy, dark mood and gloomy thoughts.

Joyfulness will not "fall into the lap" of anyone. Therefore everyone has to strive, to come, by the very developing of joyfulness, internally closer to celestial states; that is a practical path to heaven as a betweenstate on the path towards salvation from the natural, perhaps human state.

The human state is characterised by changes. It is typical for people to swing from the states of literally crazy elation to desperation again. Between these extreme inner states, there is an ideal equilibrium, which can be classified as a pure original humanness; this humanness suffers from the fact that it has to counterbalance that crazy joyfulness by subsequent desperation. What follows from that is, that to let oneself drift by the state of humanness doesn't lead to anything good. From cradle to grave, the crazy joyfulness interchanges with inner pains up to desperation and due to that it happens that a human remains only a human, from birth until death.

Emotional experience and moods are thus delimited in this way; although this delimitation is physically impalpable, it is solid, as if a person was internally enclosed by a fortress wall. Hope that an easy escape from this iron cell exists, is indeed unavailing, even though to countless people it seems like their spatial demarcation in psyche is chimerical, insubstantial.

Because of this reason, it is essential to understand the psychological setting of physical beings as very solid and starkly real, no matter how unlimited we may find our possibilities are to supply ourselves with predominantly sensory joys.

However, mystical development thrives only through a causeless joyfulness, produced and maintained by will, wanted and resisting every influence by which the Nature or worldly fate-related accidental events, would want to change this state. This kind of joyfulness is thus no longer produced by some change in the being – some feeling, some event, which then later only manifested itself by an overpowering, a carrying away of the person's psyche. On the contrary, it is a joyfulness always guarded by will, which is always ready to intervene in a moment, when, due to some outer reasons, it weakens or disappears.

In psychological terms this means that a person has internally taken hold of themselves and finally started to rule their psyche, while until then they were only a plaything of forces, which were rippling their psyche. From a straying, staggering, or 'tossing' of their psyche, a direction has arisen, whose goal is a consolidation of joyfulness, which must no longer be for them "within the reach of their psychological arm", but a state, which imprints optimism in the mind and consciousness and drives out every trace of pessimism.

Mystically, this state means the attainment of a platform of experiencing of either paradisiacal or celestial, or supercelestial beings, according to the depth and purity of his or her joyfulness, as all beings of these three supertelluric spheres are categorised by the very degree or quality of their joyfulness.

A human being has, perhaps due to their physical set-up, also a possibility to penetrate through the states of joyfulness into the superjoyous world, which is, from a mystical point of view, a state of salvation. However, this doesn't depend on their will to set this target and then to reach it, for, to leave this world is never that easy. As, the path has to be determined by the moods of the being and not by the will. All joys, which were the ideal of a person, have to be experienced, even though they were superworldly joys and no matter how remote they were from sober reality. Due to this reason, yogic or in general every method of spiritual development, shortens the way to absolute emotional satisfaction of every individual by a systematic bathing of the body in supersensory bliss; only then a person finds themselves on a so-called spiritual path, on a path of spirit, which sinuates above the level of every kind of feeling.

Those who would like to avoid this "roundabout way", marked only by mood states, the roundabout way on the so-called Direct mystical path, will be thrown down by their own being, by themselves, because they will surely cling to one of the new, and, till this time unknown joys, which are developing on the Direct mystical path.

An unwise lay person can thus think about the path of mystical and spiritual development whatever they want, but they can never avoid the fulfilment of all of their desires reaching for pleasures, perhaps sensory, perhaps supersensory, which are, despite everything, only sensory pleasures. For, this is the reality, stemming from a psychological law. From this very psychological law it follows, that a life process can never be finished by an intervention of will, but always only by living through, and perhaps even living-out everything, which was predetermined by the arisen desires.

Even the most sophisticated forms of Indian asceticism failed due to the lack of knowledge of this fact. They were conceived to suppress the driving forces of being and these forces have always slipped out of the hands of the will of every ascetic, like snakes with a slippery skin. Even when these ascetics engaged against them ardent suffering, they didn't succeed because, by that, they have only developed feelings of suffering, which were a process by which hellish states were realised, and never the heavenly or superheavenly ones.

The knowledge, which created this opinion about asceticism, however doesn't mean the approval of apolausticism. Apolausticism is only something like an allopathic treatment of the soul deeply diseased with sensory desire, and thus has nothing in common with the intended mystical joyfulness. The latter results from inner freedom or from inner freeing, the basis of which is the flight of a healthy spirit into the far-flung inner spaces. Only when a person, by admitting the influences of continual sensory stimulation will become ill in their spirit, sensory cravings unfold in them, and these will replace the inner freedom of an emotionally and mentally healthy human, uncorrupted by sensory wanting.

When a person loses this inner health, they will start to constantly seek sensory excitements, which make the body vibrate with an emotional or tactile gratification. When this happens, the joyfulness of a internally relaxed person will disappear from their memory. They will then start to believe only in a substitute of the true joyfulness, in the sensory excitements. These, as indulging in physical feelings, do not make them stronger and healthier, but are driving them into a hangover by whose repetition they will get extensively ill in mind, body and spirit.

Therefore it is common, that those who start to search for solutions of the problems of life on the paths of mysticism, first have to heal themselves from an incorrect conception of the idea of joyfulness. They have to strive for distinguishing between that substitute springing from gratification of unbridled sensory desires, and the true joyfulness, which, in turn, springs from the overcoming of sensory desires. This however requires renunciation of the world, an asceticism of its kind, which follows from a genuine absence of craving. For, those who do not overcome sensory cravings in the broadest extent of this task, will never find the mystical goal. Only those, who have cured themselves from sensory desires by their total extinguishment, will.

The joyfulness required by mysticism is thus a causeless joyfulness, and such joyfulness is a production of work, often of very hard work, since human nature does, due to its karmic set-up, neither always wants to rejoice, especially without a cause, nor, of course, to suffer. It is even so bad, that it is impossible to find out what human nature does in fact want. This was perhaps described aptly only by Buddha, who talks about lepers, who alleviate their severe suffering by burning their sores above fire. Burning above fire is pleasant for this state, but for a truly healthy person it is a horrible suffering, by which only a suffering of another kind is alleviated.

We were, however, speaking about a causeless joyfulness. A wise analyst, who will use this method in an effort to climb up to spiritual perfection, will recognise that also their body is directly resisting this joyfulness. Namely, it prefers the peace of a lazy person who, due to their laziness, agrees with repeated falling into suffering for a few, quite rarely occurring almost absolute moments of sensory pleasures.

By this, the path of necessary and rigorous applying of causeless joyfulness in the process of usual human experiencing, is indicated, and determined. When, after a shorter or longer time, a person will push through this causeless joyfulness in themselves, they will arrive at an evident finding, that they have reached that first Buddhist jhana, by the further development of which they will go through further jhanas up to the state of indifference through which the radiance of spirit glows.

To prevent someone from thinking that I am inventing new, non-traditional and therefore perhaps also untrue theories, I will quote from the canonical texts of Buddhism:

"When a monk finds out, that by efforts to maintain a virtuous life he overcame the five hindrances (sensory desire, ill will, sloth and torpor, restlessness and speculation, doubt), a feeling of contentment will arise in him. When he is content, joyfulness will arise in him. When he attains joyfulness, his body will calm down. Calmness of the body induces a feeling of happiness. Through the feeling of happiness his spirit will concentrate. And then he will dwell free from cravings and from unfortunate states in the first level of concentration, in the first jhana, which is, however, accompanied by impressions and thinking, which have arisen from solitude and are therefore accompanying this jhana by zealous interest and joyous happiness."

"When, with continuous spiritual efforts, the impressions and thinking start to cease, a monk will attain inner peace, unity of spirit. Here he will be already dwelling in the second level of concentration, in the second jhana, which is free from impressions and thinking and which has arisen from concentratedness; then he will be filled with zealous interest and joyous happiness."

"When the zealous interest ceases and the monk starts to dwell equanimous, fully conscious and vigilant and he will physically feel that joyous happiness, about which the noble monks say that equanimous and insightful monk is abiding happy, then he is dwelling in the third level of concentration, in the third jhana."

"When a monk overcomes both joyous happiness, and all suffering, when the earlier satisfaction and solicitude disappears out of him, he realises the fourth level of concentration, he attains the fourth jhana, which is experienced as suffering-free, pleasure-free and made clear by indifference and turning inwards."

However, let us return to the requirement of the mystical teaching that a human is to be joyful.

We have already said that the mystical goal is beyond the celestial worlds, which in humans are symbolised by joyfulness and supersensory happiness. Joyfulness, as well as supersensory happiness, is physically felt just like as obstinacy, pessimism, anger and other negative inner and mental states. A person formed internally in the usual way is, however, always closer to these negative inner and mental states than to the states of causeless joyfulness. He or she is even hardly able to understand why they shouldn't rather get angry than rejoice without a cause, since, for their anger they have mostly immediate and real reasons.

However, here we are talking about mysticism and its goal. As, from the perspective of mysticism, those immediate and real reasons for their anger are also relative. Even if we leave aside the fact that the anger of a person always springs from their selfishness, by their sensory cravings, a general relativity, which also includes burning personal pains, pains which are flamingly urgent and according to their manifestations real, still remains.

It is a matter of fact, that a person can laugh even at these pains and, very often, when they already laugh at them, these pains will themselves prove to be relative. As, on the other hand, we can often observe in others that there is no more reason for their suffering, but, nevertheless, they still suffer because, to speak with irony, they fell in love with their suffering. After all, a rational person can always well understand that life consists of both pleasant and painful moments of emotional experience. When they understand this, they are already close to a philosophical discovery, that suffering as well as crazy joyfulness is only a matter of spirit and thus no one needs to suffer, but only to rejoice.

However, this is not the aim of mysticism, since it is an entirely factual teaching. It only has in view the fact, that the mystical goal is even beyond the celestial worlds, into which a subject can get only by causeless joyfulness. From that follows, that, as the usual human set-up shows evidence of oscillation from suffering to some pleasant sensory excitements, this has to be altered by laying down only one line for it, a line of causeless joyfulness, which is a path to heaven.

A student of mysticism necessarily has to rejoice, because it means to get from the path of ascending towards joyfulness and then again descending into multiple hardships, to a path which is always ascending, first towards the consolidation of joyful moods and later to heavenly, and then superheavenly, states.

However, the passage from the fluctuating path, to the path which is constantly ascending requires an intervention into the innate laziness or a seeming inability to govern one's own states, one self. That is, though, difficult. Experience will, however, show that this difficulty isn't great. For, when a habit of rejoicing is created, the joyfulness will often seize a person and then it only suffices to be attentive, not to let it disappear in the flood of accidental daily events and circumstances.

When a person is able to easily watch over it, they will arrive at an evident discovery, that they have entered an ascending path in emotional experience, moving toward higher and better states of the spirit. There will be an evident finding that they are going towards heaven and this is then a result of walking a constantly ascending path through life. Even the sense of vision will develop for this perception. Those joyful states, mirrored only in feeling, will suddenly reveal themselves as a path leaving human life, which sinuates from suffering to pleasures, and then entering paradises, which, if they aren't visually perceived immediately, will begin to be gradually perceived more and more.

After stabilising themselves on the ascending path of developed causeless joyfulness, everyone will be able to clearly detect, that they are on a path into sensorily perceivable heavens. If they behave correctly, they will learn that even heavenly experience isn't in essence a desirable experience; that only peace above joys is acceptable, because it is a state of inner inexcitability, while joys occurring from the subhuman states up to the heavenly ones contain something imperfect and disintegrative in them.

But, joyfulness is not only an emotional state. It is a tingeing factor, which will take hold of a human being as an object and transform it; and this transformation of the being is actually the point. For, no matter what philosophies exist about the solving of life, psychological and philosophical problems, the unchangeable fact remains, that the mind and consciousness are only filled with that, with which the qualities of the body are filling them. In this regard, causeless joyfulness, which has filled up the body by means of will, begins to have a feedback effect. If this joyfulness corresponds qualitatively to heaven or heavenly states, however high they might be, it will always internally fill up the person. This is the basic condition of an evident certainty, that a person is already released from inner contents belonging to humanness and often literally overwhelmed by inner contents qualitatively corresponding to heaven.

No. Mysticism really isn't concerned with chimeras or some philosophy which will in the end suggest to a person some peculiar thoughts, images, convictions and other similar things of a psychological character. The point in it is only a change of the inner content, which is in the common humanness documented by fluctuation of the consciousness from sensory joys, which have a character of sensory excitements, to experiences of suffering, which are perceived as reality. Therefore, the mystical practice is about an attack of will on the existing inner set-up, which lets us oscillate from sensory pleasures of a dubious value, to suffering. The will is forcing causeless joyfulness on the being for so long till the being accepts this content and begins to have an effect with it into the consciousness, where it will then manifest itself as a new content, in this case always supertelluric and spiritual, though usually with a touch of supersensory happiness.

Because of this reason, practical mysticism can be classified into the scientific system of psychological forming, which, through the use of joyfulness, reshapes the whole inner beingness. It will change its emotional states and by means of qualitatively improved joyfulness will raise it in an objective sense, from sensuality into transcendence. The only point is thus joyfulness, predominantly a causeless one. Those who do not apply this joyfulness, because they believe that it is not the right effective means in the order of psychological things, will not be successful in raising themselves into the transcendental world, no matter what philosophical system of spiritual education they may turn to.

The means in mysticism are as simple as the lived sensory life itself. Correctly used causeless joyfulness leads to knowledge, only

out of which the philosophy known as spiritual grows. If this philosophy doesn't spring forth from this joyfulness, it is always only
a series of speculations, which will lead their wearer to a spiritual,
and oftentimes general, ruination.

Therefore, it is necessary to rejoice. The very joyfulness, in particular the causeless one, is that spiritual arrow, by which it is possible to bring down the seemingly uncontrollable human nature,
which once wants to rejoice, and then after saturation by joyfulness
again suffer, to never leave the fluctuating path and to prevent a
person from ever escaping from suffering forever.

2. Why to concentrate

Concentration serves, above all, to the obtaining of knowledge.
Thus, if even the most scatterbrained person has some knowledge,
it means that they, now and then, settle on the perceived things for
a while; only these fleeting moments of interest in something, thus
actually moments of concentration, bring them knowledge.

We can deduce from this fact, that if such fleeting moments are
sufficient to obtain some relevant knowledge, then a longer settling
on the observed things will provide one with a knowledge which
is deeper. This logic holds true in the practical psychology.

However, we have in mind mysticism – a teaching which can
be considered, in the first place, a deep practical psychology. It is
known in it, that each piece of knowledge, obtained by the settling
of attention on the outer objects, is limited by the duration of this
settling. This gave rise to the idea of concentration – how this term
is understood in its conception. The experience with concentration has brought to the light of logical considerations an idea to
use concentration for penetration beyond the curtain of the usual
sensory perceptions.

In the initial stages of the mystical training, the results in the
form of knowledge – especially outer knowledge – are not thought

of. Only the need to prevent wandering of the mind is taken into account, in order for the knowledge not to become mingled with ideas produced by the inner, and, in particular, psychological, structure of the beingness. These ideas have a direct relationship to the karmic contents of the being which were obtained by birth. Therefore, when using the concentration of thinking, the only aim is to remove the mental wandering in order to achieve the platform needed for the pilgrimage along the mystical path all the way to its highest goal.

However, this platform would never be achieved if the concentration of the mind was too intensive; the goal is only to achieve an inner stability which a mentally restless person lacks.

A mentally restless person can never be, and never will be a mystic. This statement cannot be refuted by the fact that most of the lay mystics are mentally restless people who largely speculate. These people have, also, actually brought out, to the level of the daily consciousness, their various hidden inclinations, whose excess makes them suffer; therefore their restlessness is their characteristic which makes them unable to remain with all senses on the ground. Given the diffuse character of their mind, only fantastical matters suit them. The common ignorance considers fantastical matters to be the mysticism in its true conception.

To concentrate is supposed to mean, in the first stage, retention of the reflexive functions of the mind and, in the second stage, its focusing or fastening. The initial stages of the mystical efforts should have no other aims. Therefore, by focusing of the mind, only its holding back is meant, when it tries to escape from the sober reality to fantasies. When a person succeeds in holding it back, they should let it rest on one object, which can be some place on the body; the mind's potential restlessness will not allow this state of it to continue for long, in any case; therefore this whole process is repeated over and over again.

After a long period of such constant striving to hold back the uncontrolled activity of mind, the mind will certainly stabilise.

This is already concentration, by which the mystical path begins, but not at all the mystical development, because, it is only a state of mind which allows observing with sufficient attention in order for a person to obtain knowledge about things that they see around them, which they have earlier always only seen. In another sense, it means that he or she begins to walk the path of obtaining knowledge about the world and that their spirit will no longer be benumbed by the narrowing of consciousness, which occurs so easily when the so-called powerful or intensive concentration is used – i.e. a powerful concentration of the mind on one point or a sole object.

As soon as the mind, by the holding back of its spontaneous activity, becomes capable of a continuous maintaining of its calmness, while the developed observation ability, which brings the knowledge of the phenomena of the surrounding world, does not disappear, but on the contrary, it develops further, the mind can be led to concentration. For this, caution and forethought are needed, because, with the intensity of the mind's concentration, the danger of its fixation and narrowing of consciousness grows too, both of which usually accompany it.

It has to be achieved, that the attention, which is bringing thorough cognition of the things of the surrounding world, is maintained and even intensified, but only with regard to the concentration on a sole object, because, only a mind capable of illuminative observation of the outer phenomena is a terrain on which it is possible to build an all-penetrating concentration, which is a tool helping the person to penetrate all the way to the centre of all existence, without the mind being paralysed by narrowing resulting from fixation.

Let us, however, return to the initial stages of the methodical sequence of steps towards the concentratedness of mind. Its purpose is to turn a wandering mind into a mind which does not wander. When this is achieved, a person has gained a great benefit, because, it is precisely the wandering mind that is the cause of the inner conflicts and big difficulties which one encounters in their life. A wandering mind causes one to forget what should not be forgotten and to speculate, not only unrealistically and without success, but even in a way which gives rise to damage by means of various flaws in behaviour; it causes that things, which could be useful, escape the person's attention and that this even causes a lot of inner suffering, whose basis is inner chaos.

However, even though we know that the overcoming of the wandering of mind can be the basis of successes in the usual life, still we do not pursue this goal by it. We are adhering to the intentions of the mystical teaching which has in mind, in the first place, an improvement of the subjective state of a person – creation of his or her inner peace and, in the second place, the mystical knowledge which lies beyond the border of all usual life and emotional experience. Between these two poles, one finds also, all that which can make their life successful. Thus, from the beginning of the mystical training, when one begins to strive for the holding back of the functions of the ever-oscillating mind, all the way to the results which are apparently mystical, they gain a lot of the so-called good which relates to the outer things of their living.

Due to all this, mysticism is a teaching which leads a person predominantly and all the time on the ground. It never leads them through the sphere of illusions, where live the fantasists and the seemingly mystical poets and in general everyone whose thinking, reasoning, feelings and view of life reflects their extravagant inner disposition, their idealism and ecstasiness.

However, we must complete our talk about concentration.

We correctly sense that mysticism has its goal somewhere in the transcendental sphere. It allows its followers to penetrate into it precisely by concentration. However, this only happens after the wandering of mind was overcome and when the mind has got used to a calm and factual observation of, and thinking about, everything that surrounds a person and belongs to their surrounding world. Only then it recommends using concentration of mind which, by means of the degree of its intensity, becomes a tool for penetration into the world of the physical qualities. According to the mystical teaching this means to penetrate into the world of forces which is, in another conception, the causal world in relation to everything which exists and is in the world.

What does this mean in practice?

When the mind has become accustomed to be calm and non-wandering, a person should devote themselves to its concentration. But, no matter which means to determine the aids for its concentration are used, the aim is always for it to penetrate beyond the borderline of all natural phenomena, in particular in the qualitative conception of this matter. A thorough awareness of oneself during this work with the mind is supposed to create a bridge for the consciousness; the latter one is required to, at all times, register the place and state of the mind without losing from its attention the 'I' in the form of an idea of 'I'.

After this has been achieved, a person is well prepared for the stay on the borderline of two worlds, the transcendental one and the immanent one, or, in one of them for the purpose of exploration and obtaining knowledge.

No. No one whose mind escapes to some far inner spaces where it can gather some evanescent and seemingly superworldly ideas and dreams, is a mystic. Only that person is a mystic, who is able to, with a rational conception of everything and with thinking of the same nature, move in the spheres of the so-called 'only indicated phenomena', thus actually seed phenomena, out of which the phenomena only form. Therefore, mysticism is a psychology and not at all a system of peculiar disciplines which brings peculiar results. It is thus inappropriate to judge it to be a nebulous teaching, or even a confused doctrine for spirits blundering around in the fuzzy ideas out of which nothing concrete ever comes. The concentration of mind is supposed to do the opposite – to uproot this blundering. This is clearly indicated by the fact that it is supposed to be a conscious thinking which uses its supports only to deepen the concrete thinking, to develop and improve it.

However, in the highest conception, concentration is both the Aqua regia and the analyser of the material and physical phenomena; these are means with which a person arrives at the knowledge of the universe both in the small and the grand scale, thus of the microcosm as well as of the macrocosm and by that also to the solution of the entire problem of suffering. However, I am repeating that concentration is like this only in its highest conception, because, the concentration of mind of the beginners on the path of the mystical initiation does not lead to anything like this. The reason for this is that their concentration is continuously polluted by a mixing in of emotions and various stimuli which overshadow their "observer" by inner tensions which constitute the efforts to obtain things which are pleasing for the senses and gratifying cravings.

Therefore, this mixing in has to be taken into account. When it is not taken into account, then, although a person can take up a practical concentration of mind, still they, almost exclusively, continue to create relationships to the world, or, they continue with speculations which will mix in their concentration as a consequence of the inborn emotional nature which continues to be alive. Particularly with regard to this, it is necessary to consider the enlightening concentration to be only a conscious and vigilance-full focusing of the mind on one single thing. This thing is supposed to be, above all, the state beyond both all happening and all processes, by both of which the usual living of all creatures is characterised, including such a person who strives for his or her enlightenment, and uses for it not fully understood mystical means.

Due to all this, a person must train themselves towards concentration. Initially, they must focus their mind only cautiously. It is supposed to be a concentration, by means of which they are supposed to create the necessary conditions for a thorough observation of all processes which take place in their being and, furthermore, in the entire everyday living, however, primarily in themselves. Only then he, or she, can burden their consciousness, by means of the intensive concentration, with reactions which are brought about by the direct and "hard-core" mental concentration to which they will devote themselves and by which they can attain enlightenment.

The reactions to the direct and hard-core mystical concentration are powerful. Every strained concentration has a danger contained in it that the consciousness will narrow down and then, instead of the development of the ability to obtain knowledge, only a property to become fixed will develop. This is though, a ground for the development of overwhelming emotions and drives, and also of the emotional clinging; by their action a person transfers from the path of knowledge to a path of indulging; however, in this case only a dreamlike indulging which is thus very far from reality.

This ending of, possibly even good, initial mystical efforts is quite a usual phenomenon. It is caused by the dilettantism, with which the mystical training is approached. Well, nothing can be done. Mysticism is not a scientific discipline and therefore we can find, even among the inexperienced mystics, a lot of seeming authorities whose work is now funny, now harmful and now malign. It is necessary to achieve a concentration which will become the Aqua regia and the analyser of everything that exists and which must never become the causative agent of experiences, regardless of whether they are mystical, or only emotional.

3. Why to concentrate on feet and legs

The universe in which we live is composed not only of visible and tangible phenomena but also of qualities. I mean the physical qualities – i.e., qualities that are weighable and measurable – and their psychological significance. I am though, writing about mysticism, about the spiritual development and about the training toward an inner transformation which is supposed to lead to the bringing about of new emotional, mental and conscious qualities which are pleasant or very pleasant. Therefore I will not write at length about the laboratory psychology which mostly only makes the path to liberating knowledge more difficult.

I know that science trusts the laboratory psychology and that I will be, presumably, criticised for being unscientific, but that does not matter. Those who are familiar with life in a village know very well that, for example, the psychology of rats cannot be compared to the psychology of humans, because there is always some difference between the inner life of rats and the inner life of humans. When rats are provoked to an inner life by the need for food, they 'scour' the ground with their snout for so long, till they get, for example, to a heap of grain – and then their inner life already ceases. This usually does not occur in people. I recall that in one village, there lived a person called Beerlover. He was generally considered to be a person internally underdeveloped and, precisely due to this, he was, in his inner life, very similar to rats. Nonetheless, when he learned that in the fourth village from his, a new pub had opened, he sensed that right there, he could drink beer and thought that it would be a better beer than the one in the old pub, he didn't 'scour' the ground with his snout for so long until he could 'sniff out' a house stinking of beer, but, metaphorically speaking, he stretched the thread of his thinking from his place of residence to this new pub and then went unerringly, straight to it.

If these facts of the laboratory and the usual psychology were to be judged by the ancient Chinese sage Lao Tzu, he would say that "precisely due to this difference, the inner life of humans is different from the inner life of rats". With regard to the fact that mysticism is nearer to Lao Tzu than to the "scientific", or laboratory, psychology, it rather investigates the influence of that which has an effect on a person when they occupy their mind with it, than analogies of influence of fodder on the human and animal inner life.

Mysticism is thus predominantly based on the self-evident knowledge that, when the mind is occupied with abstract things and dreaming, then the consciousness no longer abides on the ground, but somewhere in the vagueness, and this rules out the arising of a high quality mystical knowledge. However, if the mind never rises above the "soil", a person is incapable of the abstract knowledge which, by substitution of the respective terms of this equation of the inner life, becomes wisdom which is close to redemption.

Let us think simply: if the students of mysticism are to avoid the danger of development of unproductive thinking and speculations, they must not fill their mind with purely abstract perceptions, but with the concrete ones. Out of these, the closest thing is their own body.

For, it is the body that is the carrier of the animal, emotional and inner life; these psychological phenomena then correspond to precise places in the body. For example, the reason certainly resides in the head and not in the legs; the procreative drive resides at the base of the trunk; in the spinal cord, which is the very origin of the brain matter, there is a primitive sense of touch, by which the lowest of organisms react to food. The fact, that these psychological phenomena have their headquarters of awareness in the head, is not decisive. This is confirmed by research which is based on the concentration of attention. Concentration, in particular an adequately intensive concentration which is able to bring about the reactions of those places in the body, on which it is focused, always brings about only the relevant, and not various, reactions.

Concentration on feet and legs as a whole, with a special focus on their flesh, has an effect on the development of the intellect and deepening of the sensory discernment, because right here, in the legs, in the flesh of the body, the basis of the inner life is situated. The same concentration with a special focus on their bones – and in particular to the bones of knees – eliminates the instability of the usual attention; it is used to stabilise the entire inner life. This stabilisation symbolises the best image of concentration. If this concentration is pure, then, in both cases, no emotional impulses will be produced, because the feet and legs are not equipped with the relevant organs. Thus, in the sense of mystical training, these concentrations are used to train oneself in the concentration of mind, in order for the student, as far as is possible, to avoid various stimuli and inner acts which would, at this stage of the mystical education, threaten their further progress, because they would, possibly, lead them astray mystically, as well as morally.

When the gurus recommend concentration into the trunk, in particular into its base, they pursue the goal of a full emotional awakening and development of the person. This is considered necessary if a person is to be secured against a detrimental fall on the steep slopes of the mystical path. It is interesting that this issue is given attention mostly by the hatha yoga system even though it sometimes seems that the original function of this concentration is no longer known in this system. No matter how it is, a forced excitation of the subtle contents in particular in the base of the trunk, always serves to increase activity, or vitality, which is then utilised for progress on the mystical path by means of the vital factors. In any case, those who have achieved the goal in the process of excitation and development of the energies residing at the base of the trunk, arrive at the knowledge of the entire life, which is, in essence, only emotional.

Thus, it makes no sense to use the intensive concentration and focus it above this level. However, due to the ignorance of the issues of the mystical growth this happens and therefore, we will have a word about reactions to such a concentration.

When the intensity of the mental energy is focused on the belly, strange personal experiences take place. It could be said that the space, in the form of God's voice, begins to talk to the mystic, as it happened to Moses on the mountain Sinai. In any case, the astral, i.e. the invisible world opens to the mystic. It is a reflection of the material world, but it is superior to it. This fact can cause the mystic to succumb to the impression of power of this inner world, and by this, a mystical dependence develops in him or her – a dependence on God. Also due to this reason, the mystical efforts of every mystical striver are supposed to begin with being aware of feet and legs, because, in that case, the abrupt and unexplainable changes of the perceived world do not occur and, by that, neither does the mystical dependence upon an outer mystical power. However, this does not mean that the mystic should hold on to their purely materialistic conception of the outer world, because the world is not like that and therefore such a conception of the world is, indeed, incorrect.

The awareness of feet and legs – and later the concentration into them – is supposed to lead to an introversive orientation. If this orientation is carefully maintained, those forces, which so easily personify themselves, will always prove, to the practising person, to be only forces. This is the only correct understanding which creates a precondition for the striving one to reach all the way to the state of perfection – salvation.

The greatest mistake, which a mystical striver can commit, is to concentrate somewhere other than into the feet and legs. If he or she, by concentration into the belly, brings about their conscious inner inbreak into that astral world, where they can identify the existence of divine powers and abandon themselves to their dominance, then they have sunken into an equally flawed world-view, as when they do not strive mystically and they hold on to a materialistic view of the world. Due to this reason, the good mystical schools recommend concentration on feet and legs; in them, during a sufficient increase of intensity, physiological substrates of their flesh will be released. These substrates then multiply, rise up through the body and, on their way, release everything that is hidden in the psycho-physiological nerve ganglia of the trunk and of the head. This releasing is of a different kind than that provoked by a direct concentration into these psycho-physiological and neural centres. It does not become a breakthrough into the sphere of these substrates, but it remains a more natural penetration into, and transformation of, the structure of these centres. Therefore a person then enters the astral world – which is, in the microcosm, linked to the abdominal region – with their entire normal inner 'armoury'. By this, the moments of backsliding are ruled out and a person enters there as a traveller through the invisible spheres of life.

What holds true about the penetration of a person into this psycho-physiological and neural centre, holds true, as well, about his or her penetration into the psycho-physiological centres situated above the abdomen.

Let us, therefore, take notice of that most praised penetration of the consciousness into the pectoral centre – a centre in the chest, which is probably known by all mystical schools – the Christian, as well as the oriental ones.

A concentration into this centre, which is accompanied by "raising the mind towards God", brings about, with a high probability, the development of feelings which are considered to be mystical. However, from the psychological point of view, the mystical nature of these feelings is very problematic. Even in the everyday feelings, it is possible to find very ideal feelings, which can be easily mistaken for mystical ones, especially when imagination takes part in them. In such a case it is, as a rule, the sexuality that causes the mystics "concentrating into the heart" to suddenly find out that they are having a share in the divine mercy, in various states of ecstasy and the like.

We must not forget that sexuality has countless forms. Those who, due to some reasons, do not discharge sexually in the physical way, can very easily discharge in the mystical way. In such a person, the imagination then paints for them a mystical world in the form of paradises, heavens, angels, devas and I do not know what else. Behind all of this, there is a fact that the psycho-physiological neural centre was not developed by a pressure of the vital forces, released from the flesh of legs, but by an inbreak of the mind which was concentrating into the heart – a mind, which is not able to reduce the 'geyser' of feelings, related to the ecstasy of the mind, to feelings "on their own" that are, though, classified into various categories of feelings.

However, yoga does not limit itself only to concentration into the heart. It is also familiar with concentration into the neck – into the psycho-physiological neural centre in the neck. It is claimed about this concentration, that the yogi can, through its influence, shake the worlds.

Let us, however, put aside the reflections about this claim. Let us turn to the simple mystical experience with concentration. We can claim about it, that, if it is to be as effective as it is mentioned in the writings on yoga, it always has to be indirect. It must be a concentration into the legs, which must release a sufficient amount of the muscle substrates of an energetic character, to be able to develop the hidden energy, even in such a high centre as is the one in the neck. When this is successful, then the accompanying mystical experience is, in particular, an entry into the limitless space.

However, this experience and this possibility horrifies the small souls, because, such souls suffer from a constant hidden or manifest desire to always be in the company of beings, in the environment of things differentiated by shape, while the "emptiness without supports" inspires horror in them. However, the mystical development is, at the same time, a research of the microcosm, and therefore the "qualities of the neck centre" – of Vishuddha, must also be known and mastered. I claim that they cannot be known by an industrious direct concentration, because, this concentration is always of too crude a nature – it does not bring about the reactions of the subtle substances. On the contrary, the vital substrates, which were extracted by the concentration into the feet and legs, may bring the expected result and by that help a person to cross the borderline from the world of being subordinated to the natural laws to the world of power over the world of various urgencies – to get to know, by this, that the world is, on all its levels, a world of events which are subject to the law of causation and not a world of spheres controlled by gods; the lower gods do not have this power, because they suffer from selfness, while the higher ones do not have it due to the fact that they are not interested in the outer worlds. Only because of this, we live in the world of laws, in particular the karmic ones. Every yogi will get to know this, who, with a complete inner 'armoury', enters the world of the "neck lotus flower" as a being which is not subject to any suggestion invoked by a personified, or, a non-personified outer power.

Only the centre of the forehead can be opened by the yogi by means of the synergy of a direct concentration with the vital substrates released by the concentration into the flesh of legs. Therefore, the results of the opening of this centre are more obvious to everyone who practises concentration on the legs. It is, in the first place, an inner consolidation, noticeable enough to be identified even by a person with average ability of discernment. And the visions of light which occur during the concentration into this centre? – They are a portent of the realisation of the state of salvation. However, in such a case, the experience is then lacking from the path from the base of the vital, whose place is in the feet and legs, up to the top of the mental, whose place is in the head. Therefore, a simple person who, in some way, attained the development of this psycho-physiological neural centre by the synergy of both the above mentioned forces, can attain salvation without having the knowledge with which the powerful gurus, who went through all experiences of the mystical path, are equipped. These experiences teach us in an entirely factual way, that the mystical education must be based on concentration on the feet and legs in order to prevent somersaulting from the materialistic view of the world to an idealistic view, because both are false.

The mystic has to enter the empirical mystical path precisely by the concentration on feet and legs, in order for him or her to be able to identify every step of the transformation of their being, from the elementary human state all the way to an evident detection that he or she has attained an unshakeable state of salvation at which they have arrived in the same way as a person walking on the paving of a road in a city from one house to another house.

From a purely practical mystical point of view, the feet and legs very suitably represent an object, while consciousness represents a subject. If the object of a concentrating mind, and by that also of the consciousness, are the products of thinking, then the qualitative difference between the subject and the object – between the consciousness and the object of concentration – is very small and due to this it happens that the mind starts to wander. However, if the object of the concentrating mind, and by that also of the consciousness, are feet and legs, then the difference between the subject and the object is so substantial that both factors suitably represent two extreme qualities of the entire cosmic continuum. By this state of things, the consciousness and the mind will be held motionless. Therefore, the path of transformation will sinuate through all qualitative levels of existence and universe, while the substrates, which will be produced by the flesh of the legs under the pressure of concentration, will make the process of transformation of the being clearly observable, because they will make it even, and by that, also accessible to the identification of each of its levels. Due to this reason, it is necessary to avoid mental penetration into the inappropriately distant spheres of existence, in order for the mind not to become a vassal of the emotional experience and to maintain its character of an all-analysing subject.

The feet and legs are thus, from this base of knowledge, identified as the basis of the inner life, because, they are a living organism, in which the inner life dwells. A meditating mystic, who has rejected the wandering of mind through the spheres of abstract things, will always resort to directing the analysing concentration "to the bottom of life" which is quite well represented by feet and legs and then, in a higher sense, by the base of the trunk.

Thus, when the meditating mystic accepts the instruction that it is necessary to fasten their mind, which is hungry for knowledge, on his or her feet and legs, he or she has obtained a platform for both an inner deepening and an inner immovability, because in the feet and legs there is neither a place where it is possible to kindle the passionate sensory desires, as at the base of the trunk, nor the inexhaustibility of feelings whose place is the heart, or luminescence, which is irreconcilable with the usual existence, and whose place is there, where the Indians place the residence of the atman – i.e.

between the eyebrows. With regard to this, the feet and legs are a truly neutral place, even though the origins of the entire inner life can be found in them. But this is, initially, not supposed to be interesting for the mystics. The only interesting thing for them should be that an intense analysing concentration into the area of feet and legs will never kindle uncontrollable emotions which are so dangerous for a person who walks the mystical path. If it happens anyway, it was caused by an escalated intensity of thinking which was, after the period of practice, consciously or unconsciously fastened upon exactly somewhere within the trunk.

The area of feet and legs thus has to become the area of the foremost interest to a mystic, even though he or she cannot find anything interesting there, because, this area serves only to train oneself in the concentration of mind. And, just like in every scientific discipline it is necessary to adhere to certain rules, also a mystic, occupying his or her mind with their feet and legs, must increase the energy which is growing due to concentration. Besides that, he or she must keep in mind to, outside the period of training in concentration, return to the usual way of the functioning of the inner life – without an energised thinking.

By adhering to this instruction, he or she will achieve that, under the pressure of their concentrating mind, the energy contained in the flesh of their legs will start to be released. When this energy is released, it will not be irradiated diffusely, in all directions, but it will begin to rise upwards to, in case of a correct procedure, carry out its good work in the trunk.

From the point of view of yoga, this technique is hatha-yogic. It is however correct, especially for a modern person, who is, due to the character of life on our continent, a creature which is more mental then vital. Therefore, techniques other than this can further encourage their mentality and, by that, bring them to completely uncontrollable thinking and speculations – to the opposite of that which is good for them from the personal, as well as the mystical, aspect.

Hatha yoga does not care about the development of the inner life by means of encouragement of the mind to increased activity. It is based on an experience that dwelling of the concentrating mind in a part of the body which is taking part in positions, thus predominantly in the feet and legs, leads to deepened sensory discernments. These are, for an inquiring mind, the beginning of a new inner life, which is uncorrupted by a mentality which permanently speculates, or which leads to the self-confidence of those who believe that they know everything. Only those who are devoid of this mentality begin to discover the old world in new interrelations, i.e. the world as it is seen by the mystics – sages.

Nothing good stems from a base which is situated higher than in the part of the body which is taking part in positions, thus in the feet and legs. The base of the trunk reacts to an intensely concentrating mind by the kindling of passions, while the centre of the breast by kindling of feelings, which have no end or goal. By concentration into the neck and head, such stimuli arise which are only useful for a person who already can, by the help of the preceding mystical practice, identify the psychological processes and changes in the body – only then the energetic reactions of these centres enable a person to identify that he or she is travelling through the realm which is beyond the world.

Beginners are not supposed to dare to search for paths in this realm beyond the world at all. Besides, if they are searching for them, it is a proof of their disorientation. It is natural for a human being to seek paths to remove the immediate physical and emotional suffering of the common people. A habit to dwell with the conscious thinking in the feet and legs, which are either crossed according to the rules of the yogic positions or not crossed, will stabilise the mind; the mind concentrated in this way helps achieve becoming more perfect on the earthly plain, where the common person, as well as the beginner in mysticism, always lives.

The concentration into the feet and legs is considered to be a mystical development progressing in a bottom-up manner. An aphorism holds true about it that, if it is carried out constantly, it strengthens and softens the inner beingness and thus leads the practising one to the borderline between our sensory world on one side and the abstracted, the so-called astral, world, on the other side. It will be possible to cross this borderline in the moment, when the concentration into this place develops into a withdrawal of that, which a person in total is, into a single psycho-physiological point. This is exactly that 'point of uncertainty' in the psychological sphere. The awareness of oneself will then cause this point to be crossed with the entire normal inner 'armoury' and this is the beginning of an explorative path through the transcendental sphere.

It is not possible to achieve this result when the concentration is not directed into the lowest part of the body, into the feet and legs, which symbolise the immovable solid earth, because, such a concentration will determine, for a person, a path through other psychological processes; most often through the sphere of abstract phenomena. Although this appears to be mystical, in fact it is the delusory mysticism – straying through the forests of the innumerable and insignificant phenomena of the inner life or of the imagination.

Therefore, it is good for everyone not to get enticed by an idea of a path of inner development, which they mistakenly consider to be an intellectual development. A human being needs, above all, an inner consolidation; as, he or she already is unconsolidated. Only due to this reason they wander, tormented by an uncontrolled mind which can never sense the correct goal of the mystical education. It is only able to set more and more new targets, which always prove to be false and flawed.

Let us, thus, not be mistaken by the simplicity of the instruction to concentrate on feet and legs. On the "earth of life", at the lowest part of the being, in the flesh of legs, there is a gate to the transcendence, which can only be crossed by elimination of wandering of mind, which the feet and legs, as a symbol of motionlessness, attenuate very effectively. However, this gate, which is certainly everywhere – in every sphere and layer of the being – cannot be identified in any sphere which is not, or which is not made, equally immovable to the gate of earth which is symbolised by feet and legs. And what about an opinion that the concentration into feet and legs gives an impression that the inner liveliness is attenuated up to a seeming inner dullness? – There is nothing like that. The concentration into feet and legs is lively, due to the fact that it must be accompanied by vigilance and observation. Precisely by means of observation one penetrates the barrier of the solid motionlessness of the material world into the realm of life which determines the destinies of a person, because it is an inner life which is commonly unknown. By means of a mere reflexive perception, it is not possible to penetrate all the way to its bottom and, by that, nor to the origins of all destinies of the individuals. The mystic is supposed to avoid these very destinies by means of the practical mysticism.

Thus, from the point of view of mysticism and natural science, a being can be stratified in such a way that the feet and legs belong to the nature of the material formations which symbolise earth and water, the trunk, from this point of view, belongs to the nature of the physical formations and therefore it symbolises fire and air, while the head belongs to the nature of a physically not determinable ether. This ether then corresponds to the zone of the electromagnetic phenomena, chiefly to the sphere of gravitation and its various modifications, which are, in the psychological sense, predominantly the mind and then also the sense of vision, as well as other carriers of the inner life.

From the mystical point of view, and, above all, from the point of view of the so-called self-acting karma, the inner functions, in particular thinking, want to maintain their character – i.e. they want to remain qualitatively separated from the more material phenomena that are a manifestation of the elements of air, fire, water and earth. In yoga of a spiritual type, it is considered possible to obtain high quality knowledge only by connecting all of the mentioned qualities in the consciousness. However, this is supposed to happen by immersion of the consciousness into the quality of matter or earth, thus into the feet and legs, whose gravitational value is, furthermore, being modified in the mind by means of assuming positions. By that, the "matter of legs" is made lighter and the connecting of the mind as a manifestation of ether with the matter of legs is thus made easier.

When all these factors are included in an equation which is supposed to solve the problem of the spiritual development, its result is an axiom by which it is determined that the spiritual as well as the mystical development is only possible by means of concentration of the electromagnetic or gravitational factor – the mind, into the most characteristic manifestation of earth – into the feet and legs. The experience from the mystical development agrees with this.

Only a mind, which is, by means of thorough awareness, delving into the matter of feet and legs, can make the base of consciousness capable of its unidirectional raising through all layers of the being – from the earth, which is represented by the feet to calves, through the water, which is mystically situated in the thighs, and further through the fire found in the base of the trunk and in the belly, and the air found in the chest, up to the ether and its modifications which are placed in the head.

The base into which we immerse our consciousness – or, more precisely, our awareness – i.e. the feet and legs, has, precisely due to the property of the consciousness to gather knowledge from the environment in which it occurs, the possibility to pass through all layers of existence. This means from the very beginning of the creative act, which is the emergence of earth and water, and, further, the birth of the living cell and, even further, through the most elementary manifestations of vitality up to the knowledge arising from the perceptions of limitless space, consciousness and further then the emptiness of everything all the way to the extinguishment of the entire inner life without the problem of the idea of death. This holds true prospectively. What holds true immediately, is that when the mind dwells in the sphere of matter, of earth and water, which corresponds to the feet and legs, it loses its wandering, i.e. it becomes calm.

Only this kind of mind, which is, at the same time, accustomed to concentratedness, can, with the raising base of consciousness, or, awareness, transfer to the sphere of fire and air where the knowledge of the instinctive and emotional life arises; over there it will obtain life experiences which will make it wise.

However, wisdom is not a matter of an abstracted factor of being – of the mind, but a fruit of emotional experience whose elements are correctly classified and evaluated by the mind of the mystic. And because the elementary living – the emotional one, even at the level of ideals, belongs only to the trunk, the rising base of awareness or consciousness will then enable a person to experience everything that is offered by the elementary living. Having completely experienced that which the trunk contains in it as hidden experiential qualities, is an accomplishment of the state of the mystical perfection.

However, the base of consciousness and awareness can be raised even higher – above the level of the elementary, as well as emotional, living, which is contained in the trunk – up to the sphere of the abstract, i.e. intellectual cognition. It can be even raised up to the sphere of knowledge obtained by means of pure perceptions, i.e. unbiased by prejudice which is caused by the emotional clinging or aversion to the phenomena of the outer world, whether the visible, material ones, or the inner, moral and emotional ones.

The sphere of this, so-called, 'abstract cognition' corresponds to the head. When the base of consciousness or awareness is raised all the way up to here, the mystic will see life from a detached perspective. This view was obtained by the passage of the analysing thinking and awareness through the trunk. As a result of this, his or her wisdom, obtained by the state of consciousness in the detached perspective, will develop further, until the mystic will finish the entire period of life in a state of a non-violent renunciation of everything. By that, they will attain the peak of the spiritual development – a state, in which they will not wish for anything, because they will be aware of the fact that they have experienced and known everything that can be experienced and known, and so they will find no more elements of ignorance in themselves.

I can claim that this high quality wisdom cannot be obtained by other path than "bottom-up". The concentration into the breast, which is done by many Christian mystics, only develops the states of various feelings. With regard to the relationship of the feelings to imagination, this concentration can bring about visions of the most bizarre subjective pieces of knowledge; however, these pieces are not a variant of life experiences and the entire life experience is not exhausted by them – and only this fully calms down the being at the level of desires. Therefore the mystic concentrating into the breast can, at the best, die with a desire to know God or to identify themselves with him. This – if correctly evaluated – is a proof that the heat of cravings did not extinguish; this craving is perhaps more noble than the elementary taste-related craving, but still it is craving which is rooted in the insatiability of an inexperienced soul – a soul seeking the states of excitement and emotional experiences.

As far as the head is concerned, concentration into it may be recommended only by a sage knowledgeable about the entire mystical path. It is possible to generally say, that only a "soul", which is equipped with a fund of all-exhaustive life experiences, may use this concentration, because, due to its influence, the path through the life experiences is quickly finished. If this path is, by unsuitable means, prematurely interrupted, the person will finish their current physical life with a cry of the desire for life. Therefore, the wheel of karma and the samsaric life will not stop; on the contrary, it will, with a greater energy, spin further, because it will be propelled by a new force awakened by cravings.

Therefore one should begin with the practice "into the feet and legs".

4. A Warning

A mystic, who walks the path of the mystical development independently, must act wisely and not unwisely. By no means must they let their inner inspiration advise them. This inner inspiration seems holy to them and, as a rule, it appears when one reads books about the mystical practice. Even less may he or she let anyone, who is talking about mysticism, give them advice.

The mystical education must be based on the practical psychology and, moreover, on the mystical experiences of those who have already had a great success in the mystical practice. This, by itself, suffices for the advice that it is not correct to choose the mystical practices according to one's own discretion, if the mystical experience is lacking here. We have already seen results of that.

How easily did those, who were predisposed for mental illness, choose their mystical practices! The illnesses then broke out in them, because they, instead of the mental effort which would lead them to activity, devoted themselves to inner passivity which quickly facilitated the outbreak of their mental illness. Therefore, even if psychiatry claims that mysticism is a frequent cause of mental illness, it is not the case, because, in the true practical mysticism, the element of an active inner effort is always predominant. Only a dilettante mysticism does not pay attention to the difference between an active mental effort and an inner passivity. However, this mysticism does not lead to any positive results and, in general, to anything good.

The experts in the mystical development, for example, know very well that the path to the spiritual perfection can be very much quickened by means of dissociation of consciousness. Psychiatry perhaps knows about it only not more than that the dissociation of consciousness is a path to schizophrenia. However, is it really like this?

The training in concentration of the mind cannot go without a double awareness, namely, an awareness of the object of concentration on the one hand, and the outer things on the other, because, if it is not like this, the concentration very easily becomes a fixation of mind; this is, in turn, a fixed idea – a mental illness of its own kind.

Towards the double awareness, one proceeds step-by-step, in the mystical development. It is practised in such a way that the student of mysticism focuses his or her mind on a sole object which is either imagined or real and, at the same time, avoids losing the phenomena of the surrounding world from their evidence.

It is possible to practise it in this way or vice versa. In the latter case, the student of mysticism trains himself or herself in a precise perception of the outer phenomena, but, simultaneously, tries to be aware of some imagined object somewhere in their being or even only of a place on their, or in their, body.

The ability to perceive both kinds of phenomena improves with practice. When it improves, the student of mysticism will attain the ability to thoroughly perceive the outer world as well as the inner object which initially serves the concentration and later, even an absolute control over all processes of their inner life. By that, the dissociation of consciousness has been accomplished.

The results of this dissociation are very interesting. In one of the later phases of this effort, the being will prove to be some kind of receiver which is continuously tuned to all electromagnetic corpuscular quanta which are produced due to the fact that a human being exists in a living environment – in the environment of people. These quanta, which are so distinctive, precisely flag everything that produces them, thus also people and their real character. The ability to perfectly register the influence of these quanta is called the psychic clairsentience.

However, this result means nothing from the point of view of the mystical development up to the spiritual perfection; often it is only the beginning of a constant inner troubling of the one receiving these impulses. If this interference wasn't a bearer of the experiences of the mystical growth, a person would not need to work with the dissociation of consciousness at all. Therefore, it does not need to be warned against, because, this "schizophrenia" is, indeed, a methodically induced pseudo-schizophrenia, and therefore a "schizophrenia" which is well controlled by the striving mystic. The mystic, who has arrived at it, could have attained it solely by powerful inner efforts, and therefore it will not happen that they would, so easily, mistake the real world for a visual one – a fictious one, and behave in it as a person who is mentally integrated, complete, but still mentally ill. Therefore, there is no danger of mental illness here. However, this danger exists elsewhere. It exists in an unprofessional selection of the imagined objects, or places in the body, for the concentration.

Once, there existed a public mystical school in our country, in which only two mystical practices were taught – the concentration of the mind into the breast with a mental image and the so-called 'silent concentration' about whose mental anchorage I don't know.

These two kinds of concentration testified to the dilettantism of this mystical school. Due to the fascination with these two "practices" it left unnoticed a great danger which stems from a sinuous process of thinking on the one hand and from the change of the qualities of the mind on the other hand. Therefore, it used to happen that the beneficial focusing of thinking on an object, which is the body, was abandoned and, very often, a path of speculative and, eventually, wandering thinking was entered.

This speculative, as well as wandering, thinking, soon showed its evil face. Instead of mystics with a controlled and stabilised mind, mystics were occurring, who had strange views of the world and life and instead of mystics who would bear in mind the general good, mystics were occurring, who had a specific, but never a good, moral view and character.

In order for this wandering not to occur, every independently faring mystic must adhere to the effort to calm down the sinuous character of the mind, which is constantly being focused on an inner object chosen for concentration.

The best object for the concentration of mind is the lowest part of the body – feet and legs – the symbol of matter, or earth, which is the basis of the universe of phenomena. This universe must become known in its essence, if the mystical development is to fulfil its purpose – namely to bring knowledge and, by the means of it, liberation.

However, in most cases, those, who are engaged in mysticism, do not act correctly. Instead of adhering to the idea of attenuation of the mind's activity and, by that, of the entire inner life – of the inner activity, they succumb to a natural reaction of their own being to the effort to halt the inner life. They leave, in an uncontrolled way, the mystical path they have entered and then they only "train themselves" in the development of pointless thoughts, speculations, or wandering of mind.

This diversion from the begun mystical path is the most frequent. The striving for the real concentration is, often even due to a small resistance of the psyche which resists its own subordination, replaced with valueless thinking. This thinking seems to be of a higher quality, because it deals with abstract concepts or relationships instead of the usual straightforward thinking which is concerned with some material or sensorily gratifying result.

However, mysticism is a teaching which only concerns the real things. One strives in it solely for the attainment of the life experiences, in the form of mystical experiences, which will enlighten a person by an immeasurable knowledge or profound insight into the essence of things by which one also arrives at knowledge and liberation. Precisely at this intended knowledge, one does not arrive by the thinking of mystics who have left the path of the true mystical practice. By means of this thinking, they can only get to a perpetual wandering of thinking in a circle of useless thoughts. By this, the person will gradually weaken themselves so much that they will never be able to resume carrying out a correct work on the path of mystical perfecting.

Therefore, the image of mysticism, as a life in a circle of idealistic thoughts which internally carry a person away through the world of non-concretised ideas, is not valid. Those who already dwell in this "world of psyche" are, in the best case, dreamers and, in the worst case, mentally ill people who suffer from delusional ideas.

Precisely due to these two undesirable outcomes of the inner living, it is necessary to avoid the wandering of mind, into which the true spiritual or mystical effort turns so easily, if it is based exclusively on the concentration of mind. It is necessary to avoid it by consciously keeping oneself internally on the ground of reality. When this way of thinking joins the analysing concentration of the conscious thinking, one will enter the path of transformation of the entire being; only this path is the true mystical path.

Mysticism is, though, not like a practical school education. It does not have the tradition of pedagogy, methodology and school education in general. Therefore, everyone interprets its teaching in their own way and according to the imperative of his or her inborn relationship to the outer world, his or her inclinations and images of the human happiness. Internally directed by this, everyone, who strives for success in the practical mysticism, comes dangerously close to going astray in the form of losing the ability to see everything realistically and think about everything rationally. A result of this is a transparent valuelessness of their thinking, concepts and reflections.

It is thus possible to establish an assumption that only an attitude, which is realistic towards life and the world and enriched with the concentration of mind which later precisely analyses everything, is a reliable mystical path which will bring delightful results to everyone; not only in an abstract, but also in a concrete, sense.

There have been enough lunatics who were confusing the uninformed people that it is just them – these lunatics – who are the true examples of the practising mystics. However, how did they become these lunatics? – By, instead of devoting themselves to the concentration of mind by which they would attenuate its automatic activity as well as perception, they were, on the contrary, increasing this activity. They devoted themselves to thinking which was, after finishing concentration, bringing them a new kind of thoughts than those with which they were dealing before, in the period of the animal way of living. However, from the perspective of the heights of the mystical development, it is exactly the same, whether the uncontrolled and automatically active mind deals with the objects of sensory cravings or with speculations about the superworldly life and about a moral or immoral thinking and behaviour. The only thing that always decides, is whether a person brings the striving for mastering of the mind to its goal, namely to the destruction of the entire inner activity; of course, the reflexive and automatic activity, because, only in this way a person penetrates, by their perception, beyond the functional sphere of thinking and develops in him or her self an ability to discern the source of motives and to develop also the so-called direct perception, by which they penetrate beyond the curtain of illusion, which is created by the uncontrolled thinking.

However, people are internally weak and lack courage. When their effort for concentration of the mind arrives as far as to the natural reaction of their being which is defying the domination of will, or, when they discern that, by the destruction of the automatic thinking, they have arrived at the edge of a seeming abyss of inner inactivity which was brought about by the will, they run away from their original efforts and, since then, resort only to the processes of thinking of a new kind, which does not seem to have the signs of the thinking of an animal. By this, they enter the path of a valueless and purposeless thinking which will obstruct their way to successes on the path of the practical mysticism, and then, due to the fact that their thoughts are of a new kind, they conclude from it that they have achieved progress on their mystical path, although they have already gone astray.

Every student of mysticism should avoid this going astray by continuing to destroy the automatic thinking, even though they can, by that, often come to a supposition that "over there", further down this path of the destruction of the inner activity, there is just a dark abyss. The "non-thinking", which is a result of an intentional stopping and destroying of the inner activity, are the mystical depths, only in which the wisdom is born, because, wisdom is not a result of a mind which precisely speculates, but a result of the sensory discernments, purified from the mixing in of prejudice and preconceptions for, or against, something.

The mystical going astray commonly sneaks in to the mystical efforts softly and imperceptibly. The transition from a systematic stopping of the processes of thinking, by means of which the depths of the true mystical state will arise, to the purposeless thinking of a new kind – to the thinking of valueless mystical speculators – is gradual. Perhaps only an outer observer can see the, in this way, "turning aside" mystic – how the, possibly until now rationally thinking, person – a seeming mystic – becomes a speculator with abstract or even valueless contents of thinking. Therefore, there is no other option than, for every student of mysticism, to be attentive to the changes of the state of their thinking. If it is, or is becoming, speculative, it is necessary to stop the existing mystical effort, to return to factual thinking and, after its desirable correction, to begin the true mystical effort anew.

This can be understandable for everyone who insists on preserving the factual thinking and I can tell such people: the results of the mystical effort are really factual. They manifest in the everyday emotional experience which qualitatively changes to the extent, to which the moral transformation of the entire being was realised; the transformation which was brought about by thinking which completely subordinated itself to the moral and mental instructions of the true mystical teaching.

5. Nirvana

In order for us to understand nirvana, we must define samsara – the state, which evokes an image of the wandering of souls through the world of sorrowful states.

In fact, we must characterise samsara only as motion. However, motion can apply to all phenomena out of which, in "our" sensory world, the highest ones are the physical phenomena, i.e. the electromagnetic quanta, if we understand them as phenomena with a corpuscular background. These quanta cannot be considered to be unchangeable formations or clusters; they change, strictly speaking, in accordance with their predetermination which is caused by their gravitational interrelations.

We can hardly imagine that the universe of phenomena is temporary, whereas the gravitation is "eternal", so, consequently, we have to understand the universe as a universe of "eternal" motion; thus, that the universe is an exclusively samsaric phenomenon. With regard to that, every phenomenon of the universe of forms and forces is all the more samsaric. Also the creatures are exactly such phenomena; they are formations existing in the gravitational field, let us say, in some initial stage of theirs, an initial stage in the gravitational field created by the galaxies.

Beings, as the inner formations of the universe, or, of the cosmic continuum, prove to be more sorrowful formations than, for example, the galaxies which are only subject to gravity – gravitation. It proves to be this way, because, the beings, as units of their own kind, are more crowded in the given space, in which, then, the gravitational lines create an environment which is more dense and by that, thus, more subject to the "crisis of gravity".

However, strictly speaking, the beings are a microcosm which contains qualities of various kinds, of which the highest one is the consciousness.

The consciousness can be, from this point of view, understood as a field, on whose walls the picture of the "magic of illusion", which is the universe of phenomena, is generated. The ability of the consciousness to identify this picture provides evidence that it qualitatively differs from samsara – the structure of the formation of phenomena – the forms which are so obviously in a permanent motion, thus forms which are samsaric. During a constant analysis of these qualities of microcosm and their constant mutual comparing, the consciousness is, in the end, identified as nirvana in its true essence.

It does not matter that the consciousness of beings becomes a mirroring principle, reflecting only the phenomena of the universe – the phenomena which are in a process – and therefore they are samsaric, because, it is possible to rid this consciousness of this seemingly natural function, i.e. the function to reflect phenomena, thus those quanta of the physical factors. When a person achieves this, the consciousness manifests its original nature, a nature of a cosmic mirroring principle, which can then be identified only as the "nirvanic state" which is in an empirical opposition to the "eternal forming", thus in opposition to the universe of happening, to the samsara.

The idea of the spiritual development is, for the aspirant of the spiritual perfection, to realise the original state of consciousness at the level of their own being. However, this requires a work of its own kind which is called, in summary, the mystical path.

Its beginning lies in the effort to exclude from the consciousness that "manifoldness" which is created by the heavy waves of physical quanta which generate formations of their own kind. This is carried out in such a way that a person will no longer allow their consciousness to mirror everything that can have an effect on it as the phenomena of the external world, but they will only allow it to mirror states and perceptions of one kind.

This means, in practice, that an aspirant of the spiritual perfection is supposed to chose joyfulness or elevation of the mind above the world of the external phenomena, according to whether they are under the influence of the worldly mind which is inclined to melancholy or of the inner suffering whose basis is a pessimistic view of the world. Exactly the joyfulness and a constant elevation of the mind above the world of the external phenomena is supposed to become the means of keeping oneself above the world of happening, which means, above the world of ever-changing moods, changing from a deep melancholy all the way to crazy sensory joys.

When a person remains, for a long time, either in the joyful happiness, or in a state of mind elevated above the world of the external phenomena – in either case only in a state produced by the will – this state will settle in them or become a habit for them. When this state becomes to them the "carrier wave" of their inner life, they have eliminated the influence of samsara in its worst form – the influence that creates their moods, against whose pounding waves they are helpless.

From the point of view of the practical mysticism, the joyfulness produced by will and the elevation of mind above the world of the sensory perceptions are often used as realisable states. This means that a person must hold on to these states with the most intense straining of their will, until these states become part of his or her being in such a way that they are the carrier waves of their inner life to such an extent that if he or she would like to eliminate them, they would have to use an equally powerful pressure of will as when they were trying to produce and realise them. Only with the development of these states of inner forces and qualities, a person obtains a new psychological base, on which they can start to build a solid building of the spiritual perfection.

However, the way, in which the student of mysticism should act at this stage of the mystical practice, should be, in mysticism, determined by the guru. The new psychological base of being must be built from the mood elements in their precise proportion, in order to avoid the predominance of things of one or another kind and, by means of that, to avoid the arising of a situation which would, again, require an inner rebuilding, as in the first phase which was just mentioned.

It is necessary to point out right here, at the beginning, that the most experienced gurus lead their disciples in such a way that nothing is realised, but the various inner and psychological qualities of the individual are only mutually confronted in order for the "base of awareness" to move higher and higher on the level of psychological and physical qualities – as high as possible, in order for the so-called 'first realisation' of a person to be as close to the state of salvation as possible. As, the lower inner and physical states must be realised, the harder is the creation of conditions for a further progress from this newly arisen base. Those who seek then often have no more strength to get, from the states of the first realisation, higher on the still ascending mystical paths.

However, let us suppose that the student of mysticism has obtained a very experienced guru who is responsible in their field. This kind of guru can, as a rule, bring the student of mysticism to the realisation of a state which is actually just supernatural for the student. By that, the guru creates for the student preconditions for sensing even better states than those which he or she just realised and, at the same time, the guru helps them to preserve the potential possibility of, immediately, setting out further to the steeper slopes of the mystical path.

On these slopes, the students of mysticism obtain their own experience from the sphere of emotional experiencing, which means, for them, the ability to walk further alone, without "being lead by the little hand" and to avoid the realisation or getting stuck in any kind of state which does not allow them to get to know the absolute and to realise its state.

As a rule and, actually, in the best cases, the aspirant of spiritual perfection can, by avoiding all – even the very attractive – emotional states, get as far as the borderline between the immanent and the transcendental world – over there, where a living being stands at the doorstep of the absolute and, at the same time, has the knowledge of how to realise the state of absolute, i.e. the nirvanic state.

It appears, that reaching the borderline between samsara and nirvana, requires one to internally stop, i.e. to realise some relevant mystical state, as, it is necessary to have time to look around for the points of touch of these two extreme states of the cosmos as well as of the beings in their spiritual conception; for, the moment of this attainment is like walking out of the disease of the samsaric life to the doorstep of an absolute health which can be ensured only by the right way of acting. In this way, samsara and nirvana begin to be confronted in the state of humanness which, through the preceding process of the spiritual development, obtained an ability to differentiate between these two basic cosmic states, between samsara and nirvana, as the objects of realisation of every individual.

The path is unusual after this point. It is, indeed, contained in the constant confrontations of the states of samsara and nirvana, while attention is paid so that the immersion in nirvana does not distance samsara from a person to such an extent that it would not be possible to realise it again, and, on the other hand, that the immersion in samsara does not distance the state of nirvana from a person in such a way that he or she would not be able to realise it any longer, because he or she has sunk too far into the emotional experiential living.

This careful and constant mixing of the two extreme states of the universe must happen – and it usually also does happen – with a tendency for the states of nirvana to have an adequate dominance over the samsaric states. In this way, it is possible to work through to the realisation of the absolute, of the nirvanic state, at the level of the being or its daily consciousness as differentiated phenomena.

Thus, in the universe, a possibility exists for a being – a living creature, to realise the state of absolute on its own level. It is certainly a superhuman objective; however, it is adequate for the deepest suffering of the subject. When such a person, due to the great amount of life experience, no longer believes in any exhilaration that a sensory craving, brought to success, could provide to him or her, then the absolute will not be to them an all-consuming bottomless pool, but only a place of peace, which becomes perfect exactly by the realisation of the absolute.

The realisations of a lower level than exactly of the absolute are the realisations of the celestial states, because, the mystical path always begins with non-gratification of the sensory desires and therefore it cannot aim at the sphere of darkness and aversion. A person on the mystical path always looks somewhere ahead and, according to their karmic maturity, either towards the sensory pleasures – towards the heavens of a various level, or, even beyond the sphere of the sensory pleasures towards the supercelestial spheres. However, these supercelestial spheres are also more than one, so, on the lowest level it is a sphere of peace beyond the complete living out of, or oversaturation by, the sensory pleasures, and on the highest one is it the extinguishment of every trace of differentiation. From the peace beyond the complete living out of the sensory pleasures or oversaturation by them, all the way to the extinguishment of every trace of differentiation, there are various degrees of emphasising one's own 'I' of every pilgrim on the mystical path. Those, who are entirely satiated by the life experiences, have no interest in the preserving of their 'I', because they are very well aware of the fact that the world exists only in contrast to this 'I'. In this way, a decision arises, to let come to an end both the 'I' and the world – two seemingly individualised factors which are, though, in fact only one single thing in two seemingly different versions, namely the states of samsara and nirvana.

However, what about those life experiences? – During the phase of ignorance, as it is defined by the highest quality mystical teaching, i.e. during ignorance that there are only two basic states of the cosmic continuum, these life experiences must be obtained only by means of the emotional experience. However, when a person is already able to enter the path of the mystical development, then a correctly raised and nursed disciple can bridge the sphere of emotional experience by an indirect obtaining of the life experiences – i.e. by means of a profound or penetrating insight.

This insight is something that is based on an inner detachment from that which is being experienced, that which is being known and from that which exists. A person no longer rushes to explore it by two senses of the direct experience, i.e. by touch and taste, or, in other words, by the emotional experience, but only by observation. In such a case, the relative sufficiency of life experiences will not bring a person to attachment. He or she is able to constantly observe everything that exists as an external phenomenon and, by means of the penetrating insight, also to get to know the nature of it. By this they cease to toil through the world of the emotional experiencing and they only journey through the world of obtaining knowledge, by means of which the states of samsara and nirvana are precisely identified, the two "eternal" phenomena of the external world of a person.

By the identification of the nirvanic state, the possibility, as well as the ability, to realise this state arises. On the path towards its realisation, all necessary life experience is completed – they secure a person against mistaking nirvana for the highest state of samsara and he or she will be able to accomplish the nirvanic state by a continuous confrontation of the states of nirvana and samsara, i.e. they will attain the extinguishment of the will to live and by that also of the involuntary wandering through samsara.

It is thus necessary to pronounce a warning: This result will not be attained by those who are still desiring the sensory experiences and sensations, whether the worldly ones, or the heavenly ones but only by those who understand that the true mystical goal is only beyond the sphere of these experiences and sensations. If a person, who is still yielding to the "taste for life", wants to define nirvana, he or she will always only define a state of blissful emotional experiencing – the higher samsaric states. Such a person is never a spiritually perfect person and thus nor a true guru of the ones who seek.

On Breathing practices and pranayama

Yogic breathing practices may be practised only after the being becomes non-desirous, content, and the spirit of a person becomes absorbed in itself, free from desires. For, if a person is desirous or burdened by desires, then the breathing practices strengthen this very strain, this orientation towards the external things. This gives rise to a driving force, to a rushing of the spirit towards external things. This is the very opposite of that towards which yoga leads, i.e. stability of spirit, which is supposed to become capable of knowledge.

Thus, if the moral conditions of yoga, out of which an absence of cravings is the main one, aren't fulfilled, then the breathing practices strengthen the centrifugal tendencies of being, that headless activity, by means of which a person wants to achieve, exclusively, things serving sensory pleasures. This is in fact the reverse of that which is actually intended by the spiritual education of yoga.

Therefore, those who desire spiritual perfection, and are seeking a path to it in yoga, should first focus on suppression of all cravings. Only after they stop desiring both knowledge and sensory sensations – the sign of which is that their mind doesn't "step outside" of the being – they are allowed to use breathing practices in order to speed up their spiritual growth. If they do not fulfil this condition, their desires become uncontrollable, because they were intensified by concentrated power of the spirit. This momentum channels the vital energy into an undesirable direction, precisely in the period when a person is distracted due to the influence of everyday duties. This means that strengthening of energy and activity is allowed by yoga only when the being had stopped rushing towards the sensory pleasures, when it is in tranquillity. In that case, all forces of being focus on reaching, realising and learning the qualities of spirit enthroned, in fact, in the superworldly level.

However, breathing practices are themselves, a problem as well. If the spirit is perturbed by desires or cravings, organism itself seems to modify the otherwise refreshing substances of inhaled air, into igniters of uncompromising wanting. A trained yogi recognises this as fire, the rajas element. By its influence, the human spirit transforms into an animal, whose living is characterised exclusively by elementary inclinations or cravings. However, if the spirit is calmed down, without desires, without relationship to sensory things igniting cravings, then the rhythmic breathing, or breathing practices, provide conditions for a spirit of the spiritual type, to grow up. This spirit often grows out of the sphere of our world, and according to the conditions, it grows even all the way up to the transcendental world.

I am however only talking about breathing practices. This means that breathing is based on the will of a yogi to breathe in a controlled way, and control the natural function of breathing. That is not the actual yogic breathing. Nevertheless, it is its beginning; the subsequent phase of this breathing is the achievement of pranayama. The breathing practices turn into pranayama, when "breath becomes one with the body", by means of being thoroughly aware of the body during breathing, as this way, conditions are created to put rhythm into the pulsation of the life-bringing breath substances. By that, the rhythm of life force is reached, which can be characterised as reaching the state of the so-called 'unity with the breath of Nature', or, 'unity with infinity'.

By means of pranayama, the yogis bring about harmony between their inner being and the aerial actuators of the cosmos – the breath substances. Through them, it is possible to get to the physical substances of breath, which are no longer only a part of the atmospheric coat of the Earth; they are this physical field, which is also-called 'diffuse matter of the universe'. In this way, the yogis link up to the materials of the universe, and when they achieve transfer of consciousness to this macrocosmic base, the value of space and time begins to change to them. This is the boundary between the immanent and the transcendental cosmic sphere; beyond this border the yogi realises the state of transcendence. This transcendence is registered by the yogi's own vigilant personal consciousness.

Pranayama thus occurs when a yogi, whose spirit is free from relationships to the objects of craving of the sensory world, introduces rhythm of the movement connected with all factors of breathing, like, for example, the movement of lungs and perceiving of the inhaled air. If this rhythm is perfect, it is pranayama, whose identification mark is the disappearing of feelings bearing evidence about relationships of a person to the external world. This rhythm soon brings a person to the supersensory sphere, there, where people tend to be seized by ecstasy.

A yogi has to resist ecstasies. He or she has to stabilise their spirit by being well aware of their body. In this way, they are introducing into their usual experience an element of ecstasy as a natural state of spirit, state unburdened by vehement animality, which is convinced that realism in perception must be necessarily accompanied by orientation of the mind and content of the consciousness exclusively turned towards the things of our sensory world. In this way, a person reaches that spiritual freeing, the transfer of the spirit and consciousness into the sphere above the usual suffering. This new state of a person is, above all, that goal ever searched for, the goal of a life without suffering.

However, yoga doesn't have in mind this release, or, more precisely, only this release. It is considered a by-product of the yogic development, similarly to evaporation during the boiling of water. The path thus continues. When the rhythm of breathing, pranayama, has already brought a yogi to the sphere of transcendence and provided them with the knowledge of law about existence of a suffering-free living, it begins to lose its meaning. Yogis then devote themselves to an analysis of substances which made themselves known to the consciousness when the mind freed itself from the phenomena of our world which are provoking sensory cravings. This analysis helps the yogis to discover elements or substances which are more and more unfamiliar to our sensory world, until they finally reach the knowledge of that which no longer breaks apart under the power of analysis. On this level, enthroned on the top of the substances of the differentiated and discernable world, they realise that by the "sticking" of being to the highest quality of the superworld, the "oscillation" of the spirit ceases. This is the true redemption, the stabilisation of spirit, which no longer suffers from a tendency to sink into the changeful world, denoted by the word samsara.

Yoga and health

1. Foreword

It took a very long time before I decided to write about the influence of yoga on health. I was held up by several circumstances, out of which the following three were the most important ones:

1. that someone could criticise me for my impaired health,
2. that I can write about this matter only as a lay person,
3. that somebody could regard me as a dilettante who makes an occultism of yoga and, like the charlatans, promises a panacea against countless ailments which trouble the contemporary humankind.

Let the reader forgive me that the first point of criticism – which I have heard on numerous occasions but did not want to respond to it – I will answer, in the first place, similarly with criticism – that almost all people, who were wondering about the state of my health, sought in yoga a miraculous panacea against all ailments of their bodies as well as of their souls; the ailments originating in tormenting desires of the dreamers. However, I have to take into account that also people, who are more serious and less afflicted by selfishness, may ask themselves such a question and it is only due to this reason, I suppose that it is appropriate for me to answer it.

I was, actually, a pioneer in yoga and therefore I paid the necessary toll for it. Besides this, I started practising yoga at the age of seventeen, and it was after seven years of suffering from malnutrition, which made me suffer from night blindness for four years. In this state I have, after a temporary improvement of my situation, devoted myself to asceticism. I have given up meaty food and animal fats, although I have worked ninety-two hours per week: fourteen hours daily from Monday to Friday and twenty-two hours on Saturday. Four times per day I have, according to the instructions, carried out breathing practices consisting of twenty breaths each. Gradually, I needed two hours per day for them, however, before the realisation, it was six hours per day, and so, in the last phase, only two hours were left for sleep.

For a reader familiar with yoga, it means perhaps that I began with hatha yoga. While doing it, I had no idea about the physiological laws, which hatha yoga respects by ordering the novices to carry out this yoga in secrecy, in a country where a lot of alms are given, where there is a good king ruling, not at a crossing of four roads, in a country beautiful to behold, etc. However, I started to perform yoga in Czechoslovakia, in a city and exactly at a cross-roads, in a house, where everybody was tormented by difficult and undesirable insects, which was usual in old, and perhaps somehow cursed, houses.

In the usual daily life I also had to find a constant possibility to elevate my spirit and mind, because, without this factor, my yoga wouldn't be yoga anymore. This was the toughest nut, because, nowhere did I see an example; on the contrary, the environment in which I lived was only putting obstacles and resistance in my way. To remove these obstacles, I prescribed for myself a further sixteen hours of yoga practice per week. My 'working hours' thus amounted to one hundred and fifty hours per week. Ninety-two of them I spent in an environment, where I inhaled – instead of "prana" – carbon monoxide to such an extent that my skin assumed an undefinable green-yellow-blue colour. This is convincing evidence that I performed yoga under circumstances which were not quite agreeing with the calm life that the Indian yogis in general lead. However, despite being under these conditions and performing hard physical work, I have, not even for a moment, slackened in my effort to be mentally fresh to such an extent that it enabled me to precisely and objectively observe all psychological processes taking place in my own being. The reader can believe me that such a double exertion – physical and mental – is an unbearable attack on the physical health.

No matter how it may have been, the right orientation that I have correctly identified, led by a higher sense which was perhaps inborn, brought me, in one and half years, to realisation; the realisation's effect in the physical sense was so radical that from a certain perspective I could see my body in ruins, if not permanently, then for a very long time. While the fire – as a reaction to my yogic efforts – was mercilessly burning down everything in me that could be considered to be an animal health, I, already enlightened, decided that I would abandon the asceticism relating to meaty food. I did this exactly during the days when my workload dumped, after fifty-six hour working time in the four preceding working days and after a very short rest, on my shoulders a forty-eight hour exhausting physical work without a slightest break.

In spite of this entire outer burden I, exactly during this period, got to know all – perhaps the best way to say it – high-frequency currents, which are oscillating in the body as health-maintaining factors. I learned through my own body – precisely because of the most absurd contrast of the highest mental activity and the highest physical activity, exhausting the being – precisely those subtle currents, which, in my opinion, must escape any perception of which a person, equipped with a normal power of discernment, is capable. Due to this reason, I may talk about the influence of yoga on health, without feeling the duty to show the health of a predatory animal.

In any case, I am led in yoga by goals which are different to the usual ones. I am diametrically differing in view from those who are only able to understand every discipline, which causes them some harm in their life, from the point of view of their immediate gain in terms of the desirable possessions. This is because I know that it is already this attitude that represents a flawed way of living which sins against health for so long that the recovery can also happen only slowly. In this situation, the radical allopathic interventions then appear to be only plugging the holes in a rusty pot, which is already full of holes like a sieve. In this respect, yoga affects health more as the right way of living, which heals in a totally different way. But this is going to be dealt with later.

Regarding the second point – that I can only write about health as a lay person – I would like to add the following. I am well aware that the difficulty of this issue may arouse quite a number of prejudices in the people with university education, although these people, as a rule, know very little about the functional significance of the superphysical forces, which influence people's health much more than it seems. I don't want to claim that these are not forces which are the emanations of the same body which they affect, but these forces certainly are qualitatively unknown, strange to the research conducted until now. Therefore, I will probably enter a ground which is unknown to people, but not at all a ground which is too remote to the human reason to allow a person free from prejudice to follow me. Anyway, I will talk about a way of living and not about some drastic chemical means for treatment of certain diseases.

Regarding the third point I would like to say that I have on my mind the bad reputation of the spiritual disciplines, which include yoga as one of them. Yoga, due to its character, became on one hand the domain of people who believe in miracles and on the other hand a domain of the cunning ones who are able to utilise everything for their selfish goals among people who are trusting and lack an ability of discrimination. These cunning ones promise to people, who know nothing at all about the iron law of deeds, some exercise, miracles and no renunciation. Therefore, I had a hard time deciding whether to write about health in a direct relation to yoga.

In yoga, the question of health is not the primary one. Yoga is here in order to ennoble a person both physically and spiritually and, to actually bring every suffering to an end. With regard to this, in yoga, health could be considered to be an aid or obstacle on the mystical path, although health is a very important issue for people.

When they finally understand what it is all about, they become a mere observer of the processes which are classified as the bearers of good or ill health. It will depend on their wisdom whether they decide to strive to preserve their body for suffering or focus their attention to harmonise themselves internally and by that to improve their health indirectly.

2. Issue of health

If we want to correctly answer the question of good or ill health from the point of view of yoga, we must devote our attention not only to the physical functions, but also to the orientation of consciousness. A common person turns by their consciousness to their body only when it is afflicted by some ailment. Therefore, it happens that although they feel healthy, they might already suffer from small functional disorders which are doing their destructive work in the body until such a day when they draw attention to themselves in the form of a serious functional defect. Then this person visits a doctor who will either somehow intervene, or also possibly not intervene in their health; but the person will feel relieved again, and perhaps the feeling of health will return to them, because they have changed the orientation of their consciousness that they had until now. Then they will return again to the old pathways of their march through the world, where they only continue to irritate the already impaired functions of the body which may again, after some time, turn out to be defective.

If a person acts in this way for a long time, the functional disorders in their body may turn into organic ones. It does not matter whether this or that organ is affected. The causes of organic diseases lie in the lack of functional order due to a flawed way of living. This lack of order can be transmitted to the progeny, initially as a susceptibility to dysfunctions in the organism and later directly as a congenital organic abnormality.

The true cause of defects of the body is thus of a spiritual character – however, the term 'spiritual' has to be understood as organic whose character is so subtle that it is beyond the limits of possible discernments of a person with average observational abilities. I was talking about the orientation of consciousness. What is it supposed to mean in relation to the question of health? – Even though the consciousness is, from the perspective of forces, only a phenomenon – a reflection board for perceptions and thus a reality which is indefinable from the material point of view, still it is, in principle, a force, which directs the life-giving substance and therefore it is a force bringing life to the body. A person who is with their consciousness, constantly outside of their body, emits this life-giving substance outside of their body, even though this substance is, actually, the so-called 'quintessence' which is for the human health the ultimate and most decisive factor in the field of inner functions.

From what was said above thus follows, that the consciousness as the essence of vitality should continuously, by means of focused attention, fasten on the body, in order to prevent diseases altogether. However, this requires a total change in the way of living, which is, though, going to be only taken up by someone who cares about harmonising their health. But a human is weak and therefore they would rather turn to doctors to help them plug a wound from which the life-giving force gushes; a wound that they inflicted on themselves by a life oriented only and solely towards the external world.

When already talking about awareness as an important factor in the question of health, I do not intend to claim that the awareness of the physical existence is a purely spiritual phenomenon. We can also consider it to be an effect of the chemical processes of digestion, which as its highest consequence in the living world enables a person to be in contact with the etheric principle of the cosmic space. This principle already has a spiritual nature and through assimilation with the consciousness of the being, it characterises the human being as an individual, capable of objective awareness, which I would call 'an awareness on its own' or an 'impersonal consciousness'.

If we understand this contact point of the two qualities which are similar to each other, i.e. the consciousness of a being and the etheric principle of the cosmic space, and we track down that, on this place, nourishment can take place, we have worked ourselves through all the way to a place where a human is nourished not only by the coarse food, but also by the essences of the space. These essences enliven a human in a sense that their consciousness is vigilant; those who lack these contacts have a sluggish consciousness.

By this, we have arrived all the way to the level on which a person appears as a creature living on cosmic essences. If the hyper-active and unceasing thinking wasn't here, then the assimilation process, whose origin is in the contacts of the 'consciousness on its own' with the cosmic essences, would contribute to the transfer of these essences into the body. The body then would be – besides food that it has to chemically transform even into the high spiritual modifications of forces – nourished by the essential force of the universe, which would greatly contribute to the preserving of the health status in a perfect order. However, a human thinks. They think so much that they are wasting the absorbed cosmic force of the essences and thus they depend solely on food.

Food seems to be low in etheric elements and therefore a human is continuously undernourished to an unnoticeable extent. Due to this reason, the organism then suffers from aging, i.e. from the deficit of juices necessary for its proper performance. And as the essential forces are, due to an excessive thinking, separated from the organism which can, as a consequence of this, keep running only by means of chemically transformed food, the problem of health is unsolvable by the currently existing means.

No matter how you force the organs to function properly by the unnoticeable effects of the drastic medications, you will not manage – besides an immediate chemical stimulation – to force them to satisfactorily assimilate the essential forces. Due to this reason, it is desirable that a person looks at the problem of health from a different perspective than from the perspective of the mechanical processes in the physical body. It is necessary to go beyond the materialistic view of life as a series of functions and chemical processes, because by doing that it is truly possible to detect the existence of a factor determining health. A proper nourishment on the contact point of the consciousness of the being and the cosmic essences is this factor.

Thus, exactly on the contact point of the consciousness of the being and the essential cosmic forces, a process of nourishment by the energetic essences is taking place. The vibration character of these energetic essences is analogous to the thermal life force. This force gives vitality to the body and originates in the chemical processes of the material food, transforming itself into material waste products, into the lymph and finally into the etheric substances which have a gaseous nature.

As long as a person can, through the essential functional processes, assimilate the essential forces of the cosmos, and perhaps also of the nature, the health remains in balance exactly due to the fact that the functions of this kind are in order. However, if a person casts these essential forces into space by the excessive thinking, he or she disturbs the good functioning of the essential factors and, subsequently, the organism deteriorates due to the lack of life-giving forces. This fact suggests to us that it is necessary for everyone to pay attention to the 'right way of living' in thinking.

If the thinking is correct from the point of view of the way of living, the loss by emitting the etheric substances is prevented. These substances will, irrespective of the will of the person, carry out their beneficial work for health. Only due to this reason, those people who are not very interested in anything from the external world are healthier – at least on average. On the contrary, the very mentally active people are literally digesting their own body; if they act in this way for many generations, this will show itself in a fragile physical system, susceptible to numerous disorders.

It is known that the nervous people, who can not control the inner activity which is fastening upon external things, have, in general terms, a fragile health. This is because they, due to an excessive emission of the essential life forces, take the life-giving substances away from the body, which then suffers from their deficiency. If it sometimes seems that a person is nervous due to the disharmonic functions in the body, it is only because we don't know where the real root of this state is. However, it is certain that a person suffering from nervousness can, in this state, only with great difficulty start the right way of inner living. The whole thing is then a matter of will and perseverance. We have to keep in mind that the state of inner exhaustion is very advanced in all people, and what should be suggested here is a precaution and not an allopathic intervention in a crisis.

3. Field of interest of yoga

Although it is assumed that, with the exception of hatha yoga, yoga is a discipline that a person undergoes for the purpose of achieving abstract results, it still includes in itself an interest in the body, as the yogis do not only devote themselves to a method with the help of which it is possible to detach from the body, but to a method of transformation of the body, in a higher sense all the way to its undetectability by senses.

Only people who do not understand, the problem of life and its driving forces, at all, are trying to detach themselves from the body. In fact, they want to escape from a critical situation into which they have got themselves by their actions, and they do not understand that the entire question of the possible detachment or firm attachment will be resolved by their life drive itself. No matter how they curse the world, they will still not be able to detach from it, because they do not have a good alternative ideal in front of their eyes, but only a breathless abyss. And thus, wasting their forces, they try to no effect and the blackness of their pessimism is deepening further.

Such a yoga, which approves unhealthy detaching efforts, is a teaching of dreamers, of people who do not understand the subject and, perhaps, also of those who have mercenary goals, because, as far as I know yoga, I have never come across an instruction in it that those who succumbed to Weltschmerz, should spiritually detach from their body. I have always found in it, instructions about such way of evident awareness that prevents a dreamy wandering of mind and, as a consequence, an inner detachment from the concrete life.

Based on that and on the experience that I have gained by a practical effort, I can claim that the true ideal of yoga is to contain the body into the consciousness as an object requiring processing. By that we have already automatically arrived at the psychological operations, which must necessarily influence also the body.

The body is the first object which the yogi contains into their consciousness, gets hold of it by the consciousness, and influences it. It is exactly from this natural base that they proceed towards further stages of the yogic transformation. With regard to that, they do not give up the realistic thinking, even though, in the subsequent stages of the progressive transformation, their thinking departs considerably from the thinking of other people. This means, that no matter what opinion the people uninformed about yoga might have on a yogi of higher stages, it remains true that a real yogi stays on the ground of reality, because not even for a moment do they lose this world from their evidence, even if they sublimate it in a subjective sense by an analytical observation.

By this, I would like to say that yoga is a teaching which, based on the experience of its adepts, sets a seemingly impossible goal, i.e. a real transformation of that which we consider a material world, into that which we consider a spiritual world. Fulfilment of this seemingly impossible task is seen by yoga in the relative nature of reality. Experience teaches the yogis that that which seems to be a firm matter changes its appearance already face to face with the power of a mere seeing through it, at least in a subjective sense. In the face of this seeing through, the firm matter transforms into mere shadows that have exactly the value which we attribute to them by the power of the possible seeing through. This alternative opens to yogis such prospects which are undreamt-of for the common people. The entire material world, which is seemingly so firm and undestructible by the spiritual means, suddenly appears here as a set of conditional phenomena, into which a person can easily intervene by the states of their awareness. They can see that they can learn exactly from the state of awareness that the matter can, from a subjective point of view, disintegrate into moving shadows, whose previous glitter and charming forms, which negatively suggestively influence an unenlightened person, turn into a mere greyness, which is only significant from the point of view of forces. For as long as the shadows of the real phenomena of the physical world don't lose all their influence, they can incite reactions in an organism, which has not been permeated by the light of consciousness. These reactions are translated by a person, who is bound by desires for emotional experiences, into the categories of feelings.

Apart from the categories of feelings, there is no real world which would be detectable by touch. No matter how we may argue about the objective nature of the world, its subjective significance remains a fact. For, in cases where the question of subjective relationships is resolved, the world assumes a totally different form than the one it shows to those who have excessively attached themselves to the seeming individuality of their own physical existence. These people must certainly identically perceive the suggestive influence of the cosmic Lanterna Magica, because the list of the possible so-called 'material phenomena' is finite. However, beyond the borderline of these people's conscious reaches there can exist those people for whom the world is a mere shadow play of a cosmic magician, who is transcendental and impossible to be grasped by the limited perceptivity of human senses and in whose body an average person lives, thinks, feels, reasons, etc.

With regard to this state of things, we must understand yoga as a teaching which reaches the limits usually reserved for the fumbling hands of the highest level physics. Although it does not use technical aids to obtain objective knowledge of the relative nature of reality, still it solves this problem satisfactorily by the systematic guiding of a person towards power over the states of their own living and consciousness. It is precisely in the states of consciousness, where every person can obtain the knowledge of the relative character of the entire created world. Moreover, yoga will then bring a person to the possibilities of an effective operation with the states of consciousness; this in reality manifests itself as a good subjective solution of the problem of suffering, which is connected to ignorance, amplified by subjectivism.

Every problem can be resolved by operations with the states of consciousness. Although in the first phase only subjectively, still a person can, already at this point, escape from the depressing power of circumstances and that is a precondition of success on the path of slow and systematic effort for the physical transformation.

Before a person can set out on a journey of a systematic transformation of their physical being, they must arrive at the possibilities of operation with the states of consciousness, because only when they are able to perform these operations with the states of consciousness, they can, by their consciousness, take hold of the material which is spiritual, or subtle above average, and which they will be able to use for a gradual transformation of their body. The journey is certainly long. However, the horror from a progressive degeneration in the form of a progressive compaction of the structure of the beings' bodies force the person who is gaining knowledge to avert this tendency by maintaining a high state of consciousness. The high state of consciousness will then set in motion a wheel of transformation of the material structure, of the being into a structure which is imperceptible by senses, or, in other words, spiritual.

By this finding, a person suddenly realises that the state of the material nature is an automatic result of the state of consciousness, which a person or a formation has accepted as a state that doesn't force them into inner tension. From this, also an opinion on reality stems. A weakling, who does not have even the slightest influence on the states of their consciousness, is always convinced – and will also defend this conviction – that the nature is an objective phenomenon; this follows exactly from their lack of ability to influence their states of consciousness. However, those who have, in the respective stage of their inner effort, obtained an influence on the states of their consciousness, realise that the character of the nature is a resultant of the states of consciousness. That, until now uninfluenceable, nature suddenly begins, under the pressures of the deliberate states of consciousness, to transform, to soften, to sublimate, etc., so it assures a person outright that they have just arrived at a path of a great transformation, ending, on one hand, in the incorruptibility of the body, and, on the other hand, in a transformation of his or her form into a spiritual form.

It is here that we are finally, consciously standing on the field of interest of yoga. In the first phase, the point is to obtain influence on the states of consciousness, and in the second phase, the point is a structural transformation of the body. However, by this, it is said that the essence of yoga is real and the state of health is a by-product. Health here finds itself under the favourable states of consciousness and, as a consequence of that, under the favourable objective influences, which strengthen and harmonise it. A yogi thus does not seek a path to the most favourable personal conditions in their current state, as it is believed by the ignorant ones. A yogi seeks a universal solution which will manifest itself favourably, including in the partial states, if a person will not commit mistakes on such a little known path, which they are walking, after they have entered the path of yoga.

4. Directing and effects of the essences

The yogic effort does not begin with manipulations with the states of consciousness. A beginner, who is used to fastening their attention only on something external, can, also in yoga, begin with an intentional and deliberate focusing of their attention on their own body, or, possibly on inner things, contrary to outer factors, captivating their attention. The choice of an object on which a beginner in yoga is supposed to focus their attention, is thus important.

From a psychological point of view, no other object can be chosen with success except something of one's own. Every external object can arouse cravings, and therefore the external objects are ruled out. Only one's own body is an object which cannot offer anything interesting enough to arouse a craving. Thus, the body is the best and most suitable object which can be a support for a person on the path of yoga. The yogic path is, in its first phase, a path to inner harmony and inner consolidation.

Therefore, if the point is, in the first place, to focus the attention in order to suppress wandering of the mind, it is not just a simple act of observation. A person practising attention can perhaps discover that, by the act of observation, they cast their inner force towards the observed object; this discovery is based on fact.

Those who practice observation and, in parallel, gradually increase the intensity of their attention, really cast the essential life force on that which is being attentively observed. If the observed object is their own body, then this force is being actually cast on the body. The body is then being literally overwhelmed with this essential force; then it only depends on the quality of this essential force – which is given by the effects and reactions of thinking – what its characteristic influence will be like.

It is a law that a person who is internally unbalanced casts on the body, if and when they concentrate, arousing vibrations of the essential force. Therefore it was established for those who are practising such yoga which is worth this name, to become internally balanced.

This means that a person who wants to practise for the purpose of attaining the goals of yoga, must, beforehand, necessarily become internally balanced to such an extent to, by a concentrated attention, cast into the body harmonious vibrations; only such vibrations can have a positive effect on health.

Especially an internally balanced yogi, who did not reach far enough to be continuous internally focused on a quality which is bringing about the transformation, has to, necessarily, pay attention to have a positive influence on the observed object, because these reactions will later appear in their natural inner, and by that also physical, state. This means that the yogic efforts constitute intensification of the natural influences of moods and due to this reason a person must take care of the inner balance.

Thus, those who concentrate are casting the essential force – which is identical with thinking, or used by thinking – towards the object of their observation. And according to the mood state, this force has a favourable or an unfavourable effect, both in the inner state itself as well as in the object which is struck by it. In other words: the intensification of emission of this force can increase the inner arousal, and by this an unfortunate inner state is brought about. The body can be excited likewise, if we affect it by an excited concentrating mind.

Thus, if one wants to achieve desirable effects, they must, in the first place, strive for obtaining inner balance and only then they can suppose that they will, by their effort for concentration, favourably influence also their body. These are the technical conditions of the influences of concentration on health.

The entire lower stage of yoga should be imagined in a way that by concentration a person casts essences, as a material, on the object of concentration; this material suffuses the object of concentration and according to the characteristics of this material it imparts to the object of concentration either harmonious or disturbing forces, or vibrations. The object of concentration reacts to these vibrations in such a way that its basic character changes, both emotionally, as well as structurally. That would be, after all, easily understood if the force in question could be recorded by physical devices.

However, from the subjective point of view, it doesn't matter whether this force is known or unknown from the perspective of physics. The fact remains that a sufficient intensity of concentration provides a person always with the same experience. For, from their feeling states one may conclude that by means of concentration, "suffusion" of the object of concentration occurs – by a force whose quality a person recognises on their own body according to direct effects and reactions.

This experience leads to the knowledge of additional potentialities following from the energetic effect of this kind of "natural radiation". A person, aware of this fact, clearly recognises that the "flow" of the psychological material, accelerated by concentration – I call this flow of the psychological material an essential force which a person can take hold of by their very consciousness – is an effective agent from which one can expect a commonly incomprehensible result – a transformation of the material which became an object of the intentional observation and concentration of the person. And by this we have arrived at the influence of yoga on health. A person, who has understood the significance of concentration from the point of view of a psychological intensification of the flow of mental energies towards the object of concentration, will already begin to correctly and economically use the essential energy. Therefore they will, in inner peace and tranquillity, think of their own body, as a person who wants to, completely intentionally, make it present in his or her consciousness. When someone really succeeds in making their body present in their consciousness perfectly, they will affect the body by a harmonising force which gradually eliminates from it all functional irregularities and by that also disorders, manifesting themselves as health indispositions.

The functional harmonisation of the body is thus a by-product of the efforts to attain yoga. However, the by-product of these efforts is a matter-of-course. It depends only on a person, whether they will understand that this is the first level of the universal physical recovery, which can only be a product of a long-term effort. The organic abnormalities only slowly subside under the curative pressures of the harmonious effects of the inner forces which have just become active.

It is thus not possible to expect some miracle, or magical trick, which at once and against all natural laws brings about the desirable balance of the physical functions and states. What is needed is to create the right conditions for this balance to be able to develop at all. It doesn't matter whether a person created these conditions consciously or unintentionally. Possibly, an unjustified conviction can arise here that the faith in God, a suppositious devotion, a very positive relationship to yoga and other similar things affect so favourably the external life of the ignorant person.

Miracles really do not happen. Either the necessary conditions are fulfilled – consciously or unintentionally – and the result comes about, or the necessary conditions are not fulfilled and then the result does not come about. It is necessary to mention this so that no one should think that some Lord God takes care of everything and that especially to me or to you he grants his mercy, manifesting itself in good quick results, clearly reflecting themselves in our life.

A good health is thus only a by-product of the yogic effort. Whether the person striving for yoga wants it or not, they always have to use the psychological material which I have termed 'the essential force'. Then it only matters, which stand they are going to take on the desirable self-discipline which requires them to maintain an inner harmony. Specifically, with regard to this inner harmony or disharmony, one can improve or worsen their health by yogic efforts. In view of my own experience regarding this matter, I recommend everyone to be very particular about this harmony and by that to also strengthen their body by their yogic efforts, because the intrusive influences which become stronger due to the striving for yoga in a precise proportion to the inner disharmony, if a person doesn't pay attention to it, will at the end prove to them that they are walking an undesirable path. In any case, these intrusive influences have an unfavourable effect also in the later stages of the inner development, which is, in yoga, taken into consideration above all. A disturbed functional harmony more or less – according to the extent of disorders – disallows a person to realise such a qualitatively high concentration which would provide them with the necessary understanding of the highest state – the state of being aware of oneself without supports and limitations, which is the goal of the yogis.

5. Issue of nourishment

In the mechanical physical happening of the bodies of beings, the whole issue of nourishment seems to be solved by a spontaneous assimilation of the solid substances, which serve the body as food, and also by absorption of the elements of air. However, this is only the coarse nutrition, which can never suffice to maintain all manifestations of life in the body. Yet, the entire issue of nourishment appears to be solved only by this process, because all other factors serving the nourishment of creatures are not known. However, those who successfully practice concentrations according to precise instructions of yoga soon realise that they are, by concentration, gaining powers which they would never gain without following the yogic instructions.

If we thus leave aside the normal process of nourishment, and only pay attention to the effects of operations with the states of consciousness, we will find out very quickly that by certain states of consciousness we absorb many certain life-giving substances. Their subtle quality does not bother the body with a feeling of satiation, however, the effect is certainly detectable in the increase of vitality, the power of mind, the ability to fix the will etc. This knowledge enables us to draw a dividing line between the two kinds of nourishment: namely, the material nourishment and the parapsychological nourishment.

I have already said that the metabolism of food creates psychological factors as well. However, this does not mean that these factors can be maintained in operation exclusively by means of the chemical processes which process the coarse substances of our usual food. For, in yoga, a person learns that a large proportion of the nourishment, which is providing the body with the most subtle substances, comes into existence due to the respective states of awareness, i.e. by an action leading to contacts of the self-awareness with the cosmic substances which have the same, or at least similar, nature.

By awareness, a person makes the essential cosmic substances present in their consciousness. These substances, due to the existence of selfness as a state of consciousness, get into the vibration field centralised by the selfness. This vibration field is the spiritual beingness of a person, and this beingness mechanically processes the above mentioned substances, bound by awareness.

The spiritual principle of the essential element, which was until now representing the cosmic force, cannot retain its character any longer. As soon as it is bound by the power of awareness and pulled down by the gravitational force of selfness, it qualitatively deteriorates so much that it becomes a spiritual factor. This factor can no longer be absorbed by the body, because it is similar to the life force whose relationship to the body is the same as the relationship of the physical feeling to the consciousness.

From this point of view, the issue of nourishment is an issue of reactions which we can consider to enable the organs to absorb, in the critical states, substances which are qualitatively rather remote from them. However, precisely the action of self-awareness on the physical level enables these absorptions and the more (and more continuously) a person can be aware of themselves on the physical level, the more nutrients of the higher kind they can obtain for their body. Then the body will be finally also relieved, as it is not able to, despite a relatively perfect apparatus for metabolism, create those substances which grant a person inner liveliness and enlightenment.

By this I want to say that a person who is not able to obtain, by adequate contacts of consciousness, the nutrients for vitality, can have only a more sluggish consciousness and cognitive power than a yogi, who is able to obtain these nutrients by the correct conscious contacts. Apart from that, we are arriving by this at the question of decreasing the dependence of conscious living on a body, because living is a phenomenon, which has a much more dynamic nature than whichever organ of the body can demonstrate.

The nature of life is superphysical. Therefore, its disappearance after the physical death does not mean the end of existence at all. Life was not lost, only the ties between life and body were severed. Yogis have known this very well and therefore the goal of yoga is nothing less than to make life independent of the body earlier than the physical death occurs. The knowledge of the yogis, that the consciousness can also have as its support something other than exactly the body to which their consciousness has been bound until now, clearly confirms this idea of yoga.

It is exactly the supports for the consciousness which determine the entire tragedy or great happiness in relation to death. If a person has chosen, as a result of their belief which they obtained by birth, their body as the net in which they would live, they have to content themselves with the empirical phenomena as the ultimate reality for them. However, many people try to get further. In this case their net will be the infinity in time and manifestations; by that, they will, though, sooner or later, free their consciousness from the empirical reality and therefore will be able to live also without the body. What does it matter that one day it will be possible to find out that life is no longer present in their bodies? If the personal consciousness can, at all, manifest itself in a certain net whose threads are its support, then these people will, by their discipline before death, create a net which is superphysical and which can be equally suitable for their life – just as the body seems to be a suitable net. In that case it is a subjective matter, however, it does not seem that those, who have forgotten the small net called "body" and begun to live in a net called "universe", will care about the fact that the physical death marks their objective end.

The issue of nourishment is thus, in the first place, a problem of contacts – either the contacts of the physical organs with the solid substances serving as food, or the contacts of the power of awareness with the cosmic essences. Even though the contacts of physical organs with solid substances seem to be primary, still I know from my experience that they are secondary. This is because without consciousness, nothing can exist that could be called a living being. If it so happened that a person contented themselves with consciousness as a secondary existence, still it is only a matter of their choice or preference, weakness and ignorance. This will clearly manifest itself in the practice of yoga. Even though yoga begins with making the body present in the consciousness, yet this state of things later becomes natural and then the next long stage of self-discipline comes, which is called operation with the states of consciousness; this self-discipline gives the experience that the possibilities of awareness outside the body are inexhaustible.

What does the objective reality matter here? After all, it is as relative as that which we denote by the word subjective – that subjective which always and definitively decides the question of the reality as a whole. From this point of view I must consider the objective reality as a reality which is only conditionally conclusive and everyone should pay attention to stop making a 'Lord God' of it and begin to observe and examine, from an impersonal point of view, all happening of which they are a victim. It is only under these circumstances that they will realise that the objective reality is a small part of the universal reality which is waiting to be discovered in the future. And the scientists, caught in the net of prejudice, are arguing for their seeming truth, detected by the technical instruments!

6. The significance of breath

The gaseous nature of air is, to a certain extent, similar to the nature of the substance which the living organisms fix by their awareness. Due to this, the relationships among these substances have the greatest significance in the creating of an electromagnetic phenomenon which manifests itself in contact with the body as the body's vitality. The only important thing here is that at the contact place of the gaseous or even higher substances on one hand and the physical substances on the other hand, these contacts are a result of the karmic predispositions rather than of the conscious processes. Due to this reason, the creatures live under the law of predestination and the entire process of living is only a mechanical phenomenon.

The yogis, who, according to the instructions of the yogic teaching, undergo the discipline of concentration and conscious breathing, actually broaden their awareness up to the place of touch of the gaseous and even higher substances with the physical substances.

Although we can not think that, especially at the beginning of the yogic practice, the yogi can carry out the enlivening actions by acts of correct concentration, still we can be sure that the same is being carried out to a lesser extent by the yogic breathing. The instruction which prescribes that a yogi should, besides keeping themselves in the inner calmness, carry out in a precise proportion to this moral effort also the breathing practices, talks about an even breathing in and breathing out, which is supposed to be practised consciously. If the yogi carries out this prescribed breathing in and breathing out, while being aware of this activity and their body in general, they are creating, precisely by the vigilance of consciousness and by a focused attention, a link between the body and the higher factors whose most coarse representative is breath.

Thus, if someone carries out the breathing practices according to the instructions of yoga and, at the same time, they are clearly aware of what they are doing in that moment, they have connected two disparate factors – the body and the super-gaseous factors. By this they are slowly working themselves through to, one day, being able to take hold of the control over their body by a conscious maintaining of its vitality on a desirable level. This whole thing takes place in stages. In the initial stages of this effort, the yogi feels that their life potential increases. Yoga refuses the character of this life potential, because it works on the physical and vital level. Therefore, the yogi should continue further, until they learn how to bind the higher factors which allow performing operations with vitality on the causal level.

According to yoga, a yogi should, by conscious breathing, arrive at a stage where they will increase their level of vitality with a character of indifference, much rather than strengthening the vitality with animal manifestations. Admittedly, a yogi also passes through the states of a refreshing of the vitality which is crudely manifesting itself, but because they are consciously, evenly breathing in and breathing out, they are becoming anchored in the field of life manifesting itself in an increase of the vitality, which leads them to behave indifferently to the external world. This subsequently happens through the correct states of concentration. From this it is obvious that, when taking the ideal sequence of steps in yoga, a person cannot avoid the enlivening power of the conscious breathing in and breathing out. This also means that a correctly performed yoga has a favourable influence on the increase in vitality, which is, after all, an indirect manifestation of a good health. From the physiological point of view, the most interesting thing, can be that the form of breathing in question, is such a form, during which a person is internally steady, and their mind non-wandering.

This is, though, not that interesting from the point of view of knowledge which is important in yoga, because exactly the etheric substances in breath actually give rise to impulses which set the right direction and effect for the lymph. It is exactly by the correct or incorrect breathing that these etheric substances are set in rhythm or in chaotic movement; the results are thus self-evident. The guidelines for maintaining good health are therefore very simple. People should be encouraged to practise an even, deeper and conscious breathing in and breathing out, whose good result will manifest itself very markedly if they accompany this rhythmic breathing by being aware of the body. Only in this way is it possible to create the desirable link between the disparate factors of the body and life and this can be, after all, considered to be the strengthening of life in the body.

However, yoga has higher goals in view. Although for a common person it is incomprehensible that someone could wish for more than good health and perhaps a good destiny connected with it, still there are people who want to get even higher, all the way to the place where they could influence the overwhelming forces of inborn animality. In any case, it all depends on understanding. Of what use is it to be a strongly vital person when the destiny, which is created by the interaction of the individual beings, can, in the end, dictate to a person everything that is subsequently reflected in their emotional and conscious states? The enlivening influence of the coarse breathing is, only due to this reason, considered to be secondary in yoga, no matter how favourable it may be and yoga aims at the concentration-related operations, which have a higher influence.

A yogi, who has already passed through the entire phase of correct breathing in and breathing out, practises concentration. And because they are, after some period of training, able to take hold of the life force, they manipulate with this very force by their concentration. They register the life force by their consciousness and project it into the material of their body, which they enliven in this way and stimulate it by the higher substances than those that can be provided by breath.

That, which a person takes hold of, by concentration and which they have just identified as a life force, has a very high quality. In this way, they are taking hold of an enlivening force, which increases the pulsation of vitality, but it doesn't increase the animal vitality, if the person works correctly. Therefore the fixation of this, already spiritual, breath, performed by concentration, is more desirable and better from the universal point of view. A yogi, who in this way takes hold of the essential element, which is the spiritual content of breath, and who succeeds in performing this concentration in a rhythm, performs actually breathing in and breathing out on the level of the consciousness and will; this is called pranayama, or, actually, spiritual breathing.

By means of the spiritual breathing, the whole body of the yogi gets into rhythm and if the yogi introduces into the body, by means of awareness, nothing but the life force, which they have understood, they are removing from the body the stagnating waste substances, and by that they are purifying their body by the pure, vital force, of the cosmos.

A body, which a person is not able to permeate by their awareness that contains the life force of cosmos, always retains in it the essential waste products, which are the cause of the lack of functional order. Therefore, the yogi who – with their consciousness full of vitality – permeates their body well, enlivens it to a great extent, because they are eliminating by this, all essential waste products produced in the body. Therefore, yoga even in this higher stage also benefits health, because the entire yogi's body bathes in an essential substance of the pure awareness.

From the subjective point of view, matter is a mere possibility of perceptions and this is particularly true about the body. In the yogic discipline, where it is prescribed that a person should contain their whole being into their consciousness, all the material of one's own being gets into the enlivening force of the pure awareness, because the goal of yoga is for a person to turn their entire being into consciousness. Therefore one passes through stages, which mean recovery for the body, but they are really only stages. The yogi will only find a harbour in the overall transformation of the being. It can be admitted from the subjective point of view, because, if we take into consideration that matter is a special case of awareness, or the substance periphery of awareness, then, specifically, the long history had brought beings as special states of consciousness into the net of active waste products. This net became a body for the consciousness. If a yogi attempts to permeate the matter of their body by their consciousness, this is exactly the opposite process than the usual one – the so-called evolutional; this process makes the matter of the body gradually acceptable for the consciousness. If a yogi once succeeds to fully contain the matter of their body in their consciousness, the waste products, whose excess is the cause of the physical death, will never reach such a high degree that enables death to occur. This is the cause of yogi's immortality.

The immortality depends on the correct absorption of the entire being into one's own consciousness. However, it is not easy to reach this state. Nevertheless, a person, who works on the perfecting of self-awareness, eliminates the gaps of non-awareness much earlier and the continuity of the moments of awareness helps them to remove death at least at the level of consciousness, because, it is a fact that death does not arrive by a gradual disappearing of the consciousness from the body, but by the disappearing of the consciousness in a crisis. This is the reason why the yogis strive that the state of things, would not force the disappearance of consciousness upon them. The means are precisely the removal of gaps – the gaps of non-awareness.

A person, who removes these gaps, fastens their consciousness in the being in such a way that the crisis cannot mean the expulsion of consciousness from the body, but only its departure. Such a person has attained immortality at least at the level of consciousness. And once they, in the course of centuries, fill their body with light by its perfect permeation by substances which one always binds by awareness – to such an extent that the essential waste products will not be able to accumulate in it – their body will change to such a degree that it will lose the character of a sensorily discernible formation. And then the yogi disappears into nature as a spiritual formation, on the level, where the law of degeneration, which operates on the basis of accumulation of various waste products in the body, no longer applies.

7. Hatha yoga

Although yoga means creating evident contacts at the mental level of consciousness, hatha yoga is a yoga, which creates conditions for these evident contacts through the physiological conditions. In hatha yoga, the aim is, by the symbolic positions of the body, to create pressures on certain neuro-psychological centres, in which there are bound energies. These energies are released by these pressures. The symbolic positions of the body are, moreover, supposed to cause this energy, as a vehicle for the personal consciousness, to bring the self-aware person to the connection with the essential elements of the cosmos on the level of their daily consciousness.

The symbolic positions in the practice of hatha yoga thus mean conditions, which harmonise, in the first place the body, secondly the streaming life force and thirdly, they bring the consciousness into the state of freeing.

If we are not particularly interested in the freeing of consciousness from the solidifying and health disorders causing contacts, our attention can be certainly captured by further results, which, regardless of the tendencies of consciousness, harmonise the body and its other factors which strengthen or weaken health. This question is, however, independent of the special conditions which are crucial in hatha yoga. However, regarding the general influence of hatha yogic exercises on health, it can be said that all positions, breathing practices and other practices have always a good effect on health, if a person keeps in mind the basic rules of hatha yoga.

These basic rules are: a calm mind and emotional inexcitability, exercising the positions in the greatest possible inner calmness, silent and even breathing in and breathing out filling the lungs to the extent, on the one hand, to avoid overstretching, but, on the other hand, to exceed the limit of the normal filling of the lungs. Under these circumstances the maintained emotional and mental inexcitability will have a very beneficial effect on health.

In hatha yoga, one works on achieving the desirable results very purposely. However, since there are no good and genuine teachers of hatha yoga, especially in the western countries, one cannot count on a sure result, as in a school. Exercise according to the instructions of hatha yoga, carried out under the above mentioned conditions, will have a beneficial effect on health in a somewhat random manner, however, also in this case, one may count on a high certainty that it will happen.

When exercising according to the instructions of hatha yoga, under the guidance of an experienced leader, those positions are chosen which immediately release the life energy bound in organs. Since, at the same time, a certain simultaneous self-discipline in thinking is prescribed, this released energy cannot be wasted. Under these circumstances it begins to somehow circle in the body, and it harmonises energetically and with a great pressure, all functions of the body.

A hatha yogi, who works under the guidance of an experienced leader, forces the life energy to circle in the body in such a way that it creates from the body an electromagnetic field in which no functional disorder can occur. And the force circling in this way increases also the inner potency of the yogi; then the inner force strengthens the body and the enclosed and circling inner force in the body strengthens the potential, and so, a mutual benefit is achieved by the hatha yogic exercise.

If the life force, released from the organs, is forced to circle in the body for a sufficiently long time, without the yogi letting themselves be pulled down to re-enter into relations with the sensory world – this is something against which one is, in the beginning of the hatha yogic practice, strongly warned – this force will be felt as a force which is already transformed. This force gives the yogis higher life experiences by elevating their consciousness into the superphysical spheres. A yogi, who has attained this level, obtains such an intensive discernment power that they can see also that which remains invisible to other people. Gradually, also other senses develop in them, and so, even before they arrive at the physical transformation, they will move their consciousness into the higher spheres than is the level which a person can achieve by the usual ability of perception. All this occurs without the qualitative base of the perceptions and discernments being changed. Then the yogi deduces from this that the invisible world, whose existence is refused only because it is outside of the discernment abilities of the common people, is a world which is as real as the material world. It only lies higher than is the discernment base belonging to the human senses.

8. Conclusion

Yoga, which represents attaining unity of the personal consciousness with the universal consciousness, thus means a methodical effort based on real states and processes in the psyche which predominantly influence the body and only then the states of consciousness. The yogi, who adheres to the basic rules of yoga, which are: inner balance, tranquil mind and 'thinking in goodness' in general, will soon feel its good influence on health, initially in the functional sense and, in a more advanced stage, also in the organic sense. The only exception can be a resolute will to realise the cosmic consciousness. In that case a person becomes a mystic, who wants to terminate the sorrowful inner states, often at the expense of the harmonising influences on health, because they sense or recognise that the highest realisation terminates every suffering, including the suffering coming from an ill health.

Yoga and mental health

Human beings are organically equipped with the abilities of inner life – with an ability to be aware of the external world, with an ability to remember and with an ability to think within these dimensions, i.e. to think logically and to draw conclusions from. The first two inner abilities are bound by inborn predispositions; the third can be developed further, if a person is interested.

Most people live in such a way that they are primarily interested in obtaining as many sensory perceptions and impressions as possible and, via them, in "rippling" feelings, from which they demand the experiencing of pleasurable feelings. As a consequence of that, they have no regard for the necessity of conscious thinking, which is very important for mental health; only conscious thinking can become logical. They thus draw from the innate mental capacity of thinking, and thinking becomes reflexive, because it isn't under control. Such thinking only becomes active by means of stimuli coming from sensory perceptions; by this, it is subject to gradual degeneration and pathological states.

Prognostically speaking, every person who does not care about the development of conscious thinking is thus exposed to mental degeneration. A result of this is the senile mental deficiency and mental delusions of old age.

It is very difficult to determine an absolutely certain prognosis of the mental development of people who think reflexively. Conscious thinking cannot be easily distinguished from reflexive thinking, nor isolated from it. Even a mentally alert and able youth can suffer from reflexive thinking and therefore also from mental inactivity, if it is understood as passivity or laziness. It could be said that the only preventive measure against this state is a continuous effort to learn about everything. The sphere of interests of each individual has indeed a crucial role in this. Based on innate inner predispositions, these interests mostly lie in sensory pleasures, in technology or natural sciences as they are commonly understood. In such a case, a person mentally leaves themselves and then, even if thinking becomes logical, there is no guarantee that they will avoid mental disorders which occur in old age. For, by this, a person becomes a so-called 'mental type', whose pathological prospects are only different from the prospects to which those mentally inactive, lazy types without interests, are exposed; however, with an exception of those who are desirous of sensory experiences.

From the perspective of yoga, all potential evil leading towards mental disintegration or decline in old age comes from the fact that people are fascinated by the external world and have succumbed to the demands for sensory sensations. For, because of this, they are actually mentally 'stepping out' of themselves, or abandoning themselves in their own mind and by this senselessly throwing themselves into the external life; this in fact means a total absorption of their psyche into their external environment. Therefore, there is no remedy which would remove or eliminate the prospect of mental decline and it will never be discovered. An unconstrained interest in the external world develops the tendency of potentials, which constitute the inner life of a person, towards somewhere out of the sphere reserved for the idea of their 'I'. A person moves more and more away from their own self and, finally, they become dependent only on reactions arising between themselves and the external world. The worst fact about it then is, that the cause of evil is not sought in this state. On the contrary, an opinion is promoted that, only a further intensification of interest in the external world is the condition for mental and inner development and development of intelligence, whilst lack of interest in the external world is a condition for development, or at least further perpetuation, of mental backwardness – a symbol of the old times of a non-civilised and technologically undeveloped world.

Provided that we are not prejudiced against the old times and we weigh their positive and negative sides fairly and responsibly, we will always find there one immensely significant fact: that there occurred philosophers and sages, whom we have never surpassed in the field of philosophical knowledge. If we carefully track the path from these philosophers and sages all the way to the emergence of technology and "wisdom" of our age, we can easily discover the fact that they were the beginning of technological and social emancipation. However, I am speaking here from the standpoint of practical psychology and point of view of heredity. For, if a mental type of an intelligent person can beget a mentally backward child, or even one with profound mental retardation, a sage, whose knowledge springs from the knowledge of themselves, can never beget such a child. As, this knowledge can perfectly discriminate between the various phenomena of the inner and external world; it cannot happen that this discriminating ability would leave a mark of a profound mental retardation, or even mental backwardness, on its progeny. We must not forget that the mental type of an intelligent person discharges themselves exactly by their orientation into the external world, which can overrun their discriminating ability by the quality of phenomena and the phenomena will fuse into a chaotic conglomeration of unintelligible ideas.

I am not talking here about usual cases, but about those less numerous, as a human being is complicated. Many introvert and extravert tendencies often combine in it. The prospects of human mental health vary accordingly; however, orientation into the external world increases the unfavourable prospects.

In this situation, an interest in strengthening or in preservation of mental health can awaken in us, but the paths toward this are non-traditional. While medicine is trying to find help in a certain way of living and medications, yoga found this way in inner orientation. In its instructions, it is stated that we are supposed to withdraw attention from the external world and devote all our interest to our being, beginning with the body: the body, and gradually our whole being is supposed to become the object of our exploration; we get to this exploration automatically, by thinking only of the body.

Let us, however, take it step by step.

Withdrawing the attention from the world is a part of pratyahara. Attention itself might not mean anything, but because humans, as a rule, don't eliminate the sensory perceptions, the senses are working, and their functioning is increased when attention is fastened on the world. Pratyahara in this case means to undermine the usual functioning of the senses by a continuous effort. Whilst eyesight transmits a perception and then, in the next phase, an impression, this should be prevented in a way that, by the strength of will we make visual perception colourless. In other words, we are supposed to withdraw the eyesight from the seen objects which would otherwise catch our attention. Likewise, hearing should be prevented from transmitting impressions, then smell, taste and touch. When we thus put perceptions to silence, so that the sensory impressions do not take place, we must not allow ourselves to become mentally slack. In other words, we must continuously give our full attention, as if we are to control perceptions and destroy impressions. And this is exactly pratyahara in the very sense of this word. Its result is to become able to direct attention.

The attention, however, must not be directed at external things, but only to one's own body and its activities. We are supposed to be aware that we have a body in the sense of being continuously well aware of it – at times in the form of its contours, at other times in the form of a physical feeling of oneself. Besides this, we are supposed to be aware of all its actions in the present moment. This means that we are supposed to be aware that we are just walking, standing, sitting, eating food, watching something, etc. In short, we are supposed to be aware of both the body and its present activity.

We must not prematurely end this effort to obtain self-control. We must get all the way to the point when this observing of the body and its activities becomes to us as routine as was our observing of the external world until now. Only then, the mind will calm down. It will cease to wander and be active in reflexes. In other words, it will start to be able or capable of self-knowledge, as it was always understood in the sense of saying "Know thyself".

Knowing oneself is thus related to an introversive tendency of the mind. However, at the same time, a person mustn't be indolent; on the contrary, they must be acute and potentially capable of adequate human reactions. In this case, it is surely difficult to direct the mind in a centripetal way, but when we start to believe the statement that only in this way we are removing countless subjective difficulties from which we still suffer, we will obtain sufficient strength to reorientate our thinking.

By training, the mind will submit to the will, like the body of a soldier to physical discipline. It only takes to persevere. It takes the renouncing of interests in the world as an environment capable of gratifying our cravings and to continually force the mind not to run away from the body towards that which gratifies the sensory cravings. After a certain time, the mind will lose its tendencies to fasten itself upon these things. It will submit and become able to subordinate itself to our will, when we want to work with it, and change the capacity of the natural awareness. It is this natural capacity of awareness, which is the crucial factor for preservation of mental health, and even for the increase of the intelligence quotient.

Thus, when the mind becomes tractable through the practice of pratyahara and a continuous observation of the body, then the broadening of the capacity of awareness will serve us in the strengthening of mental health. For, let us not forget that psychoses are mostly accompanied by the situation in which the mind is stuck in some fixed idea about reality; if a person isn't aware of this fixation, a psychosis of a certain type arises out of it. Conscious broadening of the capacity of awareness will bring the mind to a three-dimensional view of the external world. This three-dimensionality – the capacity of awareness – is sufficient for preventing this fixation of the mind and to make the mind capable of factual thinking.

By pointing to the necessity of factual thinking, by asking a person to emotionally abstract themselves from the seen as well as otherwise sensorily perceivable things of the external world, yoga shows the way to a strengthening of the mental health, even though psychologists may think differently about yoga, based on insufficient or inaccurate information. Precisely on the basis of this inaccurate information, it appears that yoga aims only to bring new categories of feelings into the lives of people. This is how yoga is explained by those who don't know, that yoga means a continuous struggle for confrontation of the external world with a well abstracted daily consciousness, but they believe that it serves to gratify the sensory desires.

When we exclude these flawed beliefs about the mission of yoga, then, even if we don't admit that it provides a possibility to break a way through for the consciousness to transcendence with a retained ability to successfully orientate oneself in it, we may perhaps still understand that it can have a favourable influence on the mental health. This follows from the psychological laws – while a person is able to perceive everything clearly, in a three-dimensional way, they cannot fall into any of the psychoses. In yoga, this alternative of inner tendencies is manifested by an insistence on such a thorough abstraction of a person from the external world that their emotionality must drown in thinking and reason. These two mental abilities manage to observe the external world clearly, but never gain emotional sensations from it, sensations which personalise a human being so powerfully and make them narrow-minded. Already, by being able and also trained to be just an observer of the external world, a yogi will preserve a good mental health forever, because the pathological anomalies of the brain, i.e. of the mind and reason, have chemical causes which are only second place. A brain which works well doesn't offer the chance for its own chemical waste products to accumulate in it and by this to damage its function. This can only happen if the brain is not used actively, but only passively – that is, if a person doesn't try to understand the things detected by the senses, but only reflexively reacts to them.

Four outcomes of the spiritual effort

As spiritual effort, we consider practical mysticism or yoga. In both cases we can characterise this endeavour as work, i.e. expending one's energy for the purpose of attaining a specific goal; this goal is a certain skill which can be compared to a skill in a trade, science, philosophy, and the like. However, mysticism is not a paid job and therefore it often becomes dilettantism, in which case a great deal of subjective emotional considerations mix into this self-discipline. This does not happen, for example, in the course of learning some trade. Especially in mysticism, it is typical that a great proportion of its followers are people who are mentally extravagant; in the case of yoga, people are, in turn, attracted by promises that without moral and inner cost, they will achieve abilities, like those possessed by faquirs.

Followers of these flawed approaches to mysticism, as well as to yoga, aren't achieving the results promised, as well as provided, by these teachings. Among the followers of mysticism we can find many psychopathic persons, or at least people living in unhealthy "superreality"; and yoga, which has not brought these foolish people all the way to the end of their erroneous striving, they tend to leave behind later, because it hasn't satisfied them sufficiently.

These certainly are not good prospects, however, they are not contained in any flawed qualities of these teachings. Those who seek are seduced and their mind is dulled by mendacious propaganda. Many have, perhaps, approached these teachings with ideal images, but further, on the mystical path, they have succumbed, because they were dreamers who eternally search and grope in the dark, and they abandon yoga as a teaching which is unconvincing as to its promised results. In both cases, it is only in this way how the irresponsible propagandists are earning their daily bread, or at least a dubious popularity, if recognition or fame is what matters to them.

All those dreamers who search and grope in the dark should be aware that, after all, both mysticism as well as yoga are psychological scientific methods and they pursue precisely set targets, which they do by the use of adequate means. These means aren't electronic machines and apparatuses, but only the psychological equipment of living human organisms.

If we leave out the whole teaching system of mysticism and yoga and highlight for ourselves only their simple essence – work, then both god's mercy causing miracles, as well as mysterious faquir magic will drop off of them. The work itself is based on efforts concerning morality, mind and psyche. Such a work is certainly free from the nimbus of mystical "holiness" and yogic power, but definitely isn't free of the character of practical efforts nor of concrete results depending on these efforts.

I have already spoken about efforts concerning morality, mind and psyche. Only these efforts I consider as real and rational steps leading to concrete mystical results. This, however, cannot be understood by mystical dilettantism, because it is remote from the possibility to reveal the law of actions and their consequences. Some believe that if they "practise letters" à la Weinfurter*, they will attain holiness, as well as wisdom, mystical power as well as liberation – salvation.

---

* Karel Weinfurter (1868 – 1942) – Czech translator who, via his translations, has made available valuable works of foreign spiritual literature. He has also written several books on a spiritual theme himself. He was the founder and leading member of the association Psyché (1924), which was bringing together people interested in mysticism in Prague. K. Weinfurter recommended in his books, among other things, the so-called 'letter practices'. Those were carried out by placing an image of a particular letter into a certain part of body.

Some others, who devote themselves to yogic exercises, believe that either they will become powerful magicians or that that they will become successful, exhaustless managers in their daily life, or perhaps yogis equipped with abnormal mystical power and an immortal being. Precisely this belief is a delusion, which springs from a false interpretation of these two teaching systems.

I can responsibly state: nothing of that which is promised by yoga and mysticism is attained outside of the effect of the law of deeds! There are four correct outcomes of the spiritual efforts of human beings and these are directly dependent on four specific efforts, which are, of course, contained both in different kinds of yoga, and in mysticism:

1. Holiness is attained by the development of virtues, resulting from following the moral commandments of mysticism or yoga. The task of these commandments is to weaken egocentrism, selfishness and make a person fit to perform the deeds of virtue. This means that it is goodness that underlies the implementation of these commandments. Its mystical role is in dissolving the structure of a being glued together by selfish motives; a structure having, in a gravitational sense, only a centripetal effect and thus imposing psychological limits and beclouding consciousness.

Only a great abundance of goodness can transform this structure, which is glued together by selfishness, in such a way that it will shine both with a radiance of its own, as well as with eradiation, which belongs to the deeds of virtue. Under these qualities, the personality will dissolve, disappear and make room for the light, which is generally considered to be holiness.

2. Liberation – salvation, is achieved by renunciation of the world. A liberated one surely cannot be bound by the things of the world; on the contrary, he or she must be unburdened by any external thing; they must be solitary psychologically as well as in their awareness and must delight in their freeing. This is a state totally unknown to, and uncomprehended by, people attached to the world. They are seized by selfishness and understand freedom as a nonpun-

ishable ownership of countless sensorily pleasing things, with an absolute right of disposal over them. Deep ignorance and blindedness, caused by immeasurable selfishness, are exactly the things that always modify concepts and give them a totally different meaning than the one that belongs to them.

Considering this, liberation – salvation is the most difficult state to achieve. A simplified conception of attachment as a state of a natural and a matter-of-course process in which individuals are becoming part of collectives of beings or people with the same mentality, does not offer an individual the possibility to tell apart the state of attachment from liberation. People generally believe that freedom is attachment without the suffering by which attachment is accompanied.

Liberation is hidden in the fortress of a perfect detachment – renunciation of the world. A liberated one must not have anything but happiness springing from the feeling of total freeing. For this happiness to be ever possible to spring, a person must reorientate their opinion of personal needs. They must know that there simply are no needs; that needs stem from a demand for a permanent communication of individuals with the external world and that beyond this communicating, there exists a state of solitude, which has overcome the needs.

3. Wisdom, which we also expect from yogic or mystical effort, is the fruit of an extensive function of thinking. However, when I am talking about an extensive function of thinking, what I mean is the concentration of mind. For, a person may concentrate in a way that they think only of one thing, like someone who suffers from a fixed idea; or, they can spread their thinking on the whole object which serves them as an object for concentration.

Focusing on an object of concentration, which has three dimensions and is adequately large, occupies the mind as a perceiving factor. An appropriate precision of this perception is an evidence of the necessary intensity of the concentrating mind, and both together – extensity accompanied by intensity, are a direct prerequisite for knowledge or the process of cognition. A sufficiently rich cognition is wisdom.

Wisdom cannot arise otherwise than in a situation where the mind is open for lots of things and perceptive to a sufficiently large extent. An extensive concentration in the form of seeing of a three-dimensional object and being aware of it is a training in an expanded perception of all observed. That, in turn, is a condition of detecting the detailed characteristics of the observed. When there is an adequate intensity behind such observation, i.e. an intensity which does not disturb the processes of perception of a relaxed spirit, then it is in fact a concentration which is enlightening and awakening wisdom. This very intensity is changing into an analysing power of the spirit, which no longer detects only all kinds of characteristics of the outside, but penetrates into the depths of phenomena, into their spirit. Applied to people, it means an ability to detect their motives to this or that action. Only when we know these motives and are able to judge them, we are wise. Otherwise we become emotionally inflamed and forget about motives altogether, and so we then judge only the action, and action is a small manifestation of the diverse tensions in the spirits of people. This is exactly what has to be eliminated. We will then see, that every action of people is determined by countless factors, which are hidden inside, uncontrollable, like the dangerous beasts of the wildwood through which we walk. Police prohibitions will not always teach us how to avoid these beasts; such prohibitions can only break our spirit and make us unable to develop wisdom.

4. External and mystical power, and even the ability to perform miracles, springs from concentration which is intensive. For, organism is a repository of forces, which have, in their potential state, a form of coiled energies. These have to get an impulse to uncoil; an intensive concentration is this impulse. It constitutes a physical energy, which is directed by the concentration; it can be compared to an electron energy, which is accelerated by the mind, the same way as in a cyclotron.

Mental energy directed by concentration is of a neutral nature. Therefore, those who engage in intensive concentration, must pay attention, so that its intensification or acceleration of its current serves only the intended goodness and not undesirable results. This means that those who are concentrating in this way should already be able to observe the effect of the mental energy and by that achieve an ability to control its influence.

Yoga should educate its followers, who are in most cases doing only intensive concentration, by an appropriate training of extensive concentration towards an ability to detect even the smallest deviations in the potential tension of the forces of psyche. By this, they should obtain control over this entire tension and learn how to dose it. For, too strong a current of energetic potentials of being, can make from intensive concentration, a tool which is not only entirely useless, but oftentimes even malignant. Yoga aspirants should already know that intensive concentration must produce only controllable tension. Only such tension becomes a suitable tool for the development of mystical abilities and mystical power.

Dilettantes in mysticism predominantly use the intensive concentration, without knowing that it is this which brings them to 'radiate' in an unbearable degree. By this, I mean the weakening of organs by immoderate emission of their energy, which often leads to physical or mental collapse, or both.

Let us consider the organs as accumulators of physical energy, which is emitted by them in the course of their maturing (towards old age) exactly in such an amount so that everything in a being remains in balance until death. Yoga found a way how to force the organs to emit much more energy by an exact impulse expressed by the concentration of mind.

Originally, attention was paid to the emitted energy to serve spiritual purposes, or even spiritual growth towards perfection, often even salvation. However, this attention is not being paid anymore. Those who practise yoga and are fascinated by the world want to conquer the energy of organs, perhaps only for the purpose of having their external life characterised by – the most intense possible – manifestations of the vital energy. They don't know that this is a steeper path and that it leads only to premature exhaustion. The fact that the yogi – beginners feel stronger and more able does not alter this. It can be said that it is the very memento that the process of exhaustion is speeding up.

However, it is not the purpose of this short writing to point out right and wrong methods in mysticism and yoga. Its purpose is to let everyone know that the means and goals of the mystical as well as yogic efforts exactly correspond to each other. No one should think that they will attain mystical power, wisdom, holiness and liberation by a simple intensive concentration. Even the mystical power will not be achieved if the concentration is not correctly dosed to release only the amount of energy which a person can manage and is able to utilise for the growth of spirit. More probably, they will attain unfortunate results, such as irritation of the nervous system, affliction by diseases from the exhaustion of organism and from a nervous breakdown. They will not attain wisdom either, because the adequate principle of its arising – the opening of the spirit to perceptions of a detached perception apparatus, is also lacking. They will not attain to holiness either, because that is a result of deeds of virtue, which destroy egocentrism and make the being a self-radiant phenomenon, similar to the sun, which also emanates its radiance from its own inner qualities. This factor doesn't exist in the simplified approach to the mystical effort either. Of course, liberation isn't reached by such concentration either, because this requires an act called 'renunciation of the world', which means to put relations to the world down from one's shoulders, to break free from them, to enter a state of pure solitude, unburdened by anything.

Only by this effort will the four outcomes of mystical or yogic striving be found.

Eight comments

1. Aim of Yoga

I am going to express myself precisely: stupid people, who are internally worthless and fully possessed by worldly desires will never understand that the spiritual teaching or teachings will never serve the purpose of the 'old' person who is still burdened by inborn inclinations and inner values to obtain money, "love" and to "have the devil's own luck". Their purpose is for a person to transform in his or her feeling, thinking and overall inner orientation and by that to create conditions for new, sometimes a little better, at other times much better karmic and other states in life.

2. The Spiritual leader

The real spiritual teacher and leader appears acceptable to superficial people only during impersonal contact; during a personal contact, he or she does not tend to be acceptable. His or her teaching is always logical and psychologically faultless; therefore, although the superficial people acknowledge their instructions about the necessary conditions of the spiritual development, in practice they adapt the instructions for themselves in such a way that their present way of life isn't affected. – However, in a direct personal contact, a good spiritual teacher and leader requires these instructions to be observed and this, in the superficial people, gives rise to conflicts between the reason and instinctive inclinations. Therefore the real spiritual teacher and leader is acceptable only during an impersonal contact; during the personal contact he or she is not acceptable to those, who are superficial.

3. Overcoming of sexuality

Those who want to attain the peak of spiritual perfection must master sexuality even in its subtlest manifestations. By this, it is not meant the practical performing of coitus, but the elimination of idealism, of daydreaming, of the interest in figures of the opposite sex, in their inner equipment and abilities and even aestheticism. I am saying to master, not to uproot in a way which would leave bad marks in the character.

But: how to master sexuality? The best way, which in fact belongs to the 'mystical college', the 'university of mysticism', is to turn away from everything that arouses the sexual excitement, desire and lust. However, by this, neither the high, good and happy mood, nor optimism must be afflicted. Simply: the sexual excitants, i.e. women, men, their appearance, their inner equipment and abilities must be removed from the sphere of interests, from the sphere of things attracting a person's attention. By that, this question is completely solved; a person has found themselves on a "mystical path of the seraphs" and will immediately traverse the spheres of miraculous happening.

A form of control, which has to be warned against, is the suppression of the sexual want as such, i.e. the physically aggressive factor which gratifies the body. In this case a person, as a rule, resorts to breaking of the inner, so to say, robust forces: this is a cause of the formation of other moral defects which are representing a spiritual fall. I don't need to enumerate these defects, because they were, for example, projected by the writer Jan Drda into the character of the hermit Scholastik (I suppose) in a play 'Dice with devil'. In any case, the "virtuous ones" who have "won" this gloomy fight with sexuality, succumb to priding themselves on their "purity". Because of this, their moral view deforms to such an extent, that they are rather a warning than a good example for their observers. They will, however, end up the same way as all the proud ones – on a wrong track, leading towards the hellish world.

It is not easy to overcome sexuality in the way of that 'mystical university'. To keep oneself in the state of indifference to everything that we view in the world as pure and noble, and, at the same time, not to yield to sexuality which is mistaken and modified into indulging of another kind, e.g. into overeating, gluttony, mental dullness and flatness, is in fact a superhuman task. Therefore there is an opposite of this path of seraphs, the prosaic path. On this path a man may have a woman and woman may have a man, however, exactly and only for the purpose of removing, by their sexual intercourse, the aggressiveness of the sexual want which is of a physical nature and by that, to be able to give rise to any possibility at all, of an escape from an undesirable sexuality to the superworldly path which is defined by elevation of the spirit above the world of a broadened sex, manifested at that stage already by taste. Live then, husbands with your wives and wives with your husbands sexually, but only for the purpose of preventing the physical sexuality from sweeping you along to various states of the worldly sensory greed. To enable you to live, in the physical peace after the physical sexual gratification, in an inner elevation gradually up to its ecstatic form and, under these circumstances, to intensify and develop this state, until the physical lust will be overcome by a habit of states of this constant inner elevation.

We are living in the world and therefore amidst unmanageable attacks arousing sexual lusts. This is literally a misfortune, which often forever buries the conditions for experiencing a pure, simple, low – because childlike – bliss. And as long as this is here, nobody will achieve happiness, even if they would dominate the whole world with their genius, by a military, political or even financial power. Therefore, there is no other choice than to deal with the problem of sexuality, and this problem cannot be resolved at all by men having an excessive number of women, and women an excessive number of men. It requires simply to escape from the aggressiveness of the sexual drive by a forgetting of the objects of sexual desire, or by use of one wife or one husband in order to weaken this desire in a physical form; then to continuously internally elevate oneself towards the transcendental qualities, until they will be realised. This will be recognised in the victory over the sexual drive. It is not "the path of seraphs" and therefore the magical lights of mystical miracles are not dawning on a person who is on this path; however, it is a way of escape based on transformation of all forces of the physical sexual drive. According to Buddhism, such a person has to be born once again, but their path will not descend down into the hellish worlds; on the contrary, it will rise, or more precisely, it will lead to liberation in its highest form.

4. 'The Lie' as a hindrance

On the way to the spiritual perfection people encounter various hindrances. All these hindrances originate in vices; by the elimination of these a person doesn't become a simple, noble, poor little thing, as it is oftentimes believed, but a spiritually developed person. The redemption of the heart is attained precisely by virtues, concentration practices serve for attaining the redemption of the mind. If it, however, isn't based on virtues, it is a redemption, which oftentimes doesn't mean anything good at all, and sometimes it causes a vital strengthening, which can bury the redemption of the heart forever.

Yoga enumerates the hindrances which occur on the way towards spiritual perfection, but when a good and deep understanding of the conditions of the correct mystical path is missing, a person tries to overcome these hindrances by a formal adherence to these conditions.

I don't want to talk right now about numerous hindrances and the overcoming of them. The thing is, that I have just come across a hindrance called 'lie' or mendaciousness and I only want to express myself concerning this one. For this case, I would like to go back quite far into the past, namely to the year 1925. At that time I realised: if a person is given to lying, they can indulge in numerous vices, because he or she can cover them up by mendaciousness. Therefore, I have thoughtfully put mendaciousness aside, and by that I was forced to behave and act well, i.e. morally, because a principle of the yogi's actions has to be to act in such a way that he or she doesn't have to feel ashamed of anything and he or she doesn't to have to hide anything. They can simply, always truthfully, say what they were doing and how they were behaving in various situations without having to blush with shame.

Mendaciousness is a terrible moral flaw. In its final consequences, it causes a person not to see things as they are, but in a distorted way. By this, they open the way for mistaken judgements, which will show them situations in a different garment than which they in reality wear. Lies therefore lead a person to delusions. They also make him or her weak, non-resistant and cowardly, so badly vitally equipped that others see them as an unreliable weakling.

Better is life for those who act in a way that they don't need to pretend anything, nor mask anything, nor be ashamed for their actions which would be unable to withstand being seen through by the cognitive abilities of others. Therefore, it is necessary to eradicate everything that is related to mendaciousness. Thus, don't be mendacious, and you will realise how pleasant is the power which you are obtaining by that and which, upon the realisation of truthfulness, becomes qualitatively so special, that it helps a person to overcome the difficulties of life. By mendaciousness, one can help oneself only on the margin of the individual life of people. Such a person is soon forced to make so many compromises that they cease to have individuality and become a reed in the wind. Therefore, mystic, do not lie! On the path to the spiritual perfection, there are numerous hindrances and you surely will not overcome them if you would retain mendaciousness.

5. Immortality

Immortality! Immortality? Perhaps it is a matter of a subjective perception. But when I have reached it, I have found out, that the flow of the subjective time stopped in me. It was such an evident finding that I had an impression that I would stop aging. However, other circumstances urged me to cancel the conditions of this state. – Which conditions were these? – If the subjective perception of the flow of time – and therefore also mortality – wasn't connected with all relationships to other beings, who are born, live and die, including those relationships that one is not conscious of, then the question of subjective perception of the halt of the flow of time wouldn't be so complicated. However, a person is integrated into the mortal world both through conscious and even unconscious relationships and the flow of time is connected exactly with this; the flow of time, which a person can clearly detect by a thorough analysis of the processes existing in their being.

It is thus required to abandon relationships to other beings. A person must remove from their consciousness even the subtlest traces of relationships, which can be identified by a thorough self-observation, and instead of that they need to fill their consciousness with an infinite space or boundlessness or with the absolute itself in its qualitative conception. Then the "oscillation" of the energetic tensions in the being ceases and, by that, also the possibility of evident notions about time disappears; on the level of perceptions, the "now" and "then", "here" and "there" ceases; thus that which is called time, simply disappears.

The interesting thing is that it is not only the mind that reacts to this disappearance of time by its broadening and by limitless concepts, but also the organism, in which the processes accompanying time and thus also the gradual decline (dying), appear to cease and gradually, an evident perception of oneself in the state of timelessness comes about.

There is no immortality except for the ceasing of time, which is transformed in the usual states of the discernable processes. I have left this state after consideration, because I have attained it at the age of eighteen years, and only a good philosopher will understand why immortality is unacceptable at this age. However, it appears that only once in a lifetime it is possible to attain a complete freeing by the interruption of relationships to all that lives and feels. Besides that, this interruption is so immensely sensitive to the possible disturbances, that most people who climb these heights will not achieve a complete interruption. However, if they achieve it and then, even by the slightest interest in something they will destroy it, they will not be able to achieve it again. This is because it is similar to opening the floodgate for an influx of so many hidden moments of potential relationships, that no energy, nor intellect, can search them out again and eradicate them.

I am saying that I have achieved immortality manifesting itself in this way and I haven't lost it, but I have given it up: due to this I have got to know the cruelty of the state of gradual dying, but there is no regret at the loss of the immortality of this type rising up in me. It was cruel to experience the gradual disappearance of the powerful coldness which accompanied this immortality and of a gradual getting hold of the body by the physiological warmth, a hot scorching factor, which makes death so imminent and evident. My decision however, resulted from knowing that youth is not suitable for immortality. By that, an evident experience of gradual liberation started to emerge in me, one which offers immortality without the presence of the body; that which is during a gradual realisation of this kind of immortality, experienced as an absolute non-recurrability of the life process with its destinies accompanying the present state. A person thus identifies that "this moment and an experience of it" will not repeat itself again, because all preconditions for it were entirely exhausted. Thus, in place of the immortality burdening a person by its natural qualities, an immortality comes about which is unburdened and unlimited by anything, because it is arising from the realisation of the state of the absolute and its qualities, both of which are hidden in the being.

Therefore: you, who want to be immortal in the body, you can be. However, there is a condition of the abandonment of all personal relationships to everything that lives. Only in this way the relationship to dying is severed and a relationship to that which always exists is created and, on the basis of these conditions, that which always exists thus reflects its eternity in a human being as a phenomenon that has identified itself with eternity. However, this isn't immortality how it is imagined by the feeble-minded, an immortality with girls in their lap and pitchers of beer on the table, but an immortality of the immensely strong ones. Those strong ones are at risk of moral destruction anyway, because eternity contains in itself neither conscience, nor understanding for weaknesses, but it only contains its state or quality, i.e. eternity – eternity, which perhaps slightly laughs at the foolish fantasies and hopes of those who are driven and will be driven into the jaws of death, because they are living in time, i.e. in changes. If you are more reasonable you might want to be immortal perhaps without the body? – Live with your mind above the sphere of death, live with your mind in eternity – in a state of continuously reminding yourself of its qualities and do not care about the relationships to others, but only about the perfecting of morality. Then you will realise that every further step on the path of true morality broadens the possibilities of being continuously aware of the state of timelessness. Only when morality elevates you above all cravings and you will therefore not be aware of the sensory world and its objects, then the state of eternity will become to you a gradually realised quality; finally you and eternity will become one.

Mortality is a bad state. I know that well because I was immortal and I have put aside immortality. Everyone would like to escape mortality but it is not possible without the appropriate preconditions. Besides that, a wish does not mean realisation yet. Therefore, everyone, be reasonable. Avoid all dangers of the physical immortality thoughtfully; living without the moral restrictions, conscience, etc. is, in its consequences, such a horrible danger, that you cannot imagine it. Enter a more reliable path, leading towards immortality without the presence of the body. This path depends only on excluding the entire Nature from your consciousness and developing in it only the qualities of immortality, transcendental items, which will, by retaining them in consciousness, realise themselves and they, themselves will cause the miracle of immortality. In the first phase, this miracle reflects itself in the indestructibility of consciousness, and, in the second phase, in an evident detection of absence of any kind of possibility of cessation of existence, even in the sphere in which you abide through the operating feelings. This way is safe; when you sin against its rules, it disappears to you, but you are not going to detect the feelings of a spiritual fall.

6. Path of development

People do not understand yoga. Possessed by the vision of a never ceasing development they also understand yoga as a means which serves this development. When they begin to realise that they cannot keep up with the worldly people in the competitions of pursuing happiness, they think that yoga will help them to multiply their vital abilities and then, in this way, to compare favourably with others in the competition.

It is the same delusion with which they viewed technology. We can remember the times when businessmen, possessed by the vision of becoming rich placed their hopes in the automobile, which was supposed to help them to "be there earlier, so that the business as well as profit would be theirs". But, as I'm saying, businessmen! However, all that happened was many of them arrived at the same time and the vision of fast and easy profits fell apart. But in fact more things fell apart! Gone are the times when the landscape, freshly covered by snow, wasn't for many, many hours marked by human impression. Where would one go anyway? The basic foodstuffs were at home and only those, who needed salt for example, went out in the nasty weather. You might say that there was poverty back in those times. I saw a little old woman, and how she handed over her last penny to a shop assistant with a request for some scraps from smoked foods to enable her to eat something, because it would not be pension day until tomorrow. But the shop assistant didn't really understand. She handed over to the old lady an imperfectly made sausage, perhaps in the price range of this penny; that old lady was supposed to feed herself on this sausage until the next day.

Thus, we don't have the poverty of poor tables with dry potatoes for the hungry; we have a poverty of empty tables with a small sausage for one person for 24 hours. That is the gift of the redemptive technology, promising only wealth, but giving rush, which nowadays connects the snowed up landscape by cleaned roads, in order for everyone to be at work as soon as possible and create that promised wealth.

I was walking through the streets of the capital city in the wintertime before six o'clock in the morning, or more precisely at night, in a dense night full of slushy mud. Mothers were rushing, dragging their children to crèches or to some other shelter, so that they could be at work at once and perhaps build wealth. The trams were squeaking, cars were making a noise and casting the beams of their lights on the pedestrians. – Happiness, escalating happiness!

Well, we have cars, to which we quickly run at the end of the week, to quickly drive somewhere to quickly get a rest, unless we break our neck on the way because of this "quickly". This is exactly the direction of that path of development, which is seen by delusion as a perspective of happiness. But just as delusion isn't wisdom, in the same way yoga doesn't even think of such a path towards happiness. On the contrary: yoga points to a path of involution, an opposite of development. Are you protesting against it? You don't want to give up your conviction that we live to walk the path of development and not a path of self-denial? Yes! You are the admirers of the path of development and therefore hurriedly point to the prospects of a pragmatic life and you say that the meaning of life is to live, indulge, experience something. For that reason you have families, children, households. Families, in which men and women in a constant quarrel always want something contradictory; children are healthy but then again ill, the state executive assigns them a job or a profession, in which they are not interested*; children with unfortunate marriages and hunted by failures; households, which are hutches rather than housing, households, for which you have to be thankful that you have them at all, because you know that others don't even have that.

The path of development! The path hostile towards the path of involution – an extinction of that which, when objectively evaluated, is found to be suffering. In the same way we can find, on the path of development, worldly people who are blinded by visions of unattainable happiness, we can find sages on the path of involution, as the leading yogis are always sages.

When yogis have already become sages, they never think that living has any purpose; still less such a one which can be seen in the hunt for the always fleeting happiness. These yogis know that there is already enough of those hurried, eager ones; there are also enough lessons teaching that they will not reach happiness. Therefore they are not practicing yoga to be more able-bodied and by that to have a better chance of success in life, but only to still the inner restlessness, to suppress and extinguish that longing, and in place of these, to develop in themselves the calmness of beings who don't want anything.

Only a non-wanting being can be happy. A consistently non-wanting being surely does not start a household, and is not interested in going somewhere for holidays, because they are happy

---

* During the communist period, it was common for a state to assign a job to a person who then had limited word in the process. Being unemployed was considered a criminal offence. The communist period ended in the former Czechoslovakia in 1989 in the so-called "Velvet Revolution".

here, where they are, until they understand that also the physical existence itself is the basis of all suffering, which it is necessary to destroy by suppression of the desire to live or, also, to be.

We are not obliged to be, to live, to reproduce and to build "in order for the happiness to be able to come". There are already enough people for this. Therefore we can avoid the depths of suffering, deny the craving for, and drive for, life and extinguish ourselves on the spot, contented. After all, by that we will only make place for those who, confused, fear the "population explosion" and insist on a standpoint that we have to reproduce, because "the nation should not perish".

If we suppress the thirst for life, the drives, we will not be and if we, by a suppression of the drive of life, will not reproduce we will not exist in our progeny either. What kind of misfortune will that be? We believe that we do not exist after death. If we then will not exist and our survivors will not exist either, will anything happen? – We didn't exist up until our birth. Did we perhaps regret that we did not exist? Or, did any parents ever hear from their child: "I am so happy that you begot me; I was so unhappy that I did not exist."? No! There is something in us, based on the Christian teaching which was distorted, which will cover the sexual drive by a shining axiom that to reproduce is a duty assigned by God. – Now we have 'made it right'. We are saying that a human being has drives, which have to be lived out. This has automatic consequences in forming families, which need to be protected, perhaps in order for us to have soldiers – who knows?

Thus, the yogis aren't supporters of development, because they are wise and also because they know that suffering can only be terminated by putting up a resistance to one's own aggressive inclinations, to the drives in action, to the lust for life. Apart from this, there is no problem. A person will only avoid that which is viewed as happiness but which is, in practice, a deep and never ending suffering. At the same time, when aggressive inclinations are being eradicated, the consciousness of a person broadens into undreamt-of dimensions;

without fleeing somewhere after the sought recreation, a person broadens their consciousness in the middle of the village square, in a noisy town and nothing can deprive them of this broadening. This is because they have eradicated suffering beforehand; the suffering, which can so easily hunt down vacationers, even if they flee far away from their place of residence.

The path of involution and the path of development! On the path of involution a person gets rid themselves of lying ideas. But how it is on the path of development? – I was watching an anthill. It was big. I stepped aside from it. – What were its perspectives on the paths of development? A heap of needles, bigger and bigger. Let's say huge in the distant future. So huge that, in addition, problems will arise, how to feed all those creepy-crawlies. Therefore a slogan will rule there: "More of us", because strength and the guarantee of happiness are seen in that. – A running deer can jump into such an anthill and a million ants will get hold of his legs, they will pick his bones clean and he will become their prey. – Is this perhaps the purpose of the life of ants, its culmination on the path of development?

There are a lot of people. And the path of development commands us to reproduce, as that way the existence of a nation will be ensured. However, other nations calculate exactly the same way. Therefore we will probably have to count on attacking others or making food from all minerals, from everything that the animate as well as inanimate Nature provides. Is this perhaps the purpose of living, the goal of the path of development? – No! People are not wise. With the same breath they are shouting "population explosion" and "reproduce". Where then will be "happiness"? Will technology and chemistry provide us with it? – We have the means of mass destruction. This is how we are safeguarding ourselves. – Is this 'safeguarding' happiness?

No. The yogis promote the path of involution. They know: When I will not exist, I surely will not be missed by the army of people fighting for happiness on the path of development. Besides, everyone is too busy to remember me. So what is the path of development for? After all, I am striving for happiness and I surely have it, when I don't have a family, children, company, with all the negative phenomena accompanying all these, but on the other hand I have conditions for the development of the range of consciousness. Limitless awareness, which has crossed the sphere of differentiated phenomena, is itself a great donor of great happiness and the extinction of the thirst for life is an inner calmness enthroned above any happiness. Yoga turns its attention only to these things.

7. The Role of sexual awakening

A bhakti yogi has to be fully sexually awakened. This is because the positional energy of a person who is not sexually awakened is not in the appropriate place and by that, rational viewpoints are disturbed. Such a person has quite specific views about life, about events, about the world; views not as much idealistic as fantastic. However, the sexual awakening doesn't have only one single sign: sexual craving. This craving accompanies the sexual awakening only if the positional energy of a person operates only in the lower part of the trunk; this is, on the other hand, related to the interests in the things of the sensory world. Ramakrishna – a bhakta "par excellence" was, in view of the results of his bhakti, fully sexually awakened. However, the "positional energy" of his being never descended into the lowest parts of his trunk. By worship of the holy mother Kali, his sexuality broke out of the being through the heart, and so he was a person well oriented in the worldly things.

Thus, if a person is fully sexually awakened, but their interests lie exclusively in the sensory world, they have their reason in order. It is, however, a worldly reason, a reason of an entirely worldly person who believes only in the real things. If they are, however, fully sexually awakened and their interests lie in the sphere of imaginary things which are, as a result of sexual awakening, well concretised, their reason is also in order, although it isn't a reason which clings so heavily to material realities. – However, by this all possibilities are not exhausted. Since, a person may be fully sexually awakened but, they will not allow the senses to lead them only through the world of sensory, material phenomena, nor through the world of well concretised ideas and images. Then the "positional energy" of their being will ascend all the way to the upper part of their head. Out of this, a deep discernment ability of good quality arises and by that, also wisdom.

Thus, we have four kinds of people: 1. Those who are scared to fully sexually awaken themselves. These people exist as if somewhere between earth and heaven, and out of this, various illusions arise which these people allow to lead them through the world. – 2. Those fully sexually awakened, who are only interested in the things of the sensory world; these people are genuine utilitarians, who are sinking exclusively in the worldly interests. – 3. Those fully sexually awakened who, perhaps due to aversion to simple sexuality, perhaps due to an inclination to life with realised pure ideals, perhaps also due to inborn predispositions, raise their mind above the world of sensory phenomena and do not allow it to create wandering ideas. These are bhaktas, whose celestial realities are thoroughly coherent and concretised; this is a cause of a rise of wisdom of the celestial character. – 4. Those sexually fully awakened, who are able to perfectly smother the physical sexual craving, and moreover, do not allow their mind to conjure them up perfectly coherent and concretised ideas of a celestial nature. These become Buddhas, fully liberated internally and emotionally and otherwise redeemed beings.

Therefore: The lack of sexual awakening isn't a virtue, but a defeat in a fight with various inner inclinations; an inner insufficiency misleading everyone into various illusions, into fantastic beliefs, into confusion.

Yoga contains instructions for a person to be able to achieve a full sexual awakening. They are, however, only used in the case of disciples who let themselves be led by gurus and totally obey them, because not achieving the true purpose intended by yoga can manifest only as worsening of the state of the seeker, in an escalation of their craving and this no longer adds to inner peace, but to a deepening of inner conflicts.

A modified method of a full sexual awakening is the concentration of mind on precisely demarcated imaginary objects. Exactly by their precise demarcation the mind acquires rational and realistic abilities. Imaginary objects, in this case, support the emergence of objects of the mystical world and their precise demarcation or differentiation places the mystic internally into the sphere known as the 'world of concrete phenomena'. – If the mystical effort does not have this factual foundation, the mind becomes wandering and produces fantasies; that is mysticism, which is unattractive in its results, oftentimes it sterilises a person and sometimes even castrates them. Therefore it is necessary to get an accurate picture about the mission of practical yoga, or mysticism.

8. Elements in mysticism

The gurus have to relate the mystical development of their disciples to the implementation of four elements: earth, water, fire and air. In a person who is not mystically developed, these elements manifest themselves individually – which means with a predominance of one of them. They manifest themselves in a way that the dominance of the element of earth makes their mental flexibility low which, as a rule, makes them more preoccupied by a particular idea, which, in turn, decreases their mental brightness. The element of water makes thinking dependent on emotions. This, on one hand, enables a person to be bright in a precisely limited extent, but in the best case the dependence of thinking on emotions will lead them to occupy their mind with themselves more than is healthy. The element of fire makes thinking active and, in this way, biased. A person, in whom the element of fire is over-asserted, has their own thoughts without examining their value. The element of air manifests itself in its good aspect as a factor creating geniality, but in its worse aspect it creates feeble-minded people.

In the mystical development, it is necessary to bring all four elements, and in fact each of them separately, to a full development, which happens either through concentration or by an intensifying of the respective mental content. The elements have to be, though, brought to their full development in a correct order, so that mystical development leads to wisdom as an inner ability which is necessary in order to correctly evaluate the inner situation of a person and, through that, to the possibility of the attainment of a delusion-free redemption of mind in the first phase and a delusion-free redemption of heart in the second phase.

If a person is an intellectual, then it itself means that the element of air is overdeveloped in them, and this is the cause of the fact that they tend to be led astray from the mystical path by speculations. If the element of water is overdeveloped in them, they see "their true path" in the further development and application of emotions, which causes them to see mysticism as a path towards intensification of emotional experience. If the element of fire is overdeveloped in them, then they see mysticism as a method to increase their power, inner, or outer. They are admirers of power and success in life. Predominance of the element of earth makes a person dull, indolent, often incompetent in mysticism, even though the mystical thirst has already awakened in them.

Every guru has to take all this into consideration and, based on that, must conclude that it is necessary to create in each one of their disciples, a correct and firm base for the mystical and spiritual growth. If there are no special irregularities in the nature of their disciples, a guru should start with the "practice of the element of earth". The element of earth is here represented by the human body, by stability in the broadest sense of this word, simply everything that is solid, material, unmoving and entirely stable. In this respect, concentrations on the body are prescribed as "practices of the element of earth", concentrations on its most fleshy parts, that is, from the trunk to the feet; then self-observation of all one's actions, bodily shape; sometimes simply concentration on stability as an opposite of a wandering of mind. In this case, that which is qualitatively solid is the object of thinking and awareness. Through a conscious focusing of the mind, the element of air is mingling into this whole work, and it is intellectualising the earth, permeating it from the inside, and when the mental focus on these objects becomes good, it (air) will sublimate it (the earth). Because of this sublimation, wisdom is already developing in a person; the basis of this wisdom is in the "stability of an intellectualised mind". The intellectualisation of the mind is, in this case, achieved by its precise focusing on the things which are invariable, on earth and on things of an earthly nature.

"The practice of earth" takes up the largest proportion of time in the mystical practice. It involves: 1. being aware of the distal parts of the body – feet and legs; 2. self-observation in the sense of observing the processes of thinking and then 3. fastening of the attention on the shape of the body during concentration, again mainly on the shape of its distal parts – feet and legs. In the inner sphere, the mind should be forced not to be distracted, not to wander; on the contrary, to remain at the objects of observation and to watch, as a factor which is in calmness, the entire inner life. In short, in the same way as earth is predominantly motionless, so the mind is supposed to become motionless, by which the entire inner life becomes steady, unmoving, being able not to change under the pressures and impacts of environmental actions.

When a person achieves inner tranquillity by this "practice of earth", this will manifest itself by the deepening of the discernments and by an easier understanding of the meaning of all events in the world surrounding them. This is a base of the mystical development, of the growth, which will start to unfold with concrete indicators from the moment when a person will, through the "practice of earth", get to know the difference between qualities of the phenomenal and the transcendental (invisible) world. This is good due to the fact that they will arrive at a discovery that beyond the world of outer activities, there is a world of inner activities, which is a causal world at least in a sense of real events which are forming there. Thus, by means of the "practice of earth", one can arrive at the basics of the mystical life, which can be explored by the "practice of water", by the "practice of fire" and by the "practice of air".

The "practice of water" is based on an intentional 'rippling' of emotions and this 'rippling' can be successful, only after one will achieve, through the "practice of earth", inner calmness in the form of an experimentally achieved inner motionlessness, because only this motionlessness enables one to make the loving thinking and feeling, or "tenderifying", pure or unambiguous. This state, developed up to its highest level, enables the mystic to experience everything, which can be achieved on the mystical path of the Christian-type mysticism. This "everything" will provide a person with an understanding of the emotional life in all its forms. In this way, the mystic will get to know the sphere of emotional life with all its miracles, with all the complications which are created by the emotional life of beings – this leads to a mastering of emotional life and the mastering of emotional life is, in fact, a prerequisite for victory over all pains, suffering and sorrows.

However, the "practice of water" will not lead to any good result without achieving success in the "practice of earth". Therefore, even the information obtained about this practice should not tempt anyone to carry out a premature practice of this kind.

After the "practice of water" one may proceed to the "practice of fire". This practice is based on enthusiasm or raising the mind towards things of an ideal nature, e.g. towards God or some distinctive aspects of mysticism raising enthusiasm, during a simultaneous firm concentration of the mind to the centre of the chest. If the conditions of this practice are fulfilled, a fire, in the form of warming, mellow heat, will ignite in the chest. This is the foundation from which we come to the thermal phenomena, which are supposed to be used for an inner "burn-out" – to the burning down of everything which can be summed up under the concept of emotional life, because if the emotional life is not overcome in this way, a person will drown in various categories of emotional experience, which always appear as 'landless'.

By the "practice of fire", a person is supposed to burn out, a visible sign of which is a total indifference to all manifestations of the emotional life. Only by this, everyone is saved from suffering and becomes a hard realist, without having to trivialise emotional states and by that to expose themselves to the development of cruelty of their character.

Hard realism and indifference to emotional stimuli is thus a sign of a high level of mystical development. However, the "practice of water" coming before the "practice of fire" leaves intact compassion, because all this is underlain by a deep experience of the emotional living, exhaustion of all its forms; the "practice of fire" at this level then causes the emotional attachment to transform into understanding and compassion.

The "practice of air" is dependent upon an "unglueing of mind". This will be achieved by not retaining any object in mind during its oscillation, based on fastening of the mind neither on the objects of the Nature of forms, nor on the state emerging due to its mere stability. This practice can be carefully attached to the observation of the process of breathing.

However, as it is necessary to connect the "practice of fire" to the "practice of water", in the same way, the "practice of air" may only be attached to the "practice of earth". This is because the "practice of air" can be disturbed by attaching it to "practice of fire" and "practice of water", but, on the contrary, "the earth" can be "aerated" by the "practice of air" and, based on that, then put in a condition suitable for wisdom, with the help of which it is possible to find a path towards "disembodiment" – the redemption in the sphere of self-perception.

Only by means of the "practice of air" it is possible to bring the body and the entire being in general, as it is perceived in the natural inner state, to the process of disembodiment in a sense of the path towards the Buddhist redemption. Apart from that, by the "aeration" of body through the "practice of air", an ability develops to understand the issues of mystical development, of the path of wisdom. This ability leads the being towards the extinction of the thirst for life; this is a prerequisite of irreversibility of the life process, with the exception of its progressive extinguishment.

On the mystical development

The mystical development depends on the state of mind which is created by concentration. However, the concentration of mind is never properly "pure", as long as a person is still dependent on sensory experiences. Therefore he or she has to, before using concentration, overcome the inclination towards sensory indulging; only in this way their spirit prepares for the desirable purity of mind.

It is necessary to attain a complete absence of craving, without weakening of the vigilance and freshness of the spirit by that. However, this is not an easy task. Even the usual communication of the mind with the external world is a serious hindrance in the capability of the mind to perform a desirable mystical concentration; this communication can be cancelled only by mental immersion into the depths of one's own being. Then a person will realise that they are continually in relationships to the world. However, there are not only strong relationships; very indistinct relationships exist, too. It could be said that the mind is able to be worldly even in an absolute calmness and in a seeming purity and equilibrium. We can verify this by observing the mind during its passing, from calmness into activation. In this moment, clarity and purity of mind and even ecstasy dawns on a spiritual person, while on a worldly person, ideas related only to the material Nature – the sensory world, dawn.

Therefore, it is necessary to comply with the requirements of the preparatory mystical self-discipline and cancel the relationships to the world of senses and communication with this world. However, this requires a responsible and deep moral discipline. It is necessary to constantly observe and monitor the behaviour of mind, or, spirit – whether it turns exclusively to the things of the sensory world. If this is the case, it is necessary to force the mind to turn away from the world and to focus only on a state of inner contentment, which arises from freeing the mind from the world; if this contentment is absent, it is necessary to raise it by mere will and not by the piling up or acquiring of objects pleasing the senses.

Only after a person attains, by this discipline, a total absence of craving, they will be successful in concentrations carried out by a pure mind. However, it is necessary to take into account the fact that this preparatory mystical self-discipline will take years. This is one thing. Another, more pleasant thing, is that the mystical development, during the correct concentration of mind, neither stops nor interrupts itself, on the contrary, it progresses quickly, even though it is not observable in the usual way.

It can happen that a person easily finds themselves in the sphere called "the sphere of mystical heights" and then it only depends on them whether they will remain at these heights, or will be forced to descend from them, or be forced to leave them by a spiritual fall.

The spiritual fall does not only occur due to the so-called 'great sinning', but even due to a mere change of the contents of the mind. This is because, if a person purifies their mind by excluding from it the worldly, which sets in motion their sensory experience, then each return to the worldly contents means a spiritual fall, the consequence of which is an inability of the mystic to, again, find and realise the purity of mind, or, of spirit. The cause of this going astray is the momentum of every inner state, which develops from the contents of the mind. This means that, if, in the mind, purity, caused by the fact that it was rid of every worldly idea, is present, the impurity, which results from filling the mind with ideas of worldly things, cannot be present in it. Thus, if one of these things is present in the mind, the other one is so perfectly absent in it that it will not touch the consciousness of a person at all. Thus, the worldly person is separated from the spiritual world, and from a mystically perfect person; the first never discerns the contents of the spiritual world and the latter is well isolated from the worldly content of the spirit.

It is exactly this separation of qualities of the mystical and the non-mystical spirit which requires those who desire attainment of the "sphere of mystical heights" to fulfil the moral commandments of the mystical teaching. When he or she really has fulfilled them, the qualities of these heights will appear in him or her by themselves. Afterwards, it only matters whether they will forever manage to keep their mind free from worldly things, purified from the world, or not. If they do not manage to keep their mind in this state, they will forget not only these qualities, but they will also forget the path leading to their emergence and development in their consciousness.

The initial penetration of the qualities of the "sphere of mystical heights" into the consciousness does not mean though, a supreme experience and knowledge. Therefore, it is necessary to resort to the concentration of mind on these qualities. This is carried out in a way that one relaxes the body, frees the mind entirely from the contact with the objects of the sensory world and focuses their attention on the body. At the same time, one must take heed in order for the focusing of the mind on the body not to have a character of being engrossed in the material form and thus to bring about an overwhelming of the mind with darkness. This happens when the concept of the body symbolises to a person matter in the usual conception. With regard to that, thinking of the body, or being aware of it during concentration must symbolise only concretised thinking or concrete thinking with a focus on the body as a non-physical phenomenon, a focus on the body as if it was an object drawn in the air.

Under these conditions the mind preserves pragmatism without falling into material concepts or ideas. This is considered to be its freeing from the world, its liberation, and redemption. This state of mind will then last at all times or it will also develop to ever higher levels of transcendence; that is the fruit of the state of redemption of mind (not of the entire being), its enlightenment and immersion in the absolute. Nevertheless, it is necessary to know and remind oneself that this state will disappear in the moment when the mind falls back into the previously common concepts – the worldly concepts; moreover, a person will completely forget this state as well as the path leading to it, and so they will themselves perceive it as their spiritual fall, as a loss of the path walked until now, as a descent into the dark world – the human world, as it is commonly perceived and experienced.

Thus, dwelling in the "spheres of mystical heights" is conditional upon this; it is not possible to remain there, if the sensory world imposes itself on the mind. In the same way, the mystics are separated from the non-mystics; those who think as a worldly person, have not reached the spheres of mystical heights and thus belong to the people spiritually not awakened, not enlightened, to the worldly ones. If they boast about a mystical initiation, they are not telling the truth.

Thus, if a person by renunciation of the world, excludes this world from their mind, they will make the qualities of the transcendence manifest clearly in their mind. When they, subsequently, reduce the character of these qualities by the so-called "thinking in concrete concepts" (which is permitted) so that these qualities will become significant for his or her body as factors instigating a higher character of the sensory experience, their whole being slowly prepares for his or her attainment, by the implementation of thinking in abstract concepts, of the state Mahavideha, the great disembodiment. By this they will, based on a broadened awareness, realise the qualities of the absolute and create conditions for their self-awareness to outgrow the limits of their being, especially the bodily existence. This is considered a state of perfection attained from one's own will – a perfection with limitation, which is, in the Tibetan mysticism, expressed as a realisation of states of one of the Dhyanibuddhas.

The yogic working procedures are not easy with regard to these nuances in the spiritual practices and, moreover, during them, the yogi must keep in mind that they are remaining near phenomena which put them in acute danger. Freeing the mind from the world and perception of the transcendental qualities reduced by the so-called 'thinking in the concrete concepts' is sharply separated by the so-called 'thresholds', which are experienced as the thresholds of death. But, it is also quite sharply separated from the quality of experiencing of the transcendence in a state of thinking in abstract concepts.

On the first borderline between the immanent and the transcendental world, on the borderline between sensory experiencing and experiencing of the transcendence qualitatively reduced by the 'thinking in concrete concepts', a person is threatened by an inner shock. It results from the freeing of one's awareness from the world of the sensory phenomena and leaving the world of the "tranquil", in other words, material, phenomena and entering beyond its walls, into the causal world. On the second borderline, which separates the experiencing of transcendence reduced by the so-called 'thinking in concrete concepts' on one side, from a transcendence not reduced – by thinking in abstract concepts – on the other side, a person must, in this case, overcome the danger of an inner shock stemming from leaving the evident, but natural, demarcation of the world of phenomena. In both cases, this can be termed as a transfer of consciousness from the first world into the second one and from the second into the third, where the second one means the inner world and the third one means pure transcendence.

This requires a considerable degree of mental flexibility; those who have rigid opinions about the world and therefore believe that the world of phenomena has to have forms like those with which our Nature is equipped, will surely pay for this experiment with confusion. Apart from that, the transfer of consciousness from the world of natural phenomena into the world of inner phenomena, and then even more, into the world of transcendental phenomena, produces, from a momentum of interference of the forces of the being, personifications which are corresponding to atavisms and their character, i.e. provoking horror. This tends to cause forced returns of the developing mystics to the base of the elementary life. By this, the mystical world again closes itself to them. In such a case an already slightly provoked imagination presents to a person the horror of the threshold, i.e. the horror which is dwelling on the borderline between these worlds. This is because it is a law that the entrance from the first world into the second one has to be accompanied by leaving the first one, even though it is, in principle, permitted to carry over, across this threshold, also the concept of oneself as a concrete – i.e. by form equipped – being. It is actually only this transfer which is a condition for keeping the ability of an evident dwelling beyond the world and retaining the experience from this dwelling by means of a properly functioning memory.

However, the actualities of a real passage of the consciousness from one sphere into the other are more marked than it is possible to write out. Everything here depends on the extent to which a person eliminates one world from their consciousness when crossing over to the other world, and to what extent they retain the awareness of their physical existence. It is a very serious question and the least appropriate case is when a person does not pay attention to the contents of their consciousness in the form of their being and the things or phenomena of that world, which they are experimentally leaving. It is like working with explosive substances. Those who do not observe the safety regulations, may trigger an explosion, which, in the mystical sense, right at the passages from one world to another one, means visions whose influence can be devastating for the individuals.

Therefore, during the mystical development in which one, so to say, experiments with the contents of the consciousness and with the conscious passages from one sphere to another one, it is necessary to keep in mind all instructions which safeguard everyone from irreparable mistakes. The renunciation of the world is then always in the foreground; only those who are not attached to anything are safe during the transfers from one sphere to another. Those who are not destroying attachment, behave as a child playing with dangerous things.

The personified horrors of the threshold thus exist, but they are not always sufficiently noticeable. They do not reveal themselves to those whose concentration is not accompanied by awareness of themselves and the sharpest vigilance; this vigilance is supposed to be the checking factor of the intensive concentration which has to develop into an analytical concentration, breaking down the being into its basic elements. If the concentration is not of such character, it brings no results, except for the development of the play of imagination and emotional 'rippling', which manifests itself as feelings of various kinds and qualities. However, in that case the mystical research of the nature, all the way in the aspects of its non-manifest components is not taking place; what is taking place is a mental illness, even though not always an acute one. However, let this be only a reminder of that which sometimes happens during the mystical development, without drawing any conclusions from it. Let a more important fact for us be, that the concentration which breaks down the entire being to the basic elements of being, leads to the appearance of the beyond-sensory world – the transcendental world, without the personified horrors being able to prevent a mystic from entering this world as 'I' equipped with sensory abilities, i.e. with the sight, hearing, smell, taste and touch. This is considered to be a mystical initiation, which is, however, burdened by the responsibility for acting (behaviour) which will either preserve or destroy this development of the mystical senses.

It is desirable for this development of the mystical senses, i.e. clairvoyance, psychic hearing, smell, taste and touch, to be retained. Therefore, the concentration accompanied by the sharpest vigilance has to be retained even though, in the later stage, without the necessity to pay attention exclusively to it. For, this concentration has to become a permanent inner state of the person and he or she has to retain it even in the current of his or her daily life; if this is not the case, the mystical senses cease to exist again, and the mystic only retains the experience of those who have already gone through the mystical development. On the other hand, the mystical development stopped in this way provides a guarantee that one will attain the development of the mystical senses again, however, without the mystic having the advantage of the one who has already crossed, for the first time, the above-mentioned threshold which is in fact a threshold of death. He or she will not be labelled as a seraph – a candidate of immortality, but only as a human reborn from water and spirit and as such they will be burdened by the destinies of their previous existence, the destinies which are connected to their current incarnation.

From the point of view of the mystical teaching it would be good, if every mystic persevered on the path of seraphs. By that, it would be proven that death does not in fact exist, that only a transformation under the control of the never fading and indestructible personal consciousness exists. However, this path is very difficult. The humanness must not be overcome only in the first affect connected with the unbearable suffering of life, but it has to be overcome even in the relief springing from knowledge that pains and joys are only a matter of the mind and consciousness, which is able not to succumb to the forming forces of Nature – and that is determined by the desire to sensorily indulge.

A mystic should renounce the world once and for all and forever after a reflection that this world, as well as the external existence is transient. This is not common. The mystical path is being entered in the affects arisen from suffering and this makes it a complicated development, accompanied by rises and falls. A person once develops in themselves the mystical senses with all the consequences, and then, a second time, they fall again into powerlessness against the driving forces of Nature. As a result, it seems as if they never were a mystic.

Altogether it seems that only an immense wealth of life experience which is from knowledge of transience of everything – the wealth hidden in the being, also in the form of motivating forces, provides a person with the understanding necessary for them to enter the mystical path by forever turning away from everything right in the beginning. However, from a point of view of the mystical teaching, this does not constitute a precondition for its sharing and for its transfer in its highest form, i.e. the teaching which liberates immediately and forever, but only as a teaching providing knowledge from which the preconditions for a full, immediate and forever lasting liberation will develop only later.

All these facts should lead everyone to the conclusion that no level of the mystical initiation is the final one, unless it, immediately and with an ultimate effect, provides a person with omniscience, omnipotence, omnipresence and immortality. Apart from that, all levels of the mystical initiation are mere intermediate stages of initiation and a person on them needs to have the humbleness of those who are aware that they are still on the path, even if they are already able to penetrate completely all secrets of the life of others, or, perhaps, the secrets of life in general.

However, let us descend from the heights of even a modified, but still, mystical path of seraphs down to the human level, to a human who suffers from all flaws of the usual conception of life with all its phenomena and destinies. Such a person one day resists and perhaps even tries to fulfil the moral as well as intellectual commandments of yoga, but then they again fall, because they accept everything forced upon them by the world, which is affecting their usual human imperfection. However, this way, the so-called 'turning points' are created, and these sometimes manifest themselves by signs of the mystical progress, at other times by mystical states, which are usually worthless, although at times conspicuous or even interesting. From the point of view of the higher mysticism they are worthless due to the reason that they belong to the emotional experiences, i.e. emotional impulses.

The only important factors in the mystical development are the states which are in the line of a gradual change or transformation of the vital and psychological forces of being into the quality of that which we call consciousness. The real signs of this transformation are a growing clarity of consciousness and an increase in the quality of the intellect. Admittedly, this is often also accompanied by favourable emotional impulses, however, these clearly have the character of secondary phenomena, perceived by the correctly striving yogis as hindrances on the mystical path – hindrances of their own kind.

If these transformations take place during a usual attitude of the mystic towards the human life, they tend to have the character of sudden breakthroughs of the consciousness into the transcendental or pre-transcendental states or qualities; this corresponds to the mystic's strained mystical efforts on the one hand, and falling back on this path, on the other hand. This is considered to be a winding path and only the good and experienced gurus are able to correctly evaluate these sudden breakthroughs. The initial breakthroughs of this kind have no special meaning, except as indicators of the slow mystical awakening of a person. However, their constant repetition means approaching the borderline called the third Buddhist jhana. During this jhana, if we do not consider this jhana as a degree of immersion of the mind into one's own being in the form of meditation, but if we consider it to be an attainment of the adequate base of the natural awareness, the yogi or the mystic reaches a border where they will perhaps understand the purpose and, more importantly, significance of their new inner, and by that also mystical, state. They will realise that their entire previous mystical training meant only the attempts of a blind person to orientate themselves in a new land of life, while now they begin to understand that they have attained a state in which they can quite easily empty their mind and possibly fill it with new qualities. Immediately after the possible engagement of the mind in the daily duties, they are able to empty the mind and develop new contents in it – the bliss of a person entirely untouched by the world and, they are already able to prospectively understand the meaning of the so-called 'fourth jhana', which can be characterised as a total indifference towards the external world accompanied by retaining the equivalent of qualities of the absolute in their own consciousness and spirit.

Let us thus consider all states of the spirit, which are developing since the beginning of the mystical training until the attainment of the third jhana – or, even more precisely, until its further developmental stage – to be attempts whose accompanying results do not need to be evaluated at all. However, when out of these, as though confused efforts, the third jhana arises and, even more, the first signs of understanding of the mystical efforts as efforts of a psychological character arise, and when, besides that, also knowledge arises about the possibilities of easy emptying of the mind and its filling with the higher states of spirit and intellect, then everyone may think that their way towards the peak of the mystical development is fully open.

This opening of the way towards the attainment of the mystical peak in development has real signs and not abstract ones. The possibility to renew the state of mind without any difficulty, and even without purification by bliss and happiness, is the first stage of the march towards the peak of mystical perfection. The knowledge, and later the gradual realisation, of the fourth jhana as a state of an absolute indifference towards the world, accompanied by a retention of the fading happiness which is arising from a total detachment from the world, and, even more, realisation of this indifference without seeking further states of the spirit – the heavenly states, is the second stage of this march. Everything then peaks in the extinguishment of all desires; human as a tension factor of a concretised inner life ceases "without remainder", which is a technical term of the Buddhist teaching.

The progress from the states of the third Buddhist jhana towards the "extinguishment of oneself" does not mean the progressively deepening apathy of the tired and diseased. A person has here the ability to see through the possibilities of the development into various states of life, from the heavenly down to the hellish ones or even up the superheavenly ones, and they are also able to bring themselves into these states by a gradual realisation of them. However, having experienced the states of jhanas from the third one to the fourth exposes the insufficiency of every incarnation, even the superheavenly one, and that is actually a natural barrier to these realisations.

Nevertheless, it is obvious that if anyone desirous of high or wonderful incarnations would be able to realise the states of the third and fourth Buddhist jhana, they would find what they are looking for, i.e. the path to happiness in some kind of incarnation. On their path, they are only threatened by the knowledge of transience of every state; in such a case, the original intent can be modified and they will understand that the greatest happiness is "blowing out", nirvana. They will attain nirvana through the fourth Buddhist jhana. The wonderful incarnations will be attained before they reach the end or goal of the fourth jhana.

Thus, the way is open. It is not the mystical path in the pejorative sense – that fumbling and painful grasping of that which was, in the abstract world, played into one's hands by their eternal disappointment in the world of senses; it is a path which is as experimental as one may wish, with a rigorous implementation of the laws of experimental psychology, i.e. with a continuous possibility to register the entire scale of states of the gradual transformation and, this way, to gradually attain the peak – nirvana, as a person who is well aware of themselves, internally structured in the best way and intellectually well equipped. It is a path similar to walking in the sunshine; no mystical gloominess exists on it – perhaps only in the false ideas of the inexperienced, ill-informed and prejudiced people.

An Impression from Bratislava

We met there for the purpose of edification on a precise system of spiritual efforts, whose purpose is to bring about spiritual growth. This, however, isn't an issue specifically related to Bratislava, but a universal one. In the case of the group from Bratislava, though, everything has crystallised out into a precise form. Since, not only the so-called 'mystical practices' were spoken about but the whole life, the way how to live life; it thus became crystal-clear, that a question of systematic, mystical practices-based mystical development is never relevant, while people live the usual way in the society and in a normal productive age.

If a mystic is integrated in the world, in the life of society, if they are married and, moreover, have worldly ambitions and a desire to live in the usual way and to take part in the same life that is lived by all their fellows, then the problem of mystical development into the mystical powers, knowledge and realisations of spiritual qualities – from improvement of intellect all the way to consciously choosing the highest spiritual quality, which is, in the world of beings, fully analogous with the absolute – is entirely out of the question. Since those, who can choose among these qualities, make their choice and realise them, must necessarily have their whole outer being under a perfect control and power of their will and must even prove it by being more elegant, better behaved, more rational, brighter and better able to cope with every life situation than anyone else with whom they are in contact; people, with whom such yogi keeps company, must not be the lowest of humans, they should be the flower of human society with a level of inner characteristics of which I have just spoken.

If someone suffers from some deficiencies in these things, they then have to search for ways of improving themselves, in the first place in these seemingly low-grade things. Since, the environment in which a person lives surely reflects the level to which they have mastered their "outer being" – to which extent they subordinated it to their own will. Those who do not know about this context and dare to look towards the heights of spiritual qualities from intellect up to the absolute, are unreasonably self-confident fools, who are bound to be wrecked on such an important mystical path, as is this part of it.

Therefore, come down from the heights. Not you, the ones from Bratislava, but everyone in general, and improve yourselves "on the surface", in your social behaviour, conduct in the family, in acting among your colleagues at work etc., etc.! As, that part of the mystical path, where a person is already allowed to choose the qualities of the inner world and realise them, isn't for those who are imperfect "on the external level" at all.

We spoke about life the way I like to speak about it, and not about "mysticism", which is so difficult for me to bear. Even though one topic quickly followed the other one, or even interlaced with it, the situation was still so good that the necessity to tackle the problem of mystical development by a way of life, i.e. how to act in the everyday life, has clearly come to the fore. This is the only platform, from which it is allowed to start. For me it is absolutely clear. For, by this, an utterly necessary foundation, the true beginning of the mystical path was captured and underpinned. On the mystical path, if a person, afflicted by various imperfections and who is outside – in the external life – incapable in various ways, would occur among us, they would not talk about the heights of the Spirit, because, by this, they would almost always present to others his or her own horrible defects on the level of the being, their moral and intellectual imperfections. – Will this beginning, so clearly arisen from my last visit in Bratislava, be forever a matter of course for others?

People sometimes know that they have, or at least suspect themselves of having various moral and other defects. But that qualitatively non-transparent mysticism seems to them good for covering up these defects; thus it happens, that people who are really limited in the spirit, show off trying to appear as wonderful mystical luminaries. This is horrible. Even though mysticism isn't like that, these people still present it in this way to those who don't know anything about it. Then mysticism can quite well be pointed to as something to be warned against, and these people serve the world as a warning against it. Consequently, illusion leads astray illusion, limited persons the ignorant ones. Therefore I want to tell my close ones: "Do not take part in this slurring of mystical teaching." If you cannot be an example of people most developed in the external sense, work only on your betterment – this has a very good reflection on your whole mystical path. For, if you are imperfect in your social and basic private life, you cannot get more from mysticism of the "mystical heights" than just further confusion and delusions; this won't benefit you and finally, it will lead you to the path of karma of those who are also leading others astray. That, in a narrow sense, means that you shouldn't present yourselves as mystics until the moment when you can present yourselves to others as the most reasonable out of the most reasonable, the brightest out of the brightest, the most virtuous out of the most virtuous and the most socially polite out of the socially politest ones.

The mystical development has to include everything that personal life shows as its positive values. After all, it is so clear! If a person is supposed to be successful in mystical heights, they have to control themselves. They have to control themselves to such an extent that they have to be able to prove it in their external behaviour by an ability to demonstrate to others any of his or her outer faces. For, this is that mastering on the outside; if it isn't abused to delude and deceive others, it is a proof of a high-quality heart, perhaps a mystical one, which is recognisable in a will which is always good, humble and, in principle, moderate. A fully developed mystic doesn't act like a selfish person, but as the one who evidently cares about the good of others. Because, such a mystic thus has to be free from egocentric tendencies, and therefore only the others are himself or

herself for him or her. Any other behaviour of a seemingly spiritually developed mystic is a proof of their imperfection and very often
also their wickedness.

What follows from that? – Mystical development must begin
with 'self-training' on the level of acting in the external world, in
the family and society, in which a mystic – beginner lives. Even
thought they aren't selfless, they have to train themselves to be
selfless. Even though they are socially under-developed, they have
to train themselves to be a perfectly socially behaved type. Even
though they suffer from personal hobbies and likings, they have
to eradicate them in order to have a broad spirit, unaffected by
smallness. Among people who are transparent in good action and
behaviour, they have to learn to be transparent and without de-
ceit and by wishing good to all beings they have to surpass them.
When we develop this into further details in outside behaviours,
let us consider it a qualification to enter that mystical part of the
path, which is no longer concerned with 'self-cultivation', but with
a development towards knowledge of spiritually-physical qualities
and towards their choice and realisations.

A person who is imperfect on the outside will surely fall on this
second part of the mystical path, because they don't know about
the traps set before them on their way in life by the hidden factors
of the being and of the spiritual world. And surely no-one wants to
fall mystically or spiritually. I am thus talking about the necessary
security on the path of Spirit. It is not commonly known that when
a person falls spiritually or mystically, they never fall alone. Into the
abyss, where they are heading, they pull down others as well, and
by this they are inflicting upon themselves God's punishment. This
punishment no longer only means the necessity of atonement for
their own mistake, but also a punishment on behalf of those whom
they have pulled down with them, and – this punishment is much
more severe than that for one's own fall.

What else to add? As a rule, even those who are trying to perfectly
conceal that they are engaged in mysticism, or that they are a mystic,
always have someone who knows it about them; and this someone

will surely be among those who will be pulled down by the mystic's fall. And because this someone, the mystic's acquaintance, has again other acquaintances, who again know about this other striving one, a fall of one as a rule becomes an avalanche, in which many get caught. In such a way, the seemingly small sin of the spiritual fall of an individual becomes a fall of many and, all the karma for the avalanche slide, falls on the one individual who dared to fall.

This way the mystical development becomes a public, and no longer a private matter. Therefore, there is no other choice but that a person, who has devoted themselves to mysticism, is successful in the mystical development; those who are connected to him or her are raised by it, by which a meritorious karma for the help to others adds to the perfection been attained. That is usually the reason by which they manage to avoid a personal fall, even in the case of the most sophisticated temptations and seductions.

Thus, spiritual development has to be combined with goodness which begins with 'self-cultivation'. The results of this 'self-cultivation' impress others and attract them to the mystical path. Self-improvement on the level of 'self-cultivation' then helps to accumulate good karma, which makes the platform of sure success firmer, even in the places of those tens thousand pitfalls, into which those, who didn't ground their mystical development well, fall.

To have the ability to live and dwell on the level of "the sphere of mystical heights" is impossible for the unprepared ones, i.e. those who haven't known and mastered themselves on the surface of their being. Selfishness and perfection are such sharp opposites that one always excludes the other, unless one walks the so-called "black path". However, this path is safely closed to average people. There is thus, no other choice, but to start with the mysticism of 'self-cultivation', which enriches a person with virtues and with karma from the deeds of virtue, so that a person can live in qualities called "great friendly". In this way, they will gain victory over all plots which occur on the mystical path as naturally as rocks on rugged mountains. When a person has already started mystical development, they cannot stop it. They can only improve it; they have to get rid of personal preferences and selfishness and thus add to their spiritual development that which protects them from the spiritual fall, which is never small, in case someone has, without the respective morality, gained something from the mystical efforts. However, this is just a side note.

Mysticism, the Weinfurter's* one, which doesn't pay attention to the moral perfection and emphasises only the mystical development, is incorrect. When a person lives in the human society and even grows together with it by living as a human, they must start their entire mystical as well as spiritual development by the right way of life, by the moral living, as it was spoken about in the beginning. Then a person, who has made themselves more perfect on the external level, has also known the law of action and reaction – the karmic law, which they necessarily have to know if they are to successfully pass through all the way the peak of the mystical development, called redemption, salvation, spiritual perfection, and the like.

Begin thus always in life and not with the so-called mystical practices, i.e. concentrations, usage of will and especially not with those results that others can admire, like clairvoyance and similar abilities. These will, at some point, prove that the mystic has attained nothing, even that he or she has taken hold of misleading illusions, or of something by which they lay themselves open to ridicule and are approaching a general fall, i.e. a fall in the domain of a rationally thinking, reasonable, well behaved and mentally well situated person. These ends are, as a rule, worse than the mystical beginning of that person.

---

* Karel Weinfurter (1868 – 1942) – Czech translator who, via his translations, has made available valuable works of foreign spiritual literature. He has also written several books on a spiritual theme himself. He was the founder and a leading member of the association Psyché (1924), which brought together people interested in mysticism in Prague. K. Weinfurter recommended in his books among other things the so-called 'letter practices'. Those were carried out by placing an image of a particular letter into a certain part of body.

Relationship between the mystical development and knowledge

People usually think that mysticism, yoga, Buddhism, magic and any other spiritual school in general, primarily serves the purpose of development of the psychic or paranormal physical abilities and powers. Therefore, they inwardly hope that as a result of these disciplines, they will obtain better opportunities in the social world, in the society or in the material world in general. These are subjective assumptions resulting from a complete ignorance of the laws of causal relations governing the individual life. A simple, intellectually undeveloped person cannot improve their outer life, their external conditions; these are, above all, determined by the ordinary mental abilities and not by some incomprehensible circumstances which have arisen from the mystical or spiritual practices. Even a mystic, occultist or magus, obtains advantages in the external life and the world exclusively by knowledge of the laws of life and nature. This directly rules out the supposition that the advantages of a mystical initiation spring from a simple or even inept spiritual effort.

Those who are familiar with the spiritual and mystical teachings of the Orient know very well that the initial mystical effort serves, in the first place, the purpose of development of knowledge. Therefore this effort contains much more psychology than the volitional effort which is so much believed in by the ignorant mystics. Instead of a simple concentration of mind on some real or imaginary object, contentual and spatial awareness is used i.e. the same methods that are used by students when they are striving for the worldly knowledge in an effort to understand the content of their textbooks.

Yoga, and similarly other spiritual disciplines, do not provide such aids as the school textbooks. Yogis are achieving knowledge and eo ipso also the occult and spiritual power only by means of the operative activity of mind, which we can consider to be concentration of mind, only when we have removed from the concept of concentration an image of an intensive fastening of one's mind upon something. This view is incorrect, and from the point of view of the experimental psychology, it points to the fact that a person, who understands mystical effort like this, will not be proceeding to knowledge, but to the development of some fixed idea, and thus to nothing truly desirable.

The non-intellectualised fastening on some exclusive, real or imaginary object can result only in fixed ideas. The development of intellect, which is the prerequisite for knowledge and by that also the spiritual power, has to be sought for in the so-called 'extensive concentration'; the extensive concentration must introduce into the consciousness of a person as many well registered particularities of the objective or subjective world of forms as possible. From this, it has to be inferred that knowledge is a primary goal of the mystical training. A mystic arrives at knowledge by adequate comparisons of various neurophysiological electric potentials existing in the body.

In the practical sense, mystical training begins with the so-called 'right way of living'. Its purpose is to still emotional desires which are so powerfully clouding the intellect. When these desires are fading away, observation of the body, both its activities and functions as well as it itself as an object (predominantly in its natural proportions) is intensified as a factor leading to the development of obtaining desirable knowledge. This is because, in this way, the mind opens up to a better perfection and quantity of sensory perceptions, while the non-excitability from the point of view of the emotional side – which is achieved by the so-called 'right way of living' – creates conditions for the emergence and development of the necessary knowledge.

Up to this stage, the mystical training has apparently a psychological character. This deters simple seekers on the mystical paths, if they believe that the mystical training should serve as an escape from the natural sufferings of life. Such people cling to an idea that the mystical training immediately, and right from the beginning, uses secret parapsychologic factors serving for the mystical knowledge as well as the mystical power. They consider the simple, human and perhaps also worldly knowledge to be a by-product of some effect of the spiritual development, even though it is in contradiction with the common sense.

The theory of knowledge, especially of the mystical knowledge, which, though, also always has to contain the ordinary knowledge, thus follows from and is even verified by the use of operations with the conscious contents of the mind. Therefore the later mystical education, i.e. of the level of raja yoga, begins with appropriately adjusted contents and ranges of the observation bases or objects – this is what is expected to improve or perfect the intellect as well as the ordinary knowledge. Yet, this development requires a long period of time. This is because, even knowledge doesn't usually develop or penetrate the consciousness suddenly; though exceptionally it happens. In this case, also the sudden enlightenment has two phases or stages: in the first stage knowledge penetrates the being, but only in the second stage the mind absorbs it and is able to use it.

What follows from all of this, is that practical or experimental mysticism leads above all to knowledge. These are considered the prerequisites to the development of knowledge: 1. a widely-based awareness of things within the reach of sensory perception; 2. the absence of wandering of the mind, resulting from its fixation on an object, which is the person themselves. Only by that, the mind and awareness become elastic, and encompass a broad enough area. This is also the base of the mystical development on the transcendental level.

The transcendental level is of a higher order and therefore escapes the normal ability of sensory perception. By an adequate intensity of the concentrating mind, it is possible to cross the border separating the sensory and beyond-sensory world. When a person, with a spirit that is not holding on to the objects of the sensory world, starts to fasten on an object, which is he himself, or she herself, and when they intensify this fastening by a continual training of themselves in this activity, their mind, as a factor usable for exploration and analysis of phenomena, becomes more penetrative. Due to this, it also becomes usable for crossing the borderline between the sensory and the beyond-sensory world. A certain degree of this ability of penetration, depending on the intensity of "concentration on oneself" leads to the transfer of the daily consciousness into the transcendental sphere. This is the beginning of the mystical path, as the mystical path begins exactly on this borderline. The intensity of this "concentration on oneself" then also serves the awareness not to lose coherence even in the new dimensions of the transcendental world. All this together will provide the knowledge of that which is beyond the world or the superworldly, which is however only allowed under the condition that the student of mysticism has reached the peak of development of the perceptions which are enabling the development of the human knowledge.

Thus, not only the development of the ability to discern and perceive that which is really, i.e. for the senses, evidently taking place, is necessary here. It is also necessary to be able to identify the motives, causing these events. Only then the initiated ones will "open" the student's eyes for being able to perceive that which is happening in the transcendental, and by this actually mystical, world and the motives for it. However, the basic prerequisite here is that the disciples of the real spiritual gurus are able to operate with the mental images, and by this to paralyse the influences of the transcendental world which oftentimes, all of a sudden, attacks a person by visions of horrific phenomena bringing about the spiritual fall of the person.

It is very dangerous to expose oneself, through the means of dilettante attempts to mystically develop, to the influences of sensory perceptions brought about by the transcendental world. When someone, based on an unclear desire for mystical life neglects, not only the moral effort, but also the first part of the mystical training, relating to the development of intellect up to the highest degree and based on the operations with perceptions, then they violate an absolutely necessary order of the mystical works. Due to this, it can happen that they will come to the development of unfamiliar perceptions of a transcendental character. Dilettantes in mysticism will, moreover, use them in assessment of the character of outer events and (already out of their innate inability to see everything objectively) bias these events even more in their ideas. Then, instead of a mystic acquiring knowledge, we can find only a person who is prejudiced, narrow-minded and with flawed views.

It is necessary that, after a successful development of the worldly intellect, a person somehow globally develops self-awareness on a physical as well as inner basis. This means that they should concentrate on themselves in the sense of being well aware of, and by that to actually precisely analyse, everything that they in fact are. Then they will, certainly, gradually penetrate with their mind into the structure of, in the first place, their own and later the entire existence as well as into their inner contents. Eventually, they will understand that physical, mental, inner, spiritual and with consciousness equipped existence is a continuum, whose parallel with the cosmic continuum is absolutely perfect.

Only on this level will a person, as a mystic, find themselves on the platform of the physical universe, in the field of the physical forces of existence. People who are unfamiliar with mysticism think that every practising mystic must find themselves there. However, to be on the platform of the physical universe, in the field of the physical forces of existence, never means the craziness that we encounter in the mystic – dilettantes. Also the physical universe, the field of the physical forces of existence, is a universe of realities which are natural for it; if a mystic, who didn't work their way through to the highest level of development of their own intellect, finds themselves on this level, they will certainly be confused by the new kind of sensory perceptions and by that spiritually, and later also physically, destroyed.

Those who prudently arrive at the borderline separating the material world from the physical one and cross it, while being fully and well prepared for the new circumstances related to this crossing, will certainly become a sage as well as a spiritually powerful person. This state however can not be accompanied by the usual communication with other, so-called common, people. From the lower perspective, the transcendental world is perfectly separated from our world. That itself implies that, for the mystic with the so-called 'higher initiation', it is hardly possible to mutually understand each other with the common people in this world, but they will establish contacts of an entirely new kind. Sometimes it will be with people who are most intellectually developed, at other times – and more frequently – with spiritually powerful entities in the form of beings and formations of the transcendental world. Thus a high degree of alienation from our ordinary world will occur and the supposition that a mystic always lives in the conditions which are totally unknown to the common people, will be fulfilled.

These are the conditions for the freeing of mystics from the existing conditions and for establishing contacts of an entirely different kind – which is an obvious sign of the mystic's development towards new conditions and circumstances. Their company will change for another; first a company with an angelic character, later company with a celestial character, and finally the mystic will absorb themselves into the emptiness, which has a divine character, because it is self-radiant. In this realm the mystic ends their journey through the "fields of life".

No exceptions to this occur. There were never any highly developed mystics with a worldly spirit or disposed in this way, and there are even no mystics who would have mutual understanding with the common, worldly people. This is because each one of them had to go through a development, by which they have alienated themselves from the ordinary world and found the superphysical world; this has destroyed the ties between them and other people. If such a mystic has understanding for others, it only results from their previous life experience; in the present this experience has had to cease. This is because they have to exist in living relationships with the transcendental world and from them they draw wisdom, as well as abilities to live above the sphere of the usual human concerns. Therefore we can differentiate between a spiritually well developed mystic and a person mystically undeveloped, even though he or she pretends to be a mystic. A worldly content in the mind of a person bears evidence against them as a perfect mystic; also the quality of philosophical thinking can expose them as a non-mystic.

The most interesting thing about this crossing, from our empirical world into the transcendental one, is, that it is taking place exclusively through the means of the mental intensity termed as concentration, however only under the condition that this concentration has gained the needed qualities by moral efforts, expressed by a perfect inner detachment from the phenomena of the sensory world. In such case, the intensity of mind is no longer burdened by an uncompromising desire; it is only an energy, which transfers the consciousness through the threshold existing between these two worlds. Differentiating awareness is preserved here exactly thanks to this intensity and it serves for the transfer of the knowledge of the transcendental world into our world. Therefore, the mystic realisations aren't a question of a simple practice. Concentration has to be combined with moral efforts; in the first place with a gradual detaching from the world, as it otherwise leads a person to a narrowing of consciousness, which is the opposite of the process gaining knowledge, by which one can work a way through to liberation.

Problematic issues of spiritual development

The mystical teaching can bring a person into a contradiction. This is because it prompts him or her to renounce the world, and, at the same time, it urges them to be active; this requirement, seemingly, does not lead to renunciation of the world.

However, from a psychological perspective, renouncing of the world does not have to have anything to do with passivity, because renouncing itself is also an action, an effort, which requires great attention, in order for a person to be able to be aware of the renunciation of the world at all. If they do not develop this attention, they unconsciously succumb to passivity. Passivity is more related to the various attachments to the world than activity, even if a person is seemingly able to be active, solely when they are prompted by some worldly goals. However, such prompts point to the fact that a person has yielded to reflexive behaviour. This particularly is a slavery, which mystics have to overcome.

Let us not view the life manifestations of a human being through the eyes of the dilettante psychology which considers living to be a matter of inner reflexes. This holds true for the elementary types of people; those, who are internally more advanced, are able to act after consideration and simply suppress the reflexive urges. Attachment and detachment in relation to the world belongs to a different category of psychological qualities than inactivity or activity.

When the mystical teaching examines the tendencies of the whole complex of beingness, it finds out that the "serenity of spirit", as an inborn state of an internally balanced person, is always of a tamasic nature. It follows from this, that those who seek and deepen only this "serenity" walk in fact a path of decadence of the whole being, consuming their own meritorious karma, which has elevated them into the human state.

It is thus necessary to overcome inactivity connected with the state of inborn serenity and inner balance, even if it may seem that this overcoming leads to attachment to the world and even if the "inactivity" gives an impression that the problem of attachment to the world was solved. The situation is parallel to that of the universe: the evolution of the world has only a unidirectional tendency, too. As, when a phenomenon, later known as star, forms itself from the diffuse subtle cosmic material, it tends to be at first always a phenomenon made of diffusely behaving gases, the molecular clouds. Whether it is the general gravitation or also other unknown cosmic influences and forces which operate here, there is always a turning point which occurs in these gaseous molecular clouds, and, from that moment on, the gaseous clouds solidify.

Given that all necessary preconditions are fulfilled here, already the first stage of solidification of the molecular clouds brings about a tendency of these formations to shine; by this, these clouds, now as the so-called 'early stars', become suns. These suns, already as shining stars, go through a self-acting transformation process to the state of "dead" stars again – not shining, finding themselves in a state, wherein these "dead" stars crumble and fall apart by force of the general gravitation, to turn into the cosmically neutral gaseous state again.

In beings – in the microcosm, the process is analogous. When, for example, people settle for a full influence of gravitation, which, from a psychological point of view, means living which is only reflexive, they will not develop into the feeling of independence. Thus, they resemble those stars which will never develop into the state of suns. However, if they detach themselves from everything through a correct renunciation of the world, then their overall development has an ascending tendency, i.e. into the state of the so-called 'self-radiant, divine' beings. The beginning of this development is characterised by the development of activity and tension. The tension will suppress the undesirable forms of activity, namely speculation; in this way, beings arrive at the paths of intensifying active radiation similar to alpha, beta and gama radiation.

Obviously, there are no technological means to identify this gradual transformation of a human being. However, from a psychological perspective, those who are striving for concentration show more and more intense inner tension, which is also evident from the changes in their temperament, from perhaps a passive temperament into an active one, generally choleric. Then, the person in question, subjectively detects that their entire being, beginning with the body begins to vibrate; this vibration is purer and more pleasurable the more the person detaches themselves from the world and from their entire being, from themselves. This creates a state of a detached, self-contained consciousness, which is a precondition of the formation of a self-radiant being.

Only a constant detachment of the consciousness from being is able to give the body an impulse for active vibrations, for radiance, because only such consciousness produces pressures of the psyche on the body, which simply set the physical factors of the bodily existence to radiate. Subjectively, an experience is obtained by this that beings differ, from the physical point of view, by inactive and active organism. Some beings live on a "borrowed light" for example like the planets in the universe. Besides them, there are beings who are self-radiant, who, because of an inactive mind resemble the suns whose radiance is also caused by, in another sense, a transcendental compression of forces.

However, there are many states of being in the beings resembling planets, i.e. living on the "borrowed light". According to the tendency of their thinking, the light shining on some of them is a mellow light of harmonised phenomena, while on others – who are orientated towards "dead" things as are for the consciousness, for example, the material phenomena, or earthly phenomena – almost no external light shines, like they were satellites of suns which are too distant from their source of light.

All of this is a consequence of an inner passivity, of a reflexive way of life, considered to be right by the common psychologists, who consider forcing oneself into activity, including a form of precisely used tension, to be wrong. Yoga as one of the branches of the mystical teachings, except for a yoga which is wrongly interpreted, does not contain these kind of views at all. Because true yoga leads to knowledge that development of phenomena, from the darkness of ignorance towards the light of revelation, is a path of natural tendencies of phenomena. Therefore this development belongs to the true mystical teaching which requires the most resolute possible eradication of passivity, beginning with the inner one and later the passivity of all kinds: precisely through holding back the activity of mind and finally by a total suppression of the inner activity.

A yogi must thus transform, by the pressure of mind detached from being, the state of "inactivity" into a state of a continuous spontaneous activity and by that to enter the path towards the state of self-radiant beings who, in the world of beings, resemble the suns; so that he or she could, by this, overcome the state of beings which are similar to planets, i.e. living on the "borrowed light". For that reason, yoga is a teaching about the transformation of being and not a teaching about ways of how to reach pleasurable or painful emotional experiences; such yoga would only correspond to the characteristics of an entirely worldly teaching.

The awareness of those who are seeking the path to happiness by means of the spiritual teachings, should reach at least so far that they would understand that happiness can never be achieved by striving for the highest sensory gratification, even if they imagined it as "without a woman and money" like many religious penitents. They have to understand that the real and deep suffering results from covering of the consciousness with tamas, from inner, and in general an overall, motionlessness – inactivity. Hence, that happiness has to be on an opposite path, in a gradually developing activity of a being; in activity, which will erode the basic nature of all elements of existence which bring the being into stagnation. They have to understand that the activity which yoga has in mind and approves, although it begins with a physical liveliness, still it has to be increased by an inner self-control, which is to be brought all the way to its highest degree, on which the entire inner activity is fully stopped. Ceasing of the problems of happy and unhappy life is related only to the halting of the inner activity, so that then the being can develop itself into tension whose desirable degree is that which sets the physical factors of the physical being vibrating. When this vibration occurs, every being experiences feelings of happiness similar to those of young people who are unburdened by anything.

Only in this state, the boundary stone separating the immanent world from the transcendental one will be crossed, obviously into the state of transcendence. Only here the mind begins to expand to get to know what the terms "infinity of space" and "infinity of consciousness" mean, even the term "realm of entirely nothing" and also the term "borderline of the possible perception" – those so-called 'four higher Buddhist jhanas', which end in the "destruction of consciousness", but of the daily consciousness, which then transforms into a state called an "ecstatic state of mind", as it is understood in the teachings of the Mahayana Buddhism.

All these enumerated levels are accompanied by every kind of happiness which people desire for.

Mysticism and the problem of sexuality

The brain and sexual organs are, normally, separated in the mind of a person. Therefore, only the sexual liveliness, as a matter of feelings, sends impulses to the brain and the brain accepts them exactly to the same extent to which a person is sensitive to all other impulses from the body. In general, men are more sensitive to sexual impulses than women and therefore they are also more sexually aggressive. They are quite well aware what they suffer from in their consciousness, and therefore they seek possibilities for a sexual outlet to a considerable extent. Women do not suffer from sexual pressures as much, perhaps due to the fact that they are constituted to be able to bear the physical troubles resulting from ever recurring menstruation and also those connected with childbirth. In their case, everything takes place a little way under the threshold of those perceptions to which a man's organism is tuned in, and therefore they are seeking men as sexual partners more instinctively, not always with clear desires. In both cases, in men as well as in women, this state is not good, even though it might not be manifested by sexual perversion, which occurs now and then in men, or by sexual frigidity in women. In both cases, the state of men and women is determined by the Nature, in both cases it is slavery to an inner disposition or complexion.

We generally do not object to this state of sexuality, when the sexual drive in men finds its alternative outlet in the form of some technological or other hobby, we have, however, quite a lot of objections when, for men, it results in a ferocity with a goal to subjugate human society. We are, however, as a rule confused, when the sexuality of women finds its outlet in dressing up, the knitting of stockings, education of all sorts of people towards morality or, on the contrary, in "virtues" of nuns or "morally flawless" she-gossip-mongers.

When all this exceeds the limits of the personal behaviour of the "law-abiding citizens", it becomes pathological manifestations of a compensated sexual drive, which disturbs the human society to some degree. However, alternative outlets of the sexual drive do not necessarily have this nature. Sometimes it happens that people "solve" their problem of sexuality by escaping from it. In women the result is not always so bad. They become, for example, socially bearable 'pesterers' due to their nature or hobbies, because their sexual drive, when it comes to its impulses into the consciousness, is not that pronounced. However, a man, who does not want to appear as excessively sexually desirous, has to benumb himself in the brain; he will then appear as a numb, indolent person, incapable of the seemingly natural competition, which is common in the human society.

Thus, this is an image of the modified manifestations of the sexual drive. It is bad, when this modification concerns the striving of a person for political power, for dictatorship; it is also bad, when a man becomes dangerous for women because of his sexual rutting; it is also bad, when the sexual drive becomes active in women and, as a result, turns into any kind of undesirable form. However, it is not good at all, when a person, due to the incorrect handling of their sexual drive, becomes a "law-abiding citizen" in the human society. In this latter case, we can discover people who are so pliable that they have the herd morality, conforming to a current "wave of morality" or a "wave" of 'citizenship peace'.

When there is an excessive number of, in this way, "law-abiding people", morality always deteriorates because its centre is somewhere, either at some university department, or at some secretariat. This "peace" prevents people from penetrating into the secrets of teachings about the mystical development. The indolence of people who are pliable and malleable in this way proves to be laziness, which requires every teaching to serve to an increasing of their external peace; this is in a diametrical contradiction to the goal of mystical teachings, which can be called teachings about transformation of the inner nature of a person.

In practice, the mystical teaching leads a person to delve into the depths of their own being, and this can never go without escalation of the intensity, speed and thoroughness of information from their instinctive nature into their brain. Thus, it can neither go without the disturbing of a person, who appears sexually non-desirous until their body drives them into non-compromising desires, either for sexual intercourse, a glass of beer, or for banging the table with one's fist. During the mystical efforts, all these things are necessarily to be taken into account, especially at the beginning of the mystical development. Only gurus of the highest type are able to advise those who seek in such a way that their human nature will not sweep them into ill-considered behaviours, even though they are internally pushing the ones who seek towards a border where sexual discharges actually could be taking place. If the motto is "Know thyself", then it is necessary to mentally descend into oneself with analytical attention and by that to 'ripple' the level of an ever steady psyche. As those who do not, with a full self-awareness, mentally descend into themselves and stir up everything that sits there, cannot get to know themselves. Knowledge of oneself can solely relate to states existing for the consciousness, and not to those which do not exist.

There are schools of mysticism, those mercenary Indian ones which are so well trusted in the mystical circles, and these very schools show the ones who seek a path to calmness, but only to calmness of the self-ignorant ones or sleeping predators. These schools harm everyone who becomes their member in his or her present as well as future life. The reason why these schools are so attractive for people, who are nowadays sunken into false ideas about the order of things in the world, is that they actually suit the attempt of people to run away from themselves. Thus, they do not fulfil the requirement "Know thyself". Therefore they should not be thought of, nor should advice be taken from them.

Let us thus think of people who are not internally superficial and who are seeking a real solution of the problem of suffering, which springs from the very structure of typical human beings. These people should know that if they want to solve the problem of personal suffering, they have to descend into their psyche, somehow shake the structure of it and, by that they, indeed, have to expose themselves to attacks of their desirous human nature. If they proceed very prudently, they will then be able to control that which they have stirred up in themselves. When they proceed in this manner, their being is moving forward on the path of life experience, which is necessary for spiritually developed mystics if they are to avoid sliding into various delusions and into the danger of the transformation of categories of certain flaws into different ones.

We must consider uncontrolled sexuality to be the basic flaw in advanced mystics. It is sexuality that makes a person a slave, or an usurper, or a villain, or even an indolent weakling. When he or she gets rid of it, they will be able to become an example of mystical saints, as they are understood by every true mystical school.

How to combat sexuality?

When a person mentally descends into themselves with a clear, vigilant consciousness, they will certainly experience that attack of the undesirable inclinations hidden in the inner nature, the attack which was mentioned above. But if this 'stir' is properly 'dosed', a person will overcome these attacks and get to know themselves. This will provide them with the needed conditions for elimination of the uncontrolled sexuality. They will get to know not only the rough sexuality, taking place in the direct contacts of men and women, but also that sexuality which is variously transformed. If they will not sink even into the latter transformed one, they will have solved the problem of sexuality correctly. When they have solved it, they will realise that they are free and that their freedom is indestructible. And this is actually the point.

When someone searches on the path of mysticism, they are certainly looking for this freedom. However, if they dare to deceive themselves, because, being weak, they would like to solve the problem of sexuality and, by that, the problem of the entire life "on the double", they will, as a consequence, give a different meaning to concepts. Then they will, by their behaviour, prove that they did not find the true mystical goal, but only a baby's dummy, in which they indulge, without realising that they betray their real state.

A mystic must not deceive themselves, for the results of the mystical effort are concrete, even though they are being attained in a seemingly abstract sphere. The other, worldly people do not find any visible peculiarity in someone who has overcome, eradicated, the sexual drive. This is because freedom can only be experienced by each person for themselves, as a value of subjective, yet real, living – as real as when we see someone who was run over by an automobile to be injured or dead.

But be careful! Sexuality has countless aspects. I have already dared to claim that Buddha overcame it, but, even the legendary Christ, did not. That is recognisable in the inner relationships of the adept of mysticism with the surrounding world. A person, who has totally overcome sexuality, is indifferent to humankind. This is because they know that the destinies of every individual are a result of his or her wishes, sometimes expressed as a thought, at other times through actions and, in the same way, that people do not give up their husbands and wives, even though their life together is not joyful, they are unable to detach themselves either from their wealth or from their poverty. Attachment is that which for people predefines their "needs"; it can be a woman with whom they do or do not suffer, it can be conditions due to which they suffer and are burdened. A woman is all that for a man; a man for a woman usually is, as a result of transformed sexuality, socially "someone", or an enemy with whom she has to fight, or an idol with imaginary attributes. All that is a consequence of sexuality leading to suffering, which mystics who lack quality sometimes want to chase away by attaining and experiencing mystical pleasures, which are, from an objective point of view, lacking in substance, although really possible to experience.

Succumbing to sexuality thus equals spiritual darkening; finding a solution to the problem of sexuality equals spiritual knowledge and freedom. When a man no longer needs a woman for sexual gratifications, he is surely close to finding a solution to the problem of sexuality; when a woman does not need a man for sexual gratifications and is not really an omniscient person, she may be totally sunken into some unnatural form of sexuality. For, sexlessness is wisdom on one hand and inner freedom on the other.

Exactly due to the countless dangers following from modifications of the manifestations of the sexual drive, a mystic must not avoid stirring it up by mystical practices. They must, by a precisely focused, analysing mind which is intensified by means of concentration, descend into themselves and continue delving in themselves for so long until all the potential forces and characteristics of the psyche develop. Only by this process everything in the being becomes distinct and therefore also transparent and, due to its natural tendencies, also instructive. In the first moment of such efforts a person will certainly not recognise themselves as an angel; they will rather recognise themselves as an insatiable and greedy animal. Therefore, this descent into oneself, into the inner side of one's own being, has to be precisely 'dosed', because the purpose is to get to know oneself and not to terrify oneself. For, this greed will show to everyone that there is nothing divine in them; this divine is yet to be built up, created, by a moral transformation.

However, it is possible to say this for consolation:

After the insurgence of the potential forces and characteristics due to the mystical effort, they will be quickly led by asceticism again to silence, and that which remains for a person is knowledge of the inner human nature. A person will no longer judge themselves idealistically, they will judge themselves factually and then – when they will be well disposed and genuine – they will find the way to elimination of all that which is evil in them and leads them to suffering. They will also realise that suffering is not caused by the environment in which they live, but only by one's own inner complexion, which can be changed and – only that is the aim of a well understood mystical teaching.

A practical mystical teaching which appears to be right and good to an ignorant one, because it provides pleasurable experiences, is in fact harmful. The reason for that is that these experiences are brought about by becoming internally passive. This does not mean mystical development, but a decline of the being. This is because these experiences are caused by the releasing of karmic merits, which lead a person upwards only while they are being accumulated and not exhausted. In the state of internal passivity, karmic merits can only be gradually exhausted; as they are relatively volatile substances of the human psyche. The non-meritorious karma creates heavier substances, which are released less easily and definitely not by internal passivity. Internal passivity is a peace, in the background of which there can, though, be bad karma which will enter into activity always when a person starts to be active. Unfortunately, always predominantly a desirous person tends to be active.

In contrast to the path leading towards knowledge of oneself in the normal state, from which one then proceeds to higher states, the mysticism of some schools found another way. A mystic does not delve – like yogi does – into themselves over there somewhere into the foundations of existence – into the base of the trunk and initially even lower, into the feet and legs, but into the chest; they say it is there, in the chest, where the spiritual heart is placed. In the way that by delving into the lowest part of the body the forces which belong to this part of the body are kindled, similarly in the chest, the forces and properties are kindled, which belong to this part of the body.

A mystic concentrating into the chest can surely put elementary desires to sleep, because by kindling of the psycho-neural ganglia, they awake idealistic ignitions. This is certainly beautiful, but it doesn't lead to getting to know one's own qualities of the being. It is beautiful, due to the fact that a person can experience blissful feelings which, however, do not belong to a being who was not transformed by the moral efforts. A person in fact separates from himself or herself and they can even attain an abrupt lift from their inner level obtained by birth to the levels above it. However, the poisonous snake of sensuality, selfishness and desires remains in the roots of their being and, under suitable circumstances, it will find the power to return them back to their primitive and elementary humanness. It doesn't matter if it does not take place in this life. The desire for existence leads to self-renewal, re-birthing, reincarnation and therefore the snake of low humanness has enough time to finally succeed.

It is thus necessary to descend into oneself by a concentrated and analysing mind; admittedly, the lower human nature will be irritated by this, but if a person adheres to the commandments of morality given by yoga, they will arrive at a calming down again, with the good result that that poisonous snake will leave its place. Then the person will no longer be pursued by this evil enemy, but will be allowed to live in peace, in a state of redemption for all times, unless, of course, they end their own life due to the lack of desire, the lack of wish, to be and to live. This new state is no longer in that place, where a human is harnessed into a yoke of the all-controlling devil, as he was and is known by the spiritual teaching of yoga. He or she is above the Nature, above the tempting human nature, above the level of the driving forces of Nature.

The Greatest hindrance

There is no other path to knowledge of oneself, others, humankind and the whole world in general than the path of spiritual development, the mystical path; it begins with entering one's own being by conscious thinking and observation of all processes that are taking place in it. However, many do not achieve this knowledge. The reasons for this are that a person views himself or herself and the world very superficially and that they evaluate their own behaviour according to entirely wrong criteria. Especially if they are religious, they often yield to the self-deception that the decisive criterion is whether their behaviour as a citizen is flawless: they do not kill, steal, or give way to unbridled desires for erotic discharge and, perhaps, they live a harmonious family life. They think that if they behave like this, they have already fulfilled all moral requirements of the spiritual and religious teaching, and thus that everything regarding morality is, already, in a perfect order in their case.

However, I have said that the path of spiritual development, the mystical path, which really leads to knowledge of oneself, others and the whole world, begins with the entering of conscious thinking into one's own being and observation of all processes which are taking place in it. This is a matter of both mental as well as moral efforts. However, from the moral point of view, the modification of personal behaviour on the surface, the superficial virtues of the so-called 'law-abiding citizen', will no longer suffice here. The law-abiding citizen always avoids facing – wherever, whenever and in any way – the disapproval of society in whose centre he or she lives and which can constantly observe his or her behaviour.

From the point of view of the spiritual teachings, the opinion of society in whose centre a person lives does not matter at all. The only thing that always matters is whether a person practices depersonalisation genuinely and correctly. And depersonalisation? The only way to measure it is whether a person respects or does not respect their personal inclinations and desires, whether they succumb to them or even whether these may be a temptation for them, when they live a self-restrained life.

Let us assume that somebody was, since earliest childhood, infected by their family environment in such a way that they succumbed to a conviction that to seduce girls, to get drunk, to commit confidence tricks and to get into fights with other young men in pubs and other similar things are wrong. That is quite all right, however, only until the point when this conviction will bring them to break themselves in the vital sense, and become the so-called 'law-abiding citizen' unable to possibly behave aggressively, or even seemingly destructively. In such a case they don't descend into their psyche, walking the path leading to knowledge of themselves, others and the whole world, but arrive at a flawed view, that the superficial virtues of the "law-abiding citizen" mean true moral discipline. This attitude, in fact, only gives an impression that this is how an example of a true Christian, who is predestined to receive God's mercy, should look like.

In the questions of morality and especially in the question of the redemptive morality, the most important role is played by the ratio of forces, the forces of actions and reactions. This means that if the human nature has been broken by incorrect behaviour, and only because of this the morality of the so-called 'law-abiding citizen' has found its place in them, the undesirable manifestations of the vital start to run in faint pulses or below the threshold of thorough self-awareness. This is a very bad hindrance on the path of gradual descent into the depths of one's own being, i.e. on the path of knowledge of oneself, others and the whole world. A person no longer sees a reason for total purification, which is based on a complete eradication of inclinations, on the development of an absolute absence of all differentiated concepts in the mind and on destruction of all emotional experiences, beginning with the unfortunate inner states and ending with blissful ones. They have succumbed to a conviction that only those are outside the borders of the desirable morality, who seduce girls, get drunk, deceive others and get into fights with others in pubs. Nevertheless, the beginning of sinful behaviour is already present in thinking in differentiated concepts and giving importance to emotional states of any kind. In view of this, it means nothing when a person escapes from being "a Casanova" and becomes a father of an orderly family with twelve children or only with one child. Not even a childless marriage, or even celibacy, would make a person moral in line with the commandments of the spiritual teaching, if it is possible for the temptations to have a woman, or to indulge in any other emotional experience, to arise in him.

A gross violation of the moral principles of the spiritual teachings starts, though, at the moment when a person communicates at all on the inner level with the world surrounding them, even though it appears to them that they do it in a morally flawless manner. This is because, if a total inner purification is the highest moral requirement, then communication with the surrounding world which indulges in physical interests, means taking part in this way of life. Due to this, realisation of a complete inner isolation is absolutely out of the question. The sight of a person, as well as all their other senses, are no longer tuning in to perceiving various categories of emptiness, but only to obscuring perceptions of the external phenomena. From a strict moral standpoint, it is worldliness which is a reason for inner darkening.

From this viewpoint, redemptive morality is thus rooted in the effort to detach oneself from the whole world of differentiated phenomena. In the first stages of the mystical path, there is thus an effort to detach oneself from the phenomena of the material world – predominantly with regard to moments when impulses arise to get hold of them as objects of sensory gratification.

For this detachment, more is obviously needed than to just subdue the turbulent desires to the extent of allowing them to discharge themselves within the limits of the seeming external virtues of a citizen. All inclinations that we yield to, have to be therefore attacked and eradicated. All wanting has to be suppressed to such an extent, that all objects of sensory desires become nothing to a person, but at the same time a person must retain such a clarity of the spirit, even as if they would allow their wanting to run its unrestrained course.

These are the conditions of purification of the field of perception all the way to its emptying, and this also symbolises that solitude or inner solitude, required by spiritual teachings from every follower of these teachings.

The emergence of this kind of solitude is a precondition to knowledge of oneself, others and the whole world. This knowledge becomes fully flawless as soon as a person no longer mourns over the fact that they are renouncing the world. In other words, when they don't mourn over their voluntary asceticism, but they, happy and attentive, clearly see and observe the surrounding world, all that is happening in it and all the destinies of all its inhabitants. Then they will discern that there are entirely logical relationships between actions and their consequences, between behaviour and destinies following from it, as well as the fact that all events in the world of people are in an objective relation with the actions of these people.

When we are considering it from this point of view, the greatest hindrance on the path to full self-knowledge is the conscious or unconscious deceiving of oneself by a shallow or incorrect opinion about the moral flaws and virtues of people. It is necessary to know that when someone gratifies their sensory cravings, whether within the role of a father of a family or as a citizen who, for their relationships to their fellow beings or to a collective of other citizens in their community, goes for some beer, he is no longer, at all adhering to redemptive morality requiring inner isolation or solitude. He is only a social creature, to whom the knowledge of oneself, others and the whole world will never arise. The reasons are only psychological. The activities happening within these relationships are not the actions of the wise ones, which always require a distance from that which is observed, but they are actions of the foolish ones. In their background, there are always emotional stimuli brought about by participation of either the family members, or those fellow beings from their community, in these activities.

The spiritual teachings, whose purpose is to help every individual to self-knowledge and to the knowledge of the entire world and all that is happening in it, prevent the danger of getting stuck in the seeming moral and social integrity, mainly by leading their students to a systematic development of the elementary inclinations to their full extent. This seems to be in opposition to the development of the redemptive morality. However, development of these inclinations is, intentionally, interrupted by their suppression. It is similar to climbing up a ladder, where one step means sparking off even the hidden inclinations of the human nature, and the following one means their suppression, all the way to their eradication. This leads to gradation of the pressure as well as resistance, which always has to be in balance for the result – the mastering of oneself – to occur. And because at the same time, attention is paid to prevent the consciousness from being overwhelmed, during this procedure, by highly intensified pulses of the animal nature, the result of this whole process is a perfect balance of spirit which can see everything around it from a detached point of view. He or she is observing everything as a sage, who understands the whole life, because they have got to know, through this training, what do the actions and reactions of one's own inner nature, one's own spirit and through that also actions and reactions of the inner nature of all people mean. It is indeed a matter of course that it is only possible to achieve this detached point of view through gradation of the sensory temptations, which are only possible to overcome with the exertion of all of one's will.

The phrase "with the exertion of all of one's will" means that good quality spiritual teachings have the character of psychological scientific techniques which put very effective tools into a person's hands. By means of them, it is possible to achieve great good for those who have accepted them as their life directive, as well as for their fellow human beings. It is only necessary to behave according to the principles of the redemptive morality, which are always contained in these teachings and which are taught by them. In addition, it is possible to say this: the greatest enemy of a spiritually striving person are mainly their character inclinations, which force them to gratify their own sensory cravings. However, there is no other reliable solution to the problem of ignorance anyway. Neither a dull temper, nor getting swept by emotions, will ever allow reaching the peak of development of potential human possibilities. They will, however, surely be reached by stimulating the incorrectly suppressed human inclinations, or by their suppressing, according to whichever prevails: the inhibition of spontaneous manifestations of the emotional nature or their development all the way to their uncompromising manifestations.

If we observe people around us who suffer from ungratified desires, we can always figure out that there is a conflict between that which they wish to achieve and that which they are able to obtain. The roots of this conflict are developed, uncontrolled inclinations. Since, inclinations have the property of multiplication and growing stronger, and so, if they are uncontrolled, always bring a person into unfortunate inner situations. However, when a person destroys them, it is only a seeming victory over them, because they transform themselves into dream-like visions and desires; these tend to always remain ungratified and from that an impression arises that a person is facing injustice. Therefore the spiritual teachings have to go to the root of these things. This means that, in the first place, attention is paid to slow development of the inclinations to their full extent, but only whilst retaining the possibility to fully control them. And why one has to use their entire willpower for this? To desire the knowledge of oneself, others and the whole world only for the purpose of escaping suffering, requires an inner development and, afterwards, obtaining a full control over oneself.

It is never possible to achieve this result when the inhibition of manifestations of temper has already occurred, nor when a person achieved full development of their inclinations and have succumbed to their influence. Therefore, the necessary conditions of a full inner recovery have to be created. For this situation, it holds true that the criterion of full inner health is an adequate development of desires and inclinations; the criterion of spiritual perfection is gaining control over these desires and inclinations.

The spiritual teachings are, in their principle, based on the yogic method. This method is based on mental pressures on the being, because they are known to activate reactions of the physical beingness. And because the emotional vitality resides in the base of the trunk, concentration into these very parts is used in order to awaken and fully develop the desirous beingness. The aspirant of spiritual perfection, he or she who aspires to self-knowledge, the knowledge of others and the knowledge of the whole world, thus uses this concentration and, by means of it, fully develops their being on the emotional level, whilst, by controlling the inclinations of the being, they increase inner resistance. The inclinations in the form of wanting, must not overwhelm consciousness with darkness, because that would lead to a deep non-knowledge and so the ignorance would deepen even more.

From that it follows that concentration on the base of the trunk is practiced only until such a vital stimulation is achieved, which manifests itself by an increase in freshness and an overall reviviscence. Attention is then paid to the manifestations of vitality, i.e. whether desire increases or not. As soon as even a small intensification of cravings becomes detectable, will is immediately employed to perfectly suppress them. This is continued for so long until a complete inner tranquillity is achieved, a total inexcitability; only after the being fully calms down in this sense, the thrusts of a concentrating mind are repeated. In this way, further vital stimulation occurs and the stronger and stronger self-control over developed wanting must once again put everything into a complete tranquillity. This is repeated for so many times, until an evident certainty is reached – that the vital nature has fully developed and it is fully mastered.

By this, the goal of the spiritual, yogic or mystical practice is finally achieved. One's own being is identified as fully developed on the level of feelings and, at the same time, temptation cannot lead the person morally astray; this going astray is based on yielding to sensory and emotional inclinations.

The mystical practice has, in this case, led a person to the peak of fully developed humanness with concurrent and full control over all vital manifestations. However, this isn't the goal of the spiritual teachings. It is only a very important stage on the path of the integral spiritual development, whose highest goal is a "state of existence without the need of any kind of supports".

None of those whose emotional nature is covered by the state of torpefied awareness, by ignorance or by impairment of its manifestations, can reach this far. In these people, their human nature is always manifesting itself by unconscious manifestations. This is an evidence of their limited knowledge and their self is demarcated without them being able to cross its fictive barriers.

Already for this reason, the spiritual teaching which always has a character of Psychology, has to pay attention to full development of the entire human nature. However, there is a test contained in this development; a test of will, which has to prove its ability to manage everything in the field of feeling, thinking and awareness. Without this proof, there is no liberating knowledge. Therefore, a person on the mystical path – on the path of knowledge of oneself, others and everything, always meets the greatest hindrance on the true mystical path and on the path of true mystical training. The main danger of this path is that this overall self-transformation might not be genuine, it might be only seeming. It can be either based on modification of the moral surface, on the development of seeming virtues, which are rooted either in the breaking of a well developed positive temper which was ready for action, or, it can be based on self-deception, in a sense that we don't want to see our vices as vices, but we want to see them as virtues, as moral perfection. However, such 'moral perfection' is, though, getting angry with everything except its own manifestations.

Thus, from a long-term perspective, those who aspire after knowledge of themselves, others and the whole world, must be totally honest with themselves and try to obtain basic knowledge, in the first place in the field of developed and undeveloped inner life as well as animality, as the manifestations of simple vitality. Only through this honesty can they obtain understanding that the seeming morality, which may perhaps teach a person a perfectly correct social behaviour, can leave a trail of an inner destruction. Destruction of natural manifestations of temper, of the freedom of spirit which is supposed to be always free from anxiety-rousing pressures due to scruples related to the surroundings. However, if the inclinations, tastes and desires should lead a person to flawed socio-moral behaviours, he or she has to prevent it. Then they have to achieve a clear, relaxed spirit, even without behaviours showing socially flawed inclinations, and by means of this achievement, the flawed inclinations will never again be a temptation for them. Only this is the true morality, the morality of a person who is not internally deformed and who is already, at least a little bit internally free.

Knowledge of the psychological relationships and laws has to show the person the abyss of seeming morality, when he or she must, due to the effect of powerful flawed inclinations, always pretend that they are different than they really are; that they cannot show others their true face, they cannot, how it should always be, 'wear their heart on their sleeve'. In this case they lie to themselves and to others, because they can never stay in a permanent contradiction with themselves in view of their inclinations and behaviour. This deceiving of oneself is the second aspect of the greatest hindrance on the path of knowledge of oneself, others and everything.

The real knowledge, which is related to spiritual perfection and freedom, can thus never develop somewhere where there is a contradiction between that which is in the heart, and that which is in the social behaviours. For, a spiritually perfect person who has achieved knowledge of themselves, others and the whole world, never has in their heart, anything else than that which is manifest in their behaviour. This is the main foundation of the true sincerity – the sincerity to oneself, which is the true one because it does not bear the mark of contradictions between feeling and behaviour. Such sincerity is claiming the realisation of the truth, i.e. the facts which exist between the actions themselves and intentions in actions of oneself, others and all people in general.

If a person cannot detect whether, behind the actions of others, there are intentions of the same kind, they see everything incorrectly. That means ignorance, leading them astray. For, even if they would interrupt all contacts with their material environment, they will not interrupt those with the invisible environment, in whose centre they live and which also wants to deceive everybody in order to profit from it, by gaining forces leaking from those deceived ones.

And manifestations through deeds? If a person wants to observe the moral commandments of the true spiritual teachings, because they trust that it aids achievement of knowledge of oneself, others and everything, then they should enforce a balance between that which they want and that which they are allowed to when adhering to the moral instructions of these teachings; this should be only at the cost of unpermitted wanting. Otherwise they will never get out of lying to themselves as well as to others; this mendaciousness will, as the greatest hindrance on the mystical path, always obstruct their way towards the desirable knowledge. Thus, they have to be mindful of achieving of such relaxation, in which only those, can be, who have no contradiction inside of them between that what they want and what they can and are allowed to, without violating the moral commandments of the redemptive teaching. This is the way to overcome the greatest hindrance on one's own mystical path towards knowledge of oneself, others and the whole world, on the path towards realisation of the state of absolute, towards spiritual freedom.

It is therefore necessary not to lie to oneself! It is necessary to call one's own inclinations and behaviours by their proper name, so that the orientation in the labyrinth of inner life is perfect, because, if the external and visible environment can lie, the invisible environment can lie all the more. However, all this can be overcome by the power of truth and perfect sincerity – in the first place to oneself and then, indeed, to others too.

The Mystical path by means of transformations of elements

Mysticism in all its forms, and therefore also yoga, is, usually, due to people's ignorance of its prospects and goals, assessed as any other profession or job: it is expected to aid in gratification of sensory cravings, which people consider to be the criterion of their personal needs. However, this assessment of mysticism is incorrect. Mysticism, as the highest quality section of the deep psychology is guided by the knowledge that various kinds of emotional experience, good as well as bad, are directly – to a universal extent – dependent upon the inner disposition of beings and therefore mysticism focuses solely on modification of this disposition.

In line with the facts, mysticism doesn't acknowledge the conviction that the quality of emotional experience depends upon the external, material or social conditions. Both the powerful ones, as well as those who are absolute slaves to the external circumstances, can be happy or unhappy exactly according to that which their being produces into the consciousness as stimuli for joys or for suffering.

The inner disposition, which influences the quality of emotional experience, lies predominantly in the mutual ratio in the being of that which can be understood as the elemental qualities, and properties, to that which can be understood as the waste products, whose basic influence on the beings can be identified as various degrees of inhibition of daily consciousness. There are four elements constituting the material essence of the being, namely earth, water, fire and air; they correspond to the body, the feelings, the energy and the spiritual equipment, respectively.

The body is a modification of the earth element. It is composed of living cells and when we put aside all spiritual – and thus also the inner – equipment, it is a so-called 'living matter', that, which is only potentially alive, because it does not come out of itself by psychological acts, it does not manifest itself by living. Thus, from the mystical point of view, it is a factor which is solid, settled in itself, stable.

The feelings, which are an inner modification of the function of touch, belong to the life manifestation of the element of water, because they are a synthesis, provided by the perceptions to the consciousness as an experience from the abstract touches; they will thus never become a pure abstraction. The feelings are connected with the body and relate to it – they ensure chemical and physical metabolism for the body; through the physical metabolism, life experience is obtained.

The fire element, manifesting itself by energy, is in fact a waste product of the gravitational phenomena caused by the grouping of cells of the body, and thus it is a physical phenomenon, which is exclusively dependent on this gravitation. In yoga, the fire element is identified quite markedly by a carrying out of the transfers between the will as a positive factor which is dependent upon awareness and the body which is an object of this active awareness. A varying of the intensity of this transfer decreases or increases the energetic tension in the being; in a high degree of tension this manifests itself as warmth or fire.

The air element corresponds in the being, above all, to the space or field which exists or, also, is being created between the physical particles constituting the body. Under the expansion of this field by means of a stable mind and a consciousness which is not narrowed down, this type of modification of the air element behaves as an intellectualising factor – the mental factor in the matter which would always be, without the air element, just a so-called, 'dead matter'.

Precisely the mutual proportions of these elemental components of existence make the beings or phenomena animate or inanimate. From the primitive evolutionary stages up to the higher ones, these phenomena manifest themselves sometimes as mineral phenomena, sometimes as vegetal phenomena, and at other times as animal phenomena. The animal stages in turn manifest themselves either as almost lifeless, or as emotional, or as expressive (dynamic), or as intellectual according to the predominance of earth, water, fire, or air element in them.

The mystical teaching is, above all, interested in bringing the ratio of these elements into a relative harmony. Disharmonious relations are only allowed with regard to the necessity of gaining life experience, by which beings develop spiritually. Mysticism expects the earth element to impart on the being calmness of the spirit, the absence of a wandering of mind and a base for the broadest possible space of awareness. The water element is expected to erode selfishness and by that to create conditions for a constant developmental ascent, i.e. freeing from the heaviness caused by the influence of the earth element and elevation towards the development of the air element as a base of the broadest possible space of awareness. The fire element is expected to erode the structure of the being by tension, thus, from the inside. When an appropriately adapted tension in the being spatially broadens the structure of the being, the being will be adapted for a fuller absorption of the air element and, by that also, for the tendency towards spirituality – towards the opposite of the natural involution, narrowing and deadening. The air element in the being is expected by mysticism, above all, to gradually dissolve 'I' as an inner factor, which is the leading factor of a number of spiritual factors which cause the tendencies towards this narrowing, involution, or deadening. By this, the practical mysticism becomes a methodology, which, depending on circumstances, leads to the best way out that can ever arise for the living phenomena.

* * *

I hereby begin to describe this practical teaching.

1. *The path of the mystical transformation is a methodically carried out change in the qualities of being as carriers of the spiritual, moral and destiny predispositions of a person. This change is to be carried out by the person's own inner power.*

Explanation: Admittedly, a human is constantly internally shaped by the influences of the external world, but this happens only during passive attitudes. In this case, he or she has a 'herd' or collective karma. The individual karma is generated only when a volitional tension from an uncompromising desire for something arises. The external influences have little impact on this individual karma, it is a personal, and individually differentiated karma. However, the solving of this problem is actually not the aim in mysticism. The attention turns to the volitional tension, whose purpose is to change the properties of the carriers of all inner predispositions of a person. This tension must be focused on the borderline between the "thick environment" of the charges, which constitute the being, and emptiness, as the being also touches this borderline. Therefore it is necessary to explain, what is meant by the borderline between the "thick environment" and emptiness.

2. *Difficulties, that occur here, originate in the fact that the awareness of a person always kindles in the qualities of being – on its psychophysiological components.*

Explanation: Problems are purely psychological, because, the inner passivity of people causes the content of their consciousness to fully correspond to these qualities of being, and, consequently, consciousness really seems to be a superstructure on top of the physical beingness, or a product of a gradual evolution or reshaping of the material essence of being. However, in fact, this is only an illusion. Even if we suppose that the inner life is a product of this evolution, still, at some point of this evolution, the relations invert; thus, the inner life then becomes the primary factor and the whole system of being becomes a secondary factor.

It is possible that in the completely primitive stages of the organic life, the inner life is leaning on, or even developed from, the metabolism of the absorbed food. However, as soon as an adequate development of the daily consciousness occurs, the proportions invert. This is because the daily consciousness is able to contain into it being as a image. When this image precisely corresponds to the mechanically functioning organism, this consciousness is able to modify the functioning of the organism. According to the yogic experience, the influence of the organism on the consciousness changes so significantly that we can establish an axiom that we have discovered a path to making the whole being invisible.

As the senses change their abilities with the change of the influence of the organism on the consciousness – because they are able to transmit perceptions from the sphere of phenomena which is, for us, the invisible – a natural assumption arises that our sensory world, which is actually delimited by the sensory perception, is only a segment of the spectrum of reality. Discernments then constantly prove to a person that the living organisms did not evolve by a simple transformation of matter, but by a development from the primordial consequence of the interference of the physical qualities by a gradual degeneration. A correct assessment of the improved sensory perceptions cannot arrive at any other conclusion, even though there is a missing connecting link in terms of an organism which would be invisible on one hand and visible on the other hand. It is only an analogy to the problem of a connecting link from animals to humans. Rather, there is another fact detected: the arising of such evidently unchanging species (creatures) is determined by a sudden decline or uplift on the line of evolution. Somewhere in a time period of the distant past, the monads clothed in immensely subtle forms suddenly stabilised in the given forms and then their materialisation had already occurred quickly.

Besides this, we must not forget that the sensory perception is a problematic vehicle for conclusive proofs. The yogic experience can prove to us that, for example, with the systematic expansion of the process of awareness, and by that also consciousness, that 'big universe' falls into the appropriately broadened consciousness, and so, its objective dimensions are no longer valid. When the consciousness, broadened to the highest level, stabilises itself by the idea of 'I', the universe becomes something so small that it really, as an inner object of a vigilant mind, disappears or falls into insignificance.

This experience of the yogis is not based on an incorrect use of suggestion or autosuggestion. Both of these are ruled out already by the fact that a person systematically broadens their awareness more and more. Where there is an active vigilant consciousness based on work, both autosuggestion and suggestion are out of the question. It is only a relativity which applies in the world of phenomena. The universe seems to be big only when we make the range of awareness smaller by petty interests. If a yogi makes their being an object of which they want to be thoroughly aware, then a tendency towards broadening of the range of awareness arises. This broadening gradually accelerates more and more, and so, it is within the reach of the experience of a person to recognise that the whole continuum is an illusion; the range of this continuum can be altered by the very broadening and narrowing of the range of awareness. An absolute range of awareness destroys the entire universe which can no longer, in this role, prove to a person its power over them, but it will only prove to be nothing, a Fata Morgana, produced by the inner conditions, which can be influenced by every individual themselves.

3. *The being, as an autonomous carrier of the spiritual, moral and destiny dispositions of a person, thus commonly itself decides what*

kind of deeds a person will perform, whether he or she will do good or bad, whether he or she will have faith in goodness or understand evil as beneficial.

Explanation: The being is a set of psychophysiological components or elements and their ratio creates their mutual influence, which on the outside manifests itself by character and, of course, also by actions. From the point of view of the process of reincarnation, the ratio of the components of the being change. A certain grouping expresses itself by goodness, another grouping manifests itself by evil. Even though the main factor for these proportions of components is the physical influence, the physiological grouping still proves to be very significant, too. The physiological grouping does not only manifest itself in the different appearance of people, but also in small differences in their arrangement of organs. Naturally, the differences do not constitute decimetres, and, perhaps, not centimetres either, but they certainly constitute fractions of millimetres. These differences demonstrate themselves in the characters of individuals.

These differences are produced by karma as a factor identifiable by yogic means; karma, which is, in other words, the inertial force, or, even more precisely, the tension between organs. The deeds of beings leave behind a tension, which is not only a driving force, but it is also a forming force. The two effects are interrelated, so the driving force, as a resultant of deeds, manifests itself as a forming force and forming is, in turn, a state constituting a basis for the character of the driving forces. In this way karma hopelessly ties up the being and only an analysis by a mind, detached from the world by renunciation of everything that arouses wanting, can break this structure of being.

4. *In this way, the wheel of karma – the wheel of actions and their effects – is set in motion. If goodness disappears from the consciousness, even if only as the right concept, a person will walk the path of bad karma.*

Explanation: The degree of mixing of goodness and evil cannot be determined precisely. Just like the goodness is usually disturbed by evil due to the presence of selfishness, evil is usually moderated by the regard for others, by some kind of altruism, even though, in the worst case perhaps applied only to the members of one's own family. However, this is not a satisfactory state for the mystical prospects. Goodness has to be better isolated from evil by the volitional tension, leading to intentional selflessness for so long until the thinking has more interest in the welfare of others than in the personal welfare. Then the wheel of good karma will appear pure; both the inflow and the outflow of the person's activity will be only thinking in goodness. This is the removal of a non-mystical hindrance, the "clearance of the field" of prospects, which facilitates the fulfilment of the further tasks of the mystical transformation which we are interested in above all.

5. *However, the mystical transformation can only come about by the intensification, and by that, by the purification of the individual elemental principles – the earth, water, fire and air principle.*

Explanation: From the psychological point of view, the earth element manifests itself by inner stability, the water element by the feelings, the fire element by energy and will, and the air element by the inner equipment. If a person is internally unstable, the earth element is not in order in them. If a person's character is dry, the water element is not in order in them. If they are deconcentrated and pliable, then neither energy nor will is in the proper state and that testifies to a disorder of the fire element. The degree of intelligence, brightness and mental capacity bears testimony to the state of the air element. With regard to the fact that, in a common person, we can find wandering of mind or focusing of attention solely on the external things, selfishness, pliability for the purpose of keeping the best possible living conditions and prejudice, he or she must always, if they want to be a yogi, or, if they want to attain the inner and by that also spiritual perfection, pay attention to the development and intensification of the elements; this is the foremost purpose of yoga.

6. *The intensification must then be carried out in the same order, which is indicated in the previous aphorism.*

Explanation: The elemental principles of the being are been made impure by the inner passivity of a person. The inner passivity is the cause of a constant influence of the external world on the individual by an inflow of substances which are burdened by uncompromising cravings and whose influence is intensified exactly by the cravings. This can serve an easier understanding: if someone has a desire for us, they are fastening upon us mentally, and literally flood us with their life force, with something similar to a fluid, which is marked by their moral and inner qualities. Those, who are passive, are permeated by this 'something' which is similar to a fluid and due to that, their elemental principles are being clouded. However, if one is internally active, if their thinking is conscious and focused precisely on certain concrete things, then they have strengthened the dam of their being by 'concrete' of a spiritual type, so the "waters" of a fluidly character by which they are "flooded", cannot get inside them. This is the starting point towards the intensification of the elemental components of the being – this is stated in the following aphorism.

7. *The element of earth will be rid of admixtures, and intensified by means of thorough awareness of the body, primarily as a material formation, and also by an attentive observation and awareness of all physical acts and activities.*

Explanation: This is actually the "practice of earth". It is necessary to perform it as the first practice in order for the mind to stabilise, or, to become non-wandering, and for the spirit to become concentrated, or, capable of concentration. This result should never be underestimated, because, only a non-wandering mind enables one to see what is happening without bias, without the glasses of prejudice, whose absolute dominance over the human being is in a direct relation to the wandering of mind of this being. By a non-wandering mind, one can also know himself or herself.

A mystic must be able to observe everything impartially, because, no one can ever explain to them the meaning of the ever changing tension of the inner forces. These changes always escape the discernments of people fascinated by the external happening; and still, only these changes are the tendencies which lead either to critical inner states or situations, or to the calmness of spirit as to the victory over the circumstances of each subject.

Thus, this is the purpose of the "practice of earth". By an attentive observation and a perfect registering of all physical acts and activities, everyone will develop an ability to detect the changes of inner states already at their very beginning, when the person still is able to change these inner states – and one has to be able to perform this very change. For if we, based on the worldly indoctrination, rule out the possibility of attaining the transcendental mystical experience, still, in the high quality mystics, we will always discover that they control their inner states and by that also, to a great extent, the situations in which they occur.

However, the mystics do attain the transcendental experience. These are, though, not a gift of some God's mercy, but a result of the stabilising of spirit, a result of attainment of the state of a non-wandering spirit, which is able to discern that which a wandering spirit never discerns due to its restlessness. For, everything that happens has its causes somewhere in the motives – in the hiding places of spirit, where a spiritually well-developed mystic can detect them, because the calmness of mind is, for the awareness, a level where the motives emerge, or, originate.

Thus, the "practice of earth" must not be underestimated. A perfect calmness of mind resulting from this practice are those 'grounds of existence'. In it, there is the sphere of origination of all dynamics, which is called the origination of everything; a perfectly calmed down spirit of a person will get there by means of the "practice of earth", to obtain there, within the framework of the logical inter-relations, knowledge of, and to experience, the miracles of creation and of all that is related to them.

8. *By the "practice of earth" the mind becomes steady, i.e. non-wandering, unwavering, non-distracted, concentrated and – by that the element of earth is ready for a gradual mystical transformation.*

Explanation: A sine qua non condition of the success on the further mystical path is the accomplishment of the "practice of earth". Only a stabilised mind and consciousness can guarantee a perfect orientation in the inner processes as well as in the current spiritual states, which will start to run with the "practice of water". Therefore, we must not imagine mysticism as becoming sentimental up to the ecstatic dimensions, but as a method, by means of which the order-bringing will obtains control over the 'rippling' of feelings. For, the mystical education wants to bring feelings to the state of a complete satisfaction of the person and only then to the so-called 'burning out', which no longer gives feelings the possibility to pull the person down into uncontrollable inner states. However, before a person works through to this, they must get rid of the opinions of the European and American psychologists. A person must not imagine that wanting, renamed as 'personal needs', is here only for the purpose of gratification, because, in this case we would no longer need the police, which establish a limit to the requirements of our desires. Thus, it is better for a person not to let the desires develop, but to overcome them, because by that they arrive at the inner calmness which brings to completion a perfect control of all actions of the body.

It is thus necessary not to complicate the situation in the field of spiritual development by an unreasonable non-adherence to the sequence of steps, which is always supposed to begin with earth and end with air; by air, the development at the level of the natural awareness is brought to a close. It is related to a psychological law. The "practice of water" sets the entire inner beingness into 'rippling', chiefly in the emotional domain, and a restless mind, which always clouds consciousness, then disables registering of the inner processes. This constitutes the increase of confusion and increase of the inability to free oneself from ignorance, from prejudice and pre-conception. The processes that occur in the inner beingness, which are, in addition, accelerated by the mystical practices, are the sole indicators of how the whole beingness of a person tends towards the bliss of freeing itself from the driving forces given by the inner predispositions. Therefore, one must not invent which practice, from the general practical mystical instructions they should chose, because they, as a rule, only get more entangled by this into the unfortunate state of slavery based on succumbing to these driving forces. This is because the various desires always lead all thoughts towards the way of how to intensify the orientation toward the objects of desires. By that, the inner balance becomes increasingly disturbed; in such a case mysticism does not serve a person to solve the problem of suffering, but to worsening of the suffering.

Thus, the reflections of where and how to strain one's force by means of the mystical practices, must not follow from desires. In the beginning, it is always necessary to "only practice the earth" by a more perfect observation of all that by which the being manifests itself in action. It is necessary to maximise the self-observation all the way to a perfect self-control and an ability to control every manifes-tation of the being. Only then the stability of mind appears, together with the impartial perception and thorough awareness of all that is happening, and so do the first signs of the ability to fully control one's actions; by that the "practice of earth" is accomplished.

9. *The mystical transformation of the element of earth and by that, of the by birth inherited, structure of the physical being is attainable in particular by the so-called 'washout' of the body by means of the spiritual water.*

Explanation: The washout is achieved by a methodical "movement of the spiritual water" which is determined by inner activity; the most important form of this activity is the vigilant observation, but not the formal observation to which people quite often resort. It is necessary to state this beforehand, so that nobody who will "work with water" according to the following aphorisms sinks into an idea that the formal observation is sufficient. By the formal observation, it is meant such observation which ceases as soon as an insufficient control of all acts representing the mystical work occurs. By this a person falls into passivity, which 'ripples' the feelings. This is a worse state than when a person is carried away by cravings which make them vigilant and externally active.

10. *The water will become crystal clear. Its effect will intensify by attentively observing the body, while practising an inner relaxation, and by a slow and systematic development of pleasant feelings which cannot occur during a high-quality observation without relaxation, because this very observation of the body prevents it.*

Explanation: The requirements on the mystic thus gradually increase. One is supposed to thoroughly register everything that their body does, but they are supposed to perform it in inner relaxation, because it is necessary that the observer – the vigilant consciousness and the observed object – the entire being are sufficiently separated from each other. By that the observation becomes analytical. Besides that, the required relaxation must, in turn, enable the feelings to flow or oscillate – this stops whenever the will is strained to perform a pure observation. These feelings are another component of the being, they are its astral nature, and in the mystical practice it is necessary that everyone thoroughly and completely processes the natural activity of all components. Only in this way, he or she can attain that which we call perfection.

11. *Intensification of pleasant feelings is an increase of the power of the spiritual water.*

Explanation: These feelings must not be based on inner excitements, because that would be only sensory excitements. By feelings, here it is meant the state of emotions, the inner state of the one who does not suffer from anything, the one who does not grieve for anything, the one who is not tormented by the sensory desires. The state in question we denote by the words, "he or she is happy". The intensification of the pleasant feelings thus means such an inner tuning which is only possible if a person is devoid of desires. This tuning is not necessarily positive if a person is showered with sensory enjoyments. Therefore, the required good state is achieved by giving rise to unconditional joy. If this state is permanently applied, it can be classified as an inner elevation of a person above the external world. The intensified spiritual water is supposed to bring this inner elevation.

Although water, in a spiritual sense, best symbolises the ability to feel, we still cannot understand this feeling as a completely isolated manifestation of the inner life, because, in its other aspect, feeling is the sense of touch, which, in a broader conception means the sensitivity of the organism – the perception, which shapes the whole organism into the form called 'the inner life'. Thus the aspects of feelings are atavisms, drives, emotions, and even noble ideas. The body on the lower level, and the reason on the higher level, are qualities which are different from the feelings: the earth, which constitutes the body and the reason, which constitutes the air. With regard to this, "the water" can be considered to be the entire inner life of a person. This water has a tendency to deaden if all manifestations of life are determined by cravings for the sensory experience, or it has a tendency towards transcendence, as soon as the leading manifestations of the inner life are selfless joy, desires for an inner uplift above the world and noble actions in which egocentrism, or selfishness, is absent.

Thus, those who "practise the water", take care that their emotions and their feelings in general are unambiguous, good in moods as well as in deeds. Unstable emotions are a manifestation of disorders in the nature of water. This water is, in fact, rippling, which makes its manifestations ambiguous; it is a swaying from pessimism to an unreasonable optimism. Also, the sphere of an individual is limited by this swaying. The limits of this sphere do not enable the consciousness to penetrate into the zone of the infra-red and ultra-violet phenomena. This is the poverty of a person, whose world is clenched into the firm borders of the common, ordinary experiences, as well as knowledge.

12. *By that, the process of the mystical washout by the spiritual water is correctly introduced. Constant feeling in goodness changes the spiritual waters into divine.*

Explanation: That, which is of the spiritual nature, has a nature of light; that, which is of the divine nature, has a nature of light with a tendency towards goodness. According to this, the divine is actually of a lower order. However, it is necessary for a person to realise the spiritual values only after the divine, because divinity is in antithesis to the primitive animality, which is the nature of everything that is physical, whether this nature is manifested objectively, or only potentially.

Thus, when a person rises, by the spiritual development, above the states of animality, they must do it initially by the development of the divine qualities. They must thus walk the path which is on the right from the middle, in order to be as remote as possible from the danger of relapse into the animal living. Those, who have underestimated the development of inner states of the divine nature (love, goodness, altruism and constant, causeless joyfulness), were, on the path of development of spirituality, i.e. on the path of knowledge, seized again by egocentrism. Selfishness narrows the mind and the spirit of a person and by that it, of course, leads again to ignorance, and, on the spiritual path, then mostly to preoccupation with some idea of a lower order. It is a fruitless effort, which leads the efforts again back into a narrow sewer of aggressive cravings.

Thus, in the plan of the mystical development, there must be an idea that a person should be, at first, brought to a freeing from the elementary qualities, but then, he or she must be put to the development of the divine qualities for so long until the tendency towards elementarism fades away. This means, for so long until they will have lived out everything that the development of the divine qualities can provide him or her with at the highest level, i.e. at the level of the divine living. Then they are allowed to return to the development of the spiritual values of the spirit. These are correctly placed in living, if knowledge arises, together with a total indifference to everything that can be provided by the external world to a human as a being.

13. *The process of the mystical washout ends in a feeling of a deep inner balance and calmness.*

Explanation: The mystical efforts are usually classified as an intentional, or even inborn, development of the feelings brought about by an inflaming of the mystic towards that which we call God. However, the emotional nature takes up almost the entire human inner beingness, which is, as a consequence, sometimes an aid, and, at other times, a hindrance on the mystical path. In most cases, this beingness is brought, by this emotional inflaming, into an uncontrolled, wave-like motion which oftentimes becomes an insurmountable hindrance of the further mystical development, because it begins to suppress the necessary inner strain and activity. If a person sinks into the inner passivity, it might be subjectively convenient for him or her, because it provides them with a possibility for the states of an emotional carrying away to come to the fore. However, then they have to pay for this by a paralysis of energy and disintegration of the inner nature as like we know it in the chronic drug addicts.

An equivalent to this unfortunate state is, usually, also the development of the mystical emotions of those seeming inner contacts of a human with the God, which were experienced by countless mystics. In principle, the feelings resulting from these contacts are simply the heavy waves of emotions, which can paralyse a person at the level of their usual human nature. This is an unfortunate phenomenon, even though it results in a pure sensitivity of the mystics "seeing God", because, it is a sad fate of a human that, for him or her, even God is always an imaginary factor. A human is always exposed to the law of action and reaction and therefore a constant overview about everything that the being is, and that it produces, serves them better. Admittedly, by this a person does not have the prospect to become or to be the child of God, but he or she remains a being responsible to oneself. If they adhere to goodness, they make the burden of responsibility for oneself lighter. Only in this way one can achieve a victory over their own destiny, a victory, which can never by achieved by a mystic who is, reportedly, dependent upon God.

A true mystic must be washed out by the spiritual water. However, the washout becomes useful and good for all times only under the condition that the mystic will never again dip their feet in the egocentrism and selfishness. Therefore, the mystical washout by the spiritual water is supposed to be planned together with stepping forward towards the higher mystical goals. If this is absent, the mystical effort becomes trial and error and will end up in the same state from which a person actually started the mystical path only for the purpose of escaping their unfortunate state forever. In such a case it was thus a futile striving and a completely unsuccessful work.

A good practical mysticism leads to no uncontrolled carrying away by feelings. Even though it is necessary to 'ripple', or, even, to inflame the feelings of a higher type, it is always only for the purpose of a proper "processing of the water element" in the being. The water element actually constitutes almost the entire inner life of a person. Therefore, the development of emotions and feelings of the best kind, which rid a person of selfishness, is prescribed. When these emotions and feelings consolidate, i.e. when they become enduring – like the elementary, or animal feelings were before, the absence of cravings and, later, inner calmness begin to appear in the character of a person. Then it is relatively easy to impart a character of an ecstatic calmness on this inner calmness.

14. *The process of washout is supposed to last for so long until the person becomes a "sodden wood".*

Explanation: The state in question is a state of the development of mystical feelings, which is, in a figurative sense, the development of constant contacts with a quality which we call God. In terms of the categories of emotional experiences, this constitutes the development of such feelings, by which those people are led, who love their fellow beings – people who are able to sacrifice themselves for others. This is characterised, in the subjective states, by a nearness of the state of ecstasy, of experiences, that we know as bliss in some Christian mystics. However, the Christian mystics have achieved these states of bliss as a result of their devoutness and their spiritual efforts. Those, who are walking this mystical path, are supposed to attain these states by a methodical development of the favourable emotional states with a tendency – in the form of a desire – to unite with the highest quality of the universe, which we denote by the word God.

The "sodden wood" is thus, in a metaphoric sense, the state of a mystic, who feeds their body, and even their entire being with the waves of an elevated mind and with a joyful mood and, possibly, also with inner vibrations of a transcendental nature. It is the opposite of the way the worldly person acts – they feed their body with the waves of a desirous mind and with sensory desires; this in turn manifests itself in an arising of unfavourable inner states and possibly also by an unfavourable inner quiver, by which the desirous people of an elementary type, are usually seized.

The "sodden wood" thus symbolises a positive inner state, which is a result of good and elevated moods. It is necessary to consider this state, just as any other state, to be a reflection of the active emotional nature, which is classified as a manifestation of the mystical water, or, in another sense then, as a manifestation of the element of water, and, in the psychological conception, as a manifestation of the entire inner nature. It should be deduced from this, that during the advance towards the mystical goal, "the entire mystical water must be processed" – the entire emotional nature. The mystic must process it by the implementing of favourable feelings, based on an inner uplift, so that he or she emotionally elevates themselves above the common humanness; only in such a case the further works will make a good and sound mystical sense.

15. *Then the element of fire may be intensified.*

Explanation: The fire element is, in a living organism, a phenomenon which is produced by a confrontation of the psyche – which is regulated by the vigilant consciousness, or, simply, by awareness – with the body as an object of this psyche. In the first phase, the fire element serves a drying of the spiritual water, or in another sense, of the lymph, and, in the second phase, it serves the burning down of waste products produced by desires. If this fire is used towards an earth which is not consolidated by a stable and non-wandering mind and towards impure water which is not developed by the development of the adequate feelings, the state of the mystic will worsen. This happens by a mechanism in which, from a mystical point of view, by the effect of the mystical fire, inner ashes are created; inner ashes, from which the "bird of life" rises to life again – the consciousness, which did not find a new world by previous works; it only found it's own old world. By that the entire previous striving proves futile. However, if the mystical fire is used towards well-developed mystical feelings, as they were described in relation to the works with the water element, then the drying by the mystical fire produces enough humidity, or, vapours, which will purify the earth and prepare it in such a way that a bird of a transcendental life will rise from the ashes produced by the effect of the burning fire; a bird – a divine spirit of a human being of the mystic, thus, a spirit reborn in relationships to the divine life.

If we translate this explanation into a more understandable common language, we must emphasise that the mental concentration, which is the root of the rise of the mystical fire, is not supposed to be used without due consideration and, in particular, not earlier than when the mind becomes completely stable and the emotions become purified by the development of feelings, which can be perhaps approximately described as altruistic. These feelings are an opposite of the natural selfishness – of feelings, which are characterised predominantly by self-love. If it is like this, the mystic will create by their concentrations a spirit with consolidated selfishness. By that, tendencies are created towards the narrowing of spirit, i.e. towards a general intellectual worsening, towards a spiritual as well as psychological decline.

16. *The fire element of a mystical type will strengthen by means of a sharp, or even the so-called 'pointed', concentration, focused on the being, on the body and on the peace attained by the "soaking in the heavenly water".*

Explanation: The ignorance of the psychological laws makes mystics concentrate not only on the body, but also on various ideas. In this latter case the person, without knowing it, strives for a preoccupation with a fixed idea, or, for going astray both on the mystical path as well as on the path of life. From the point of view of the mystical psychology, it is very important upon what kind of symbols created by the imagination a person mentally fastens. The symbols of earth, i.e. the body itself and, in the inner sphere, the stability, make a concentration an analytical process, by means of which it is actually a natural science knowledge that arises. However, the symbols of abstract character, i.e. some idea or an uncontrollable desire, modify the effect of concentration in the sense that thinking becomes wandering and easily sinks into preoccupation with fixed ideas. Due to this reason, the works with the fire element must be imbedded in a precise psychological and being-related context; otherwise they bring only damage.

The mystical efforts must not be approached in a dilettantish way – from impulses behind which there is a mere idea, not based on facts. This holds especially true for the work with fire – with the concentrations of mind. The fire affects the body as an agent which is loosening, or even destroying, its structure – the set of its components; this leads to a physical weakening. The effect of fire on the psyche not consolidated by a mental stability will provoke even greater inner restlessness, which, in a better case, leads to the abstract thinking and abstract speculations, i.e. to daydreaming; in a worse case it results in pathological manifestations.

17. *In the process of the mystical transformation, the sharp concentration of mind, must serve, above all, to the evaporation of the mystical waters of the being.*

Explanation: Those, who did not practice feelings which belong to the work with the water element, will, by means of the concentration used with a wrong timing, evaporate the lymphatic substrates of the being which have a positive influence on the inner beingness. This usually becomes the cause of development of the emotional dryness, which will be more inclined to the fulfilment of personal cravings than to the development of friendly contacts with everything that lives. However, if a mystic, before the use of the mystical fire – the concentration, multiplies the mystical waters, they will, by their evaporation, 'wash the being out' in a sense that they will either diminish, or eliminate even the potential tendencies towards selfishness. By the "warming up" of the mystical water, the mystical earth – the body – is thoroughly soaked and by that, the destruction of passions gradually comes about. Therefore, the concentration – the work with the mystical fire must be used in an adequate time, or, according to a correct psychological schedule.

There must be an appropriate amount of water – emotions – in the being, and this water must be incessantly purified by a constant development of the noble emotions, because passions, drives and the manifestations of attachment to the worldly things are also a modification of the water element, however, they make this water impure. By this, it is modified into the so-called 'astral beingness', into a double, who, independently of the physical being seeks taste gratifications; this then manifests itself in life as irresistible urges for sensory pleasures. The noble emotions, especially the emotions of love leading to the deeds of virtue, to the love for everything that lives, disable the "water of existence" to transform into this low astral double. Instead of this a, so-called, 'etheric beingness' arises, which gradually grows into the air element. This is a transfiguration of beingness equipped with consciousness, into a spiritual beingness. It is a product of a seemingly natural development in the structural sense; therefore one does not pass through the fire developed by the mystical practices.

The water, which actually represents the entire inner beingness in the being, has so many modifications in the sphere of resulting manifestations that the seeking mystics can only rarely and by chance fulfil the necessary conditions of advancement. Due to this reason, a guru – a spiritual leader, is needed. However, the relationships between the leader and the disciple of mysticism are, in turn, influenced by the attitudes of the students of mysticism, which is an issue beyond the scope of this writing.

18. *By the use of the mystical fire, a feeling of increase of the bodily temperature appears – a state of drying up which must result in the destruction of the spontaneously arising elementary emotions and feelings, and in the deadening of all passions.*

Explanation: The feeling of increase of the physical temperature is not only connected to the concentration of mind, but also to the presence of the inflammable substances in the being. These inflammable substances are contained in the "spoilt" water which was not intensified and purified by the mystical works, in the so-called 'astral waste products' which create the elementary astral double of a person, or in other words, in some kind of personified characteristics which are manifesting themselves by sensory cravings. Precisely these characteristics are those inflammable substrates which, when they are exposed to the mystical fire, in the form of a sharp concentration of mind, they start to burn down. This manifests itself in subjective feelings of increase of the physical temperature and, then, in drying up which is related to the dying away of the emotional, i.e. astral nature, burdened by the sensory wishes or cravings. Contrary to this, the second aspect of the astral nature in the form of an etheric body begins to strengthen. This etheric body can be simultaneously also burned down in the course of incautious manipulation with the mystical fire – with concentration. However, in such a case the mystical effort does not bring any positive result.

Thus, the work with the mystical fire – the work with concentration, is the most responsible work. Flawed work with the mystical water can facilitate the development of feelings of one who succumbs to emotions. Flawed work with the mystical fire – with concentration – can mystically cripple a person, so that they will no longer be able to develop the transcendence of inner life, an ecstatic mind and thus the precondition for the development of wisdom, either; wisdom, which is the only thing that can bring one to the spiritual liberation. Thus, it is safer if a mystic, who does not have a good guru, only develops the superworldly feelings; in other words, if they only work with the mystical water, because in this work, the precondition of understanding of the essence of mystical effort is never destroyed. Thus, the prospect of the way in which it is necessary to work with the mystical fire does not fade away either – the mystical fire by means of which a high quality mystical beingness is created with which one will already arrive at the mystical goal, at the spiritual liberation.

19. *After the "evaporation of the mystical waters", a person must already be emotionally dead; they must be forever elevated above the state in which their being spontaneously reacts to the stimuli from outside. Now the mystic may react to these stimuli only intentionally.*

Explanation: The "emotionlessness" of a mystic who has arrived at the spiritual perfection is not an expression of an emotionlessness of the selfish people, but an indifference to, or detachment from, the world as a complex system provoking emotional impulses and activities resulting from that. Compassion, giving rise to the deeds of virtue, remains; it is not impaired at all.

This result can be considered to be a major improvement of the subjective state of the mystic. From the point of view of yoga, the state of succumbing to the so-called 'irresistible urges', which are always brought about by the stimuli from the external world through the atavistic human nature, is a very unfortunate state. According to yoga, no personal happiness exists for those who do not eliminate the relationships to the world which is gratifying the sensory cravings on the basis of an inner attachment or its opposite, the inner aversion.

The pleasure of those who have advanced very far on the path of mystical transformation, and they have, by means of an adequate mystical effort, burned out, stems from an abiding of their consciousness in the sphere of the very origin of the sensory world; this will later be understood by the mystic as a consequence of their own sensory desires, too. When they put an end to these desires, they will rejoice in the contact of their own personal consciousness with the central quality of existence. Even later, when the relationship towards their own entire being ceases in them, an indifferent state of the one who only lives within themselves, without any kind of relationship to the external world, will arise in them. It is a state of the one who only lives within themselves, in a quality otherwise known as consciousness which will, to them, turn out to be the centre of everything that exists. However, this is a result which rarely comes, seemingly, by itself. It is usually necessary to proceed to the work with the air element.

20. *If a person is already emotionally dead – indifferent to everything that provokes the sensory impulses, they can accomplish their mystical work by intensification and purification of the air element.*

21. *This is done by perceiving an imaginary emptiness – a blank space or its emptiness, as represented by looking at a clear sky during the day.*
Explanation: Mysticism does not understand air as the wafting of air, but as the pulsating or undulating space, which is able to have an intellectualising effect on the consciousness of a person and, in

another aspect, it is a factor enabling the organism to carry out the necessary chemical metabolism. Therefore, this work is not a system of breathing, but a series of operations with awareness. By means of the awareness, it is necessary to "expand the space" for the physical charges constituting the body. This means that this is a system of awareness, by which the being no longer manifests itself as a compact matter, but as a "dense oscillating or pulsating environment", in which the yogi's consciousness abides, and the yogi tries to impart on it a character of a thinner environment.

This in practice means, that the concentrating yogi does not consider their body to be a space in which their mind comes across substances giving an impression of a state of firm or hard elements, but he or she only considers their body to be a space in which they fix their awareness by an awareness of a place, i.e. by finding an imaginary aid, which is necessary for the consciousness to lose its tendency to disperse.

When the body of the yogi becomes to them a space where their consciousness is firmly settled, and when they find in it the environment for the intentional movement of their non-wandering consciousness, they "practise the air". The air is practised exactly by means of the ability to move the non-wandering consciousness. When a yogi does not move such consciousness, they practise space. This leads to completely different results than those intended. However, in order for the practised air to be utilisable correctly, the blank space must be perceived to such an extent which still enables the perceptions of the worldly things to draw attention of the yogi's consciousness to themselves. This is because these perceptions still potentially exist in the being, or, more precisely, in the being there are dispositions for arising of these perceptions, even when a person is burned out. The perception of the pure and empty space in the form of a clear sky during the day is supposed to become the source of new kinds of perceptions, which must cover up the hypersensitivity of the being to the sensory perceptions and bring about a mechanics of new kinds of perceptions; these mechanics arise from the intentional perception of an empty space. This intentional perception of en empty space will turn out to be transcendental perception.

22. *This practice is successful only if the body refreshes by it. This refreshment is not flawed if it is not accompanied by any recurring unintended emotional reactions to the external world.*

Explanation: This lapse is possible, because the lower being must not be killed, but only mastered. This means that the functions of the animal nature are conditionally overcome, but the spiritual transformation of a person will only take place after the new kinds of perceptions – the transcendental perceptions – prevail even at the level of the potential phenomena, thus, even in the domain of the rudimentary sensory perceptions. Therefore, the path is not problem-free at this stage. The calmness of mind, achieved by accomplishment of the "practice of earth", and the killing of the emotional nature by the "practice of fire" must always bring the mystic to a qualitative change in awareness which then has to persist in their conceptual existence, which is qualitatively changed by burning out, i.e. by the destruction of all, functions of their emotional nature, including the automatic ones.

23. *By that, wisdom will be born; the more a person is internally dead towards all external stimuli, the higher the wisdom is in the qualitative sense.*

Explanation: However, wisdom is not a matter of the mind and its activity, but a matter of the sensory discernments. If the mind is wandering, then the discernments are imperfect, as if we watch the riverbed through the river's turbulent flow. Only an absolute inner continence, which is another form of the inner burnout, provides the inner stability that improves discernments. The prejudices and biases do not interfere, and so, in front of the observation ability, events begin to present themselves not only as something to which a person has an inner relationship, but as the happening, or even happening which is precisely motivated by the one who causes it.

Only motives are the cause of happening, both the happening related to beings as well as the physical happening. Therefore, wisdom recognises that these happenings are not always a full life, as those, who are seized by delusions, believe. It is often also purposeless or absurd changes which rather burden living by suffering instead of making it blissful. Only wisdom reveals that a happy living is enabled solely by the indifference towards the world, by an absolute inner calmness which always stems from the contacts of the consciousness with the central quality of the world and of life – with the absolute, as we can understand it as humans.

From what was said above, it follows that wisdom is dependent upon the application of the air element whose quality was increased by the stability of a conscious observation as a concentration which is thoroughly registered by the consciousness and by the mind. This registering, which is dependent upon vigilance, must thus dominate over the "movements" of spirit, which are caused by the adhesiveness of the feelings, or emotions. The mind will then be able to observe and analyse everything that happens. This state of the mind will deepen the discernments to the extent which we assume in those who are equipped with the supernatural abilities, in particular with clairvoyance. This means that a well stabilised mind, which is out of reach of emotions – feelings, by means of which people cling to or feel repulsion to the things of the surrounding world, is a tool for discernments which we admire as clairvoyance, or, clairsentience.

24. *The concentration of mind, enriched by wisdom, on the body, on the feelings and on the inner states, thus, on the entire being, leads to a deep qualitative change of the mind, which thus becomes stable and, by that, ecstatic, because it was made non-worldly by an inner detachment of a person from the world.*

Explanation: By an 'ecstatic mind', a fantasising mind is not meant. When the mind has been stabilised and purified by the "practice of space and air", the processes on the path of transformation have not rid it of realistic opinions; only its position, direction and contents changed. If we would thus compare this mind to a static charge of the electric energy, the tendency of its possible spikes is no longer towards the objects, gratifying sensory cravings, but towards the qualities of the transcendence. Such a mind is no longer mystical in a sense of turning to the world of its own abstracts ideas, even if they were pure or ideal, but it continues to be active in a higher sense – in the investigation into the broad and deep domain of the spiritual life, into its happening and the causes of its happening. If the mind obtained, besides that, a habit to carefully attend to all inner movements, thus, even to the subtlest ones, it will convey discernments from the zone, lying perhaps even beyond the red line, as well as those lying beyond the violet line. In any case it will convey the perception of silhouettes and phenomena of the so-called 'invisible world', however not as phenomena completely out of touch with the phenomena of the sensory world, but as their another, factual aspect, which is existing in another octave of things.

25. *By this the path of transformation of the evident factors of the being ends.*

Explanation: The path of transformation leads from the state of uncontrolled reactions to uncontrolled perceptions and impulses arising not only from the emotional part of the human nature, but also from the atavistic part of the human nature, in other words, it leads from the state of being subordinated to the external world, to the state of freeing from the state or environment of necessities, i.e. to such an inner freeing which has the character of an absolute inner freedom. However, this does not mean that this freedom is a more advantageous position for a more perfect or even unrestrained gratification of the sensory cravings. Gratification of sensory cravings means dependence on feelings; this dependence is a force of existence which overcomes the inner forces of a person. However, only these inner forces can be the giver of this freedom, which is ruled out by the power of feelings. The gratification of the sensory cravings even causes the consciousness to become constricted and clouded by the processes of emotional experience; however, wisdom, which is directly related to the possibility of an evident feeling of an, even absolute, inner freedom, is possible only when the consciousness is not constricted and not clouded.

From this point of view, a person, whose spirit is not broad, whose reason is not excellent and whose intelligence is not high, is neither spiritually free nor mystically perfect. These faculties cannot be replaced by the mystical experiences, which are valued by the usual mystics; these experiences are the reverse-side of the worldly emotional experience and in fact constrict the spirit just like the various kinds of drugs. Thus, if someone classifies these very experiences as the qualitative improvement of their own being, they only prove that their spirit is cramped and their consciousness is constricted, like the spirit and consciousness of everyone who has sunk into some kind of a sensory indulgence.

26. *However, mysticism does not deal exclusively with the questions of the mystical transformation of the evident factors of the being, but also deals with the creative potentialities of the spirit which is progressing towards the transcendence of existence.*

Explanation: However, this second stage can only follow after the first. The first must not be skipped. This is because it is necessary to master the being and to register all processes taking place in it, because in the second stage, the processes completely escaping the usual perception are coming even more to the fore. However, mysticism aims at transcendence and therefore the second stage logically follows from the first one.

It would be the greatest mistake to believe that mysticism means only a superworldly life or only a worldly life, improved by greater and miraculous possibilities. In the initial stage, mysticism must certainly lead to the stabilisation of conditions and to an improvement of the situation of the person, but this is only a start towards a more hopeful superworldly path. The very improvement of the situation of the striving mystic is a proof that they are not driven to the further stage by worldly desires and by a general outer dissatisfaction, but that they are led by higher goals, following already from the knowledge of instability, impermanence and nothingness of all that exists.

If these preconditions are present, the mystic will fasten their attention upon the knowledge by which all suffering is eradicated. This suffering necessarily continues, as long as the primitive desires keep bothering the mystic. However, the knowledge, eradicating suffering which stems from the existence itself, lies somewhere beyond the borderline of our world with all its details, peculiarities, and nuances of the impressive moments. It lies in the sphere of transcendence, there, where one can get exclusively by means of a mind liberated from the world, of an ecstatic mind, which is, however, objectively thinking about everything and evaluating everything. In the sense of the applied elements, it is a path of a developing effect of the so-called ether – akasha, the principle of the air element. This is dealt with in the following aphorisms.

27. *This method is based on the manipulation with space and with the density of awareness.*

Explanation: With regard to the fact that people succumb to an attraction to the things of the external world that can gratify their sensory cravings, their consciousness becomes, proportionally to this interest, constricted and by that it, metaphorically speaking, 'thickens'. However, a yogi must, in the first stage of the mystical path, overcome this interest by not letting the things of the external world provoke them to wanting. By that, their consciousness is freed and obtains the prerequisites for its broadening and by that, indeed, also for becoming clearer, for the decrease of its density. Only by that he or she becomes able to proceed to the second stage and to develop in it.

28. *The awareness must step outside of the space delimited by the body.*

Explanation: Usually, a person is not able to be aware of anything but the body and that which interests them in the world. By discipline of thinking – a thinking which is registered by awareness – they can also learn to be aware of the entire sphere of that which lies between their body and the things that interest them. If they begin to be aware of this sphere, their mind has obtained the ability of analysis of the processes, which take place in this sphere. By this, they will learn about the "third dimension" of the subjective world – about that which is between them and the things that they may want. Here is the beginning of the mystical path in the transcendental sphere, the beginning of the path of the mystical knowledge. This knowledge is of good quality only when thinking does not begin to wander, but when it remains able to register all concrete perceptions.

A peculiarity of the usual awareness, is that it is able to flow only in a narrow stream towards the external things that interest a person, or, to passively accept information from the body, and this takes place only when the body is affected by a health disorder. However, this state is completely different from the yogic state. A yogi of a higher type must increase the volume of their awareness. By being aware of the body as a three-dimensional object, initially in its original outline, he or she must achieve the ability to register perceptions from many information sources. Later, they are supposed to achieve that these perceptions will also be coming from the abstract sphere, i.e. from the spheres outside of the borders of their being and outside of the reach of their senses.

These changes of the volume of awareness depend on practice, because, in the line of the usual development determined by life experiences, there is no indication of a tendency towards the broadening of the contents of awareness. It is the opposite. In particular, by upbringing and education tending towards the increase of the interest in the external world, the awareness "specialises", or, actually, narrows down in such a way that a "well educated person" is not able to do anything more than to be intensively interested in the particularities. This is a path to the narrowing of consciousness, and to the decrease of the intelligence quotient as a base of a broad and high quality education. By effort focused on the perception of the whole object which is one's own body, the consciousness becomes capable of, as well as, open to the manifold information which is based on the process of perception. When the "breadth of awareness" appropriately increases, the consciousness will also gather perceptions from other dimensions of phenomena which, in case of due elevation and purification of emotions, belong, in most cases, to the transcendental world.

29. *Object and subject will then be thoroughly separated, and so a person will become able to perceive impartially.*

Explanation: While a person is a slave to emotions, they themselves, as 'I' merge with the things that impress them. Thus, they view and judge everything, and take stands on everything, partially. Out of this, their poverty, subservience to the world, and a narrow outlook on it, arise. Such a person is not a yogi, even if they may practise yoga. All their mystical efforts only reinforce their slavery; because, whatever they do, they are only strengthening their inner bonds and ignorance.

Thus, the object and the subject must always be thoroughly separated. The freedom of the subject is based only on this, and this freedom is absolutely essential for a successful advancement towards the high mystical goals.

30. *When a person is not attracted to the external objects, he or she can make their own being an object lying inside of their observation and awareness.*

Explanation: It is necessary to achieve this. On the one hand, one's own being will be known as a microcosm which offers the necessary partial knowledge to the analysing mind, and, on the other hand, one attains by this the possibility of the empirical liberating which is exclusively dependent upon the dissolving of the being by the power of a systematically applied opinion about this being.

31. *If the being of a person, or even their entire existence, becomes an inner object of awareness, i.e. the object of concentration, the consciousness begins to transform.*

Explanation: In the usual case, the consciousness of a person is a subject, while the external world is its object. This state symbolises both slavery as well as incapability of knowledge. However, if the higher task of the yogic training is accomplished, the consciousness will see, or, understand one's own being as an object inside of awareness and that is already an attainment of liberation of one's own consciousness. However, it does not all end here. As soon as the consciousness ceases to be the content of being and, instead of that, being becomes the content of awareness, the consciousness obtains the ability to grow, to expand into space, while all its previous objects, the Nature, the world, and the infinite space of the universe, begin to, literally, fall into the spaces of self-awareness. In this way, the yogi attains a total victory over the Nature – its overcoming not only by a simple expansion of their consciousness, but also by being aware that the Nature is subordinated to him or her.

However, the expansion of the self-awareness does not stop at this simple victory over Nature. In the end, it swallows up the entire universe which becomes its inner object. This is connected with an awareness that the yogi has outgrown everything; that all this is a gradually mechanically transforming Nature, which is therefore uninteresting, undesirable; it is an illusion, which impresses those who have not attained this freeing, but not on the yogi, to whom the entire world became completely colourless, worthless. It became a Fata Morgana with the yogi's awareness on the background of it, that it is a nothingness which cannot delude them by an illusion of reality.

32. *In this way the yogi arrives at the work with akasha, with the space, which has to be gradually set to a rhythmic motion, in order*

for the non-existence of their being to be sealed, i.e. for their liberation to be complete.

Explanation: Only awareness of emptiness, which cannot be disturbed by external influences, reinforces the absence of the desire to be or to live. This perhaps commonly appears to be a sad result of the yogic training. However, every being proceeds to this blowing out. It is not a sign of wisdom to cover one's eyes in the face of this and plunge into a foolish substitute with false contents by trying to live, be, act, build and impart by will, a semblance of reality on a constantly dispersing existence. Nothing wise can result from that, anyway. One delusion follows another. Those who expect to live eternally will have to be prepared for disappointments, for the dashing of hopes and expectations, for the complications of karma. In striving for existence, a person commits not only foolish, but also evil actions, to which the world reacts with evil, too. A person thus yields to evil and pain.

It is not necessary to add anything to life. Those who, not being seized by the desire to be and to live, do not perform evil for their rescue, which they will not attain anyway, live in a calm and attentive effort to live and let live, and will finish their days just as those who want to impart a different character on their life. However, they will finish their days in an inner peace. They will live in peace and die in peace, which is more valuable than to live torn apart, or even only in a great distress caused by innumerable and unfulfillable desires.

The work with akasha also serves to overcome the Nature in another way. When the yogi is already able to perceive space as a set of substances that can be inhaled, he or she will bring themselves into the harmony with the Nature, or, into a rhythm, which is classified as unity with the breath of the Nature. If they "breathe this way" constantly, they will attain a feeling that they have won over the Nature, as well as over their emotional nature. In this case, they are no longer resisting the influence of Nature by their will, or by their consciousness outgrowing everything that exists by its expansion, but they are resisting it by the emotional states of the original existence; these are blissful in a way that only the feelings of those can be, who have just begun to develop into an individual life without obstacles, to which those, whose life is endangered by destruction, are exposed. These emotional states are, due to the previous life experience of a yogi, identified as episodes on the path of return to the very origin and by that also as a practical solution of their, actually, unfortunate current state, the state of humanness, which they are abandoning, overcoming, or, in other words, destroying.

Thus, a yogi on this level "breathes space". By this they are acquainting themselves with the physical causes of the origination of everything that exists and they are, by this, also obtaining knowledge of how to prevent their being from arising again and by that to seal their perfection – the spiritual perfection, the perfection of the being, and, the general perfection.

33. *With the completion of the works with akasha, and with the knowledge of the conditions of the origination of existence, the yogi halts the entire mechanical inner activity of the being.*

34. *By that the yogi rises above the sphere of elements, into the transcendence, which they will already recognise as the absolute.*

Explanation: If there was nothing in the Nature besides the sphere of the elements, namely earth, water, fire, air and akasha (ether), there would be no escape from suffering. Humans would be, just like the inanimate phenomena of the Nature and of universe, condemned to cycle through the processes of progression and retrogression, and their consciousness, as an abstract factor, would be subordinated to all this. However, the consciousness is able to make the things, composed of elements, its objects, by that to abstract itself from them and by that to free the self-awareness in the form of selfness from everything.

However, this option is a negative result. It only becomes positive after the yogi imparts on the self-awareness a rhythmic wavy motion – the breathing, by which they will come to life in this abstraction of theirs, in a freeing outside the sphere of all happening, mechanically taking place. Thus, they become a "living soul", which once commenced the path towards involution, towards the sorrowful state of humanness, which is subject to the power of the phenomena of the external world. And because they become a "living soul" on the path of return to their very origin, they recognise the difference between slavery – being subordinated to the Nature – and freedom, which is based on a continuous detachment from the processes governing the Nature. The awareness of this abstraction, of this freeing, is a powerful adversary of the return of the state of being subordinated to the natural happening; by this a precondition arises for preservation of the liberated personal consciousness all the way to the moment of death. By this, the creation of conditions for repeated coming into existence, for reincarnation, ceases, by which the spiritual freedom becomes complete and independent from the dimension of time.

35. *This is the end of the path of transformation with the use of the elements.*

On four Buddhist jhanas

Yoga is a system of mystical efforts. This is not commonly known, because, in the western world there are a lot of practical yogis whose understanding of the idea of yoga is that it is the exercising of positions, or mental effort concretely expressed as concentration of mind on one entirely exclusive object out of the commonly known objects. From this, indeed, an opinion stems, that the yogic development is fully in the hands of people and that the only important thing is whether they will or will not fulfil instructions, concerned mainly with either physical, mental, or both types of, practices.

This is, however, not in question in yoga. Someone said that yoga is a struggle for quality. This can be understood by it been a struggle for the best inner state, for the clearest state of consciousness, for the highest vigilance, for a state of mind without ill will, hatred and for development of its clarity, for the best emotional states, etc. – for states of a purely positive character. As a rule, it is not possible to achieve such success only by mental effort. This is mainly because those who believe only in this effort are obviously not interested in the religious ethics of yoga, but only devote their effort to achieve that, which they desire emotionally. When striving spiritually, this moral flaw has to be removed by adhering to moral commandments of yoga.

"Struggle for quality" thus means to exclude vices and replace them by virtues, which are reflected in thinking. In another sense, it means to constantly exclude from inner states negative manifestations like, precisely, ill will, hatred, prejudice of mind against someone and something, or its darkening; further then to constantly exclude negative inner states, sleepy torpor and bad emotional states. If a person does not strive precisely in this direction, then no – however strong – desire and concentration of mind, will solve either their problem of a happy emotional and mental state, or even the question of a good health. For, the "struggle for quality", especially if accompanied by a correct yogic morality, constitutes the right way of living – a way of living, which, by itself, causes that the being of a person will be gradually led to inner tranquillity and will be producing happy states, even enlightenment, and everything that accompanies the development of a superworldly mind.

The right way of living is thus an action, by which the restlessness resulting from a desirous mind will be subdued and, by that, also its introvert tendency will be brought about. This tendency is then a self-acting concentration of mind, it is the mind's concentration on one's own being or on the existence of a yogi. By this, his or her disturbance by irritative sensory perceptions and reminders which so powerfully ignite the taste for trying something, for tasting something, for some experience, will be excluded.

To once and for all interrupt this complex of psychological inter-relations and processes causing inner restlessness and ending, as a rule, in some orgasm of varied kinds and natures, is indeed already a great success on the mystical path. It is a great action of renunciation of the world and the beginning of a deep moral discipline, leading to mystical growth, to mystical development. The pounding of waves of cravings and sensory impulses thus ceases and the person devoted to yoga then must get used to, to a great extent, new inner and emotional conditions and conditions related to awareness.

Correctly evaluated, the new inner orientation which came into existence in this way, can be considered an arena where a person struggles in a difficult fight with himself or herself for increase and improvement of the inner tranquillity. The momentum of the previous orientation, actually constantly and immensely aggressively, forces them to again return to the previous way of life and – by this, that "struggle for quality" is characterised. For, if a person does not resist the evil, selfish urges, they are seriously damaged on the mystical path of yogic nature.

This very fact indicates that the mystical development induced by yoga is, in the first place, a matter of a right way of living. Only in the second place it is a matter of mental practices of the type of simple concentration of mind, or of the hathayoga exercises which are popular nowadays. Inversion of the mental vibrations or discharges, which is brought about by withdrawing the mind from the world, its focusing inwards, is continuously disturbed by a desire to repeat earlier feeling sensations – experiences. This fact makes practising concentration or positions, in the first case, devising plans how to get to emotional or sensory experiences, in the latter case restless sitting, from both of which nothing good will result.

To keep setting the inner being robbed of the, until now unlimited, emotional experience into tranquillity, requires a great deal of inner strength. Generally, it takes years until a person arrives at a complete tranquillity of their "psyche". Only this tranquillity becomes the true mystical concentration, it becomes those Buddhist jhanas, which are so closely connected with the degree of inner peace arisen from the absence of wanting. Only the degree of tranquillity arisen from the absence of craving brings the mind from the first to the fourth Buddhist jhana; other goals that a person on the path of yoga sets for himself or herself serve nothing good. This is because these goals do not exclude continuation of the inner restlessness, that eternal 'cycling' through existences, through reincarnations of the life process, and now – in this life – they, as a rule, claim their price in form of inner decadence, disorders or loss of health. Thus, something totally different than that which a person expected from yoga or hoped for.

Let us, however, return to the development which leads to those four Buddhist jhanas. I would say this about it: when a person, by means of a massive struggle for quality against strongly developed sensory cravings, finally withdraws their mind from the world, they will be overcome by rejoicing, similarly to that of a slave freed from chains. This is the first jhana, which can be disturbed by cravings which surge again and again.

The struggle for the overcoming of these, again surging, cravings, deepens the rejoicing which comes about as a result of the first Buddhist jhana. The struggle disrupts the shallowness of the first Buddhist jhana and, at the same time, it also deepens the mental tranquillity, which can be characterised as a tranquillity arisen from joyfulness. This is the beginning of an emerging impartial view of the world, which can be characterised, due to its accompanying joyfulness, as the second jhana.

When a person, from the second Buddhist jhana, no longer obtains joyfulness as something opposite to the ceasing feverish state of a harsh and uncompromising desires, but being aware of the fact that this joyfulness is easily disturbed, they begin to fight for undisturbable tranquillity, slightly tinted by this, it can be said, causeless joyfulness, they are entering the path of realisation of the third Buddhist jhana. When they succeed in developing this undisturbable inner tranquillity, they will finally achieve equanimity, accompanied by bliss of joyfulness, which is at first developing, and then slowly fading away. This is the third jhana, not achieved, evidently, by the concentration of mind, but by the right way of living. It is the first state to lead to "opening of the eyes".

This has to be understood as the beginning of a correct comprehension of the whole question of spiritual development, as it is regarded by yoga; comprehension of a fact that the life process can only be stopped by a way of life, i.e. by a systematic, life-practice based, an extinguishing of the not only thirst for life, but – and mainly – the life drive itself. A person will thus understand that only, and repeatedly only, the right way of living leads to the extinguishing of the life drive, working in life as a consuming, burning, bad fire. The technical yoga, understood as practices independent of the modification of the external life, never leads to this. Not even knowledge, no matter how developed, and even though a superworldly one, leads to this. A person starts to understand, that knowledge is only a product of the correct mystical effort. Thus, it is a factor, which makes the extinguishment of the life drive understandable and by that also realisable, but altogether unrealisable by the technical yoga.

However, the third Buddhist jhana is a *process*, similarly to both of the previous ones as well as the following fourth one; it is even an inner life process and not an inner state. Therefore, if a person pays attention to fulfilling the conditions of the development of states of the third Buddhist jhana, they are maturing towards the realisation of the fourth jhana. Even the slightest traces of a tinge of emotions disappear from the state of enlightenment. Even the slightest traces of a tinge of emotions, which is inherent in the third Buddhist jhana, disappear from the state of enlightenment. The state of enlightenment gradually develops and an indifference of the enlightened one to the sensory life in the broadest sense of this word begins to emerge. The ignoring of suffering of the samsaric existence and living, as well as ignoring of the celestial states, comes about. An increasing introspection, and leaving everything around oneself behind, is accompanied, solely by an utter absence of craving. Therefore the lust for life ceases to exist, as does the life drive, and a person becomes ready to entirely pass beyond without a single impulse of the desire "to live" or "to be".

The force that keeps the incarnation process running thus ceases to work, and a person is ready to extinguish themselves like someone, who has lived their life out until the ultimate trace of a touch of desires. The terrible "then" with a horrible conglomerate of sufferings, interwoven with only exceptional moments of pleasures, stops for them. A landless clear emptiness, welcomes the realiser of the fourth jhana. The others, who haven't eradicated the life drive down to its root, are only welcomed by dazzling hopes for future pleasures; but instead of these, only sufferings occur.

Therefore, yoga doesn't mean concentrations without a right way of living going hand in hand, contrary to what uninformed people believe – those people, who are picking from the yogic teaching, only the promises of power and victory over their life difficulties. Yoga is, in the first place, a right way of living, which can, indeed, be properly expressed only by that "struggle for quality", as it was said above. Those who are able to struggle for quality without the modification of the moral orientation which is prescribed by yoga, will fulfil the conditions of the right way of living without modifying their living according to the moral commandments of yoga. However, is not easy. Those who are full of cravings, as a rule do not struggle for quality, they only struggle for emotional experiences. Therefore they miss the target. The right way of living accompanied by yogic effort does not miss the target.

From Hradec Králové

Apart from myself, doctor Kovář, J. Studený and docent* Bajer were present. They have attained the third Buddhist jhana exactly in this order. Doctor Kovář reiterated that the third jhana gives a person an understanding of the purpose of mystical efforts and a good orientation on the mystical path. He also stated that the third jhana removes all inner suffering stemming from sensory cravings, because it brings a person to a state which is attainable by overcoming of the five hindrances according to the Buddhist understanding. He has stated again, that their overcoming gives rise to joyfulness and happiness, both of which then gradually disappear when a person is passing through the third Buddhist jhana.

I want to add that when this joyfulness and feeling of happiness disappears, the person will no longer return to the suffering of their previous state, but they are attaining "equanimity" which enables one to have an overview of the causes of all suffering which afflicts people, detect them and thus to learn which measures to take in order to prevent the inner suffering, originating in adversity of fate, from occurring at all.

When a person has already attained the possibility to avoid this suffering, they begin to clearly discern how to go on, farther towards the removal of all causes of this suffering. They have joined those who know that the causes of this suffering can be removed by further deepening the states related to the third Buddhist jhana, because it is precisely during these states that one encounters a landmark

---

* Higher academic degree (transl. note)

where an understanding dawns on a person that retaining even the smallest or subtlest traces of worldliness is a hindrance to accomplishment of that "happiness" belonging to the fourth Buddhist jhana. This happiness springs, as I have added at this meeting, from the development of a total indifference towards everything that may arise during the communication of an individual with the external sensory world.

In general, it holds true that the third Buddhist jhana means, in the first place, an attaining of the state called "the place of rest" and, then, the ability to repeatedly and easily find this "place of rest" when the conditions for its occurrence have changed. This is also our common (i.e. doctor Kovář's, Studený's, docent Bajer's and mine) finding. I am not losing the "place of rest" at all, or, I am rediscovering it immediately after I, for example, like that Ramakrishna's chandala, stop arguing with others in the course of the struggle for existence. Doctor Kovář finds this state as one which is surpassing all other states, but he generally doesn't disrupt the conditions for its arising in the consciousness. St. is able to find it easily after each storm caused by his place at work and in life. Docent Bajer also reaches it easily after he ends his daily duties – and even during carrying them out – but to achieve this, he has to internally rise himself, as if towards God. When I mentioned docent Bajer, the point was that he should try to find this place of rest without the, currently perhaps still indispensable, inner elevation.

Then we have already arrived at the unfolding of talk about the fourth Buddhist jhana. I have drawn the attention, especially of docent Bajer, to the fact that the fourth Buddhist jhana is supposed to be attained at the level of an entirely usual state of consciousness in order for a redemption "on the spot" to occur. With regard to this, it is necessary to add that also for St. the fact is becoming urgent that the deepening of the third Buddhist jhana may be – and as a rule really is – connected with elevation of the person's spirit and mind above the usual level of natural awareness, because he or she is used to it from the previous stage in which they had to, in order not to be swallowed up by the five Buddhist hindrances, develop that Sursum Corda. *

In this way we have arrived at an explanation that indifference, which is connected with the fourth Buddhist jhana, must be developed in a natural state of awareness, without elevating the spirit or the mind towards God. This sometimes equals to redemption attained on a human level, often even in the state of a non-complete burn out of the sensory desires. However, it can even happen that a person also learns how to descend to the levels under the human level, and so, they can be redeemed by a developed fourth Buddhist jhana, even on the hellish level.

This level is always present in a person, too. If they do not let the fact of non-manifesting of the hellish states fool them, and, by means of descent into their being, they will discover this lowest point of their being, then they will surely try to carry out the action of redemption exactly on this base. This is what I had in mind when I said that when a person develops the state of the fourth Buddhist jhana on their lowest level – on the hellish level, what more can still put them down from the spiritual height they have obtained – the pre-nirvana height – the state of redemption during life?

Those present at the meeting have understood this. In particular, J. Studený "begun to scent" that he also reaches the third Buddhist jhana in the state of inner elevation and probably well understood that he must remain longer on the painful path of asceticism – on the lower base of the mystical path, although this state which is currently in his sight is incomparable with the suffering of the state in which the five hindrances are not yet overcome. Docent Bajer has clearly understood all of this, however, so far only theoretically. Therefore this whole discussion has served its purpose – the explanation, as doctor Kovář stated, that the inner strain, or the elevation during the development of the third jhana towards the fourth one, may be a cause of attaining realisation – in this case a state, which in fact closes for the mystic other mystical possibilities.

---

* Sursum Corda: Latin for "Lift up your hearts" (transl. note)

It thus appears that this discussion has served an understanding by means of which the limitation, which stems from realisations related to the third Buddhist jhana, i.e. from realisations which are relatively high, will be overcome by all those present. They already know, and doctor Kovář also from his own experience, that what is needed is to prevent any kind of 'anchoring' even in high levels of the mystical path in the form of realisations; that the opposite is necessary – to constantly and further deepen the delving by the consciousness or mind into one's own being – in order to attain an uncompromising descent of the consciousness all the way to one's own lowest inner level, and by that also the lowest level of one's being. By this, the conditions arise for such redemption which is impossible to be endangered by any personal impulse even in case the impulse would be the highest one – a heavenly one.

What remains to be added? It is pleasant and relatively also quite easy, to attain redemption by inner exaltation, or ecstasy. However, a person can easily accept this only as long as he or she searches for their happiness somewhere else than inside of themselves – in their natural, or even "undernatural" state. Nevertheless, when they stop fantasising about the nature of reality and consider their state completely objectively, then they will understand that redemption attained by exaltation, by ecstasy, is not a definitive solution. It is necessary to uproot the entire base of an automatically forming anchorage from which uncontrollable existence maintained by an inertia force arises – an anchorage for the occurrence of a new existence. This is only possible through beholding the truth, through knowledge provided by the fourth Buddhist jhana, which was attained at the real lowest point of oneself, somewhere there on the level of atavisms, where the basis of unfolding of life lies together with its uncontrollable destinies. Then a person realises that they have reached redemption which has no outer endangering; they evidently recognise that the wheel of their samsaric existence stopped. They know that they have attained irreversibility on the level of forces of one's own being, which is termed by the Buddhists as "no return after death".

Initiation and self-initiation

These terms are usually not understood. As a rule, people suppose that it is possible to obtain initiation with the help of a guide or a leader through a mysterious mystical world, with which the initiated one acquaints the one being initiated and gradually teaches him or her how to obtain the mystical or magical power. People never think that initiation is only related to self-transformation; however, they admit that it usually involves examinations without knowing what kind of examinations.

This lack of information in the common people, tempts the charlatans to make the initiations associated with theatrical performances whose role is to have such an effect on the minds of those being initiated which weakens their sober, or critical, reason. In the end, the teaching is turned into a hollow ritualism. Its purpose is to help its representatives to get now popularity, now income, now self-aggrandizement.

No theatrical performance captures the process of a real initiation, even though it sometimes happens that this initiation involves a formal procedure. However, it is a rare case and I know only about Ramakrishna, who has initiated Swami Vivekananda in this way. I have to add, though, that in this case there is an underlying readiness of the one being initiated there; it is necessary to understand it in a way that the one being initiated has already attained the initiation, but that it has not worked its way through to the surface, to his or her daily consciousness. In this case, the real initiated one, as a guru, must recognise this state of his or her disciple and then possibly use the power which is able to lift this potential initiation up into the consciousness. In this way, the guru suppresses and annuls, in the one being initiated, a possible mental disorder which sometimes leads them, due to a hidden hysteria, to paralyse themselves by a mistaken attitude to a highly regarded person – to the guru. This mistaken attitude often ends up, in such persons, either in them being unhealthily carried away, or in something that is similar to ecstasy, or by a series of peculiar inner experiences which are then judged by the one being initiated to be the initiation into mysticism. The real initiated ones are aware of this and therefore will prevent the people of weak mind to finish the mystical things in this way.

I want to give a concrete case of the process of a real initiation only for information, in order for the true seeking ones to be helped.

It was yesterday, on the day of 26th January 1972, when I spoke to S. Kulovaný about the result of his spiritual effort and I managed to find common understanding with him. The matter in question already dated back perhaps nine months; he has obviously already attained this result back then, but without himself being able to discern it, although I have drawn his attention to it several times. Only yesterday, when he spoke with me again about how he, in regard to his requirement to abide with his consciousness firmly in the body – to be aware of it, always slowly works his way through to the purity of consciousness (mind); that although, by this, his mind abstracts from the physical, his body does not disappear from his attention. This is, according to his statements, usually a cause of arising and development to another inner state which he termed "elevated".

That enabled me to build on this, his own term, and add that I have, already for a longer period of time, considered exactly this state, which he termed in this way, to be a good result of his spiritual effort and an important turning point on his mystical path – to be that third Buddhist jhana – this is a term which is related to an arising of a new inner state, which was unknown before. This term has gained ground in our circles lately. Then we already have quickly found common understanding. Nevertheless, in order to properly characterise his state, he has quoted from A. Ghose for me, that it is something that develops into the mind as a quality of another world, a quality which seizes a person; something positive which is neither controllable nor inducible, something that comes and goes by itself, as a reaction to a bhaktic attitude of the one who seeks and something that can be qualified as a divine state.

I had the opportunity to explain to S. Kulovaný that what Ghose is talking about is exactly that quality which I had in mind when I was persuading him that he has attained a substantial mystical result. However, because I, due to my approach to mysticism, belong to the old mystical schools, it is for me a matter of course that this quality can be both intentionally brought about and operated with. This is the way in which it is understood in the old schools of mysticism which always brought their disciples to the attainment of this something, intangible for Ghose, and to the ability to fully control it. For, only in this way the mystics used to attain the ability to reach the spiritual perfection from their own will, thus, independently of chance or of special conditions whose origin they would not know. Then I have added that the ability to bring about this state from one's own will and operate with it, is specifically a result of initiation which Ghose apparently did not attain if he believes that this state appears in a person by itself, and it does not allow to be operated with.

Already since my youth, I hold the view, which is based on experience, that initiation means the ability to operate with an adequate state which is serving self-initiation. The only difficulty is to identify this state and even more difficult is to learn how to operate with it in order for a person to direct, from their own will, their development towards spiritual perfection. As a rule, it is almost necessary to obtain a mystical leader who will thoroughly acquaint the disciple with this state and who will teach him or her how to employ this state in the being in the decisive moments of a practically, almost uncontrollable, pulsation of the life forces.

What is meant by these moments, are periods of a relative balance of qualitatively diverse forces, in form of tension, which are emerging in the being. In these very periods, the one being initiated must, by the force of will, apply this state as a dominant state in his or her being. By repeated acts of this kind, the pulsation of an overmastering effect of the life forces will be gradually overcome, which leads to a victory of this state over all other states. When this state completely dominates all other states, the one being initiated arrives at an evident knowledge that he, or she, has crossed the realm of nature with its total domination over all living creatures.

Only this evident discovery is a sign of a real initiation by methods of the old mystical schools. They do not accept any accidental spiritual events on the developmental spiritual path. From the moment when the introducing of this state to the disciple is successful, the disciple's initiation proceeds with routine skill and the spiritual perfection is also attained with workmanship.

This can be seen as that key to the mystical initiation which was lost because those who were seeking initiation were weak and insincere and they dared to pretend the mystical knowledge and experience. Thus, this key was completely lost. Therefore mysticism became a path of those 'groping in the dark', who are deceived by not being prompted to overcome the usual outlooks on life. They are neither taught about the unlimited power of human beings who arrive at the peak of the mystical initiation, nor about the fact that the decisive force is karma – the mechanically acting law of actions and their consequences, and not a superior divine power.

However, that is one thing, which is seemingly transforming, or even destroying, the idea about the values of the outer and inner world. Another thing, which is leaving the divine things with their divinity, the worldly things with their worldliness and the subhuman things with their demoniacality, is, that before a person attains their own redemption and a development of the state about which we were talking with S. Kulovaný, they have to be educated not to themselves destroy the state, attained by a successful initiation, by their worldliness which is rooted in their mind. They must be already able to recognise in this state a potential, as well as structural, transcendence and, only as such, use it for a gradual elimination of the imperfect humanness from their consciousness and for a development of the state of superhumanness. For, the world is just like that: immanent and transcendent. However, the "consumer" or "consuming" humankind does not recognise it as such, because it has succumbed to an animal view that only that is real which can be, in various ways, devoured.

I have said above that this true key to initiation was lost. However, I have found it myself by means of a precise analysis of the entire conglomeration of the inner states which are arising completely mechanically in the emotional sphere and, moreover, I teach how to use it. From this, it can be deduced that everyone can find it; but only if they will strive the same way I did. However, I am aware of the fact that the present-day people do not value things that must be valued. As a consequence of this, they either do not recognise that state, or they degrade it by their opinion, and by that it ceases to be a correct tool for self-initiation. With regard to this indisposition of people I behave to everyone in a quite specific way. Many whom I lead can certainly complain about it; however, I must keep in mind that the students of mysticism recognise this state poorly and that therefore its loss in a multitude of other inner states of a worldly character occurs. How else could it happen that the achievers of this state do not recognise it?

It has already happened that one person has reached this state and he has also correctly assessed it within an intact quality of his daily consciousness which he was using. However, because his thinking was not, in the period of his preparatory moral mystical self-training, rid of the last vestiges of worldliness, he perceived this state as a well controllable tool, which is, however, only usable for his own outer good. He did not understand that this is a tool which one may use *only* to attain spiritual perfection, and therefore he was deluded by both the Nature and the mythical guards of spirituality. Through the influence of Nature and these guards, he has later anchored in his original inborn state of the low daily consciousness with only one small difference from the state of the common people: he believes that he has obtained and retains a consciousness of a superhuman, despite the fact that he has been a human again since long ago.

Therefore, although this state is realisable just like any other ordinary state of consciousness and not like something that is a "wind which blows from where it itself wants and where it itself wants", still its achievers must be, already during their mystical path, trained to assign to it its right place in the order of states. Only by that they will obtain in this state a factor, usable for a conscious departure from this world, for attaining of the state buddho, or, for attaining the initiation into the state of the so-called living buddhas – for an ability to disappear into Nature.

S. Kulovaný has attained this state and perhaps identifies it, with my instruction, correctly. Therefore, it is possible to judge that by its use he will attain a real initiation, unlike A. Ghose, about whom it is supposed that he was an initiated one; however, because he has considered this state to be a "wind which blows from where it itself wants and where it itself wants", he was not an initiated one.

The initiated one must never be mistaken in the classification of the qualities of "chidakasha" – the spiritual universe. Otherwise they will end up as a slave of the nature which they were already earlier, from their birth. The prize of the spiritual effort will be, in the last moments of their life, snatched away from their hands as well as from their mind and consciousness, and this will plunge them into the state of the common people again. But one must not overestimate themselves either. When they are able to make the quality of this state something, with which it is possible to operate, they must never degrade it by considering it to be something ordinary – to be one of the inner forces which they are using to fulfil their sensory greed. In that moment, this quality ceases to be a tool serving self-initiation and becomes only a factor which paralyses the person, for example, by awakening spiritual pride in them. The spiritual pride is enough for the initiated one to be forced to descend again to earth as its slave.

It is certainly not necessary to make the quality of this state a "wind which blows from where it itself wants and where it itself wants". If it happens, it is a proof that it wasn't an initiated one who expressed themselves. However, another profound error leading to a spiritual fall is when the quality of this state is considered to be one of the completely usual or ordinary states or phenomena. This judgement testifies to an undeveloped discrimination ability which every mystic has to develop by the respective mystical efforts if they are not equipped with it since birth. Otherwise they will never enter the path of self-initiation.

Thus, there are enough problems around this state and its correct classification. Therefore, the gurus must initiate their disciples in the gloom of their ignorance until the moment, when it is certain that those who are being initiated will not degrade this prospectively attainable state by the usual moral corruption; such corruption, which suggests to them an opinion about everything that exists outside of their person as things that are supposed to serve their sensory greed. Besides that, the guru must always avoid crippling his or her disciples by avoiding suggesting to them a thought that this state is a sacrament which as a rule manifests itself by an aureole. He or she must know the qualities of the cosmos, and must also know which of them spiritually kill and which spiritually revive.

S. Kulovaný is now another cornerstone in the mosaic of that which is called the liberating mystical teaching. He has crossed the stumbling blocks where there is a danger of discrediting the physical qualities of the spiritual life, and he has crossed it without accident – like those before him with whom I have worked. Therefore I judge that the count of the "partially initiated ones" has reached a number which assures that the true teaching exists and that I know it well. It is a wonderful teaching which knocks the thought up gods down from their thrones and, by contrast, it raises the devils created by inquisition if they deserve it.

Thus, I am not of the opinion that the qualities, which make a person an initiated one or an animal human being, are divine if they are not in the power of the person or non-divine if they are in the power of the person. I would even say that these are forces of Nature which can be identified through a thorough analysis of all tensions in the being; only there are more of the non-divine qualities for a person who lives their life in an animal way. However, mysticism is an inner training, by means of which we reveal everything in ourselves; only the lack of discrimination can cause that we evaluate valuable qualities as not valuable and – by that an aid for attaining spiritual perfection is lost.

With regard to the fact that the loss of this aid is irreplaceable, almost every individual needs a mystical leader. This leader is supposed to help them to identify the desirable quality, and explain to them that it is one of many; however, it is necessary to imprint it into the consciousness, develop it there and finally use it for mystical operations, whose aim is self-transformation which is primarily of a psychological type. The identification of this quality, its isolation from other qualities, its imprinting into the consciousness and its development in the consciousness – all this belongs to the admission of the disciple by the guru, thus, to the first stage on the path to initiation. Operating with this quality all the way to the attainment of self-transformation is the second stage and it means the process of initiation of the disciple by the guru. The attainment of special properties in the field of self-transformation is the third stage on the path to initiation and it actually means self-initiation. The reaching of a limit where the disciple evidently discerns that, "there is no further knowable land" – as this state is described by the Tibetan mysticism, is the fourth stage and it in fact means the accomplishment of the self-initiation.

If the initiation by means of "communication of the power of initiation", i.e. by a transfer, exists, then it is an exception which only proves the rule, because, this initiation requires that the one undergoing initiation has already attained the initiation, but they have not yet become aware of it, or, that he or she is a suitable tool for the guru to achieve his, or her, intended spiritual goal. We have an example in Ramakrishna and in his relation to Vivekananda. However, this process of initiation excludes an idea that the initiated one convinces the one being initiated by magic in a sense of the pulling of living rabbits out of an empty pocket, or money from the empty pocket of the disciple to put it then in their own pocket; it is also not possible to require from the true guru clairvoyance in the usual conception. The guru must save his, or her sight by protecting its purity in order to be able to detect the mystical progress in their disciples; the clairvoyance, foreseeing the external destinies in others which can change by their efforts, belongs to witchcraft which will surely deprive the quasiguru of their spiritual sight. This means that we do not carry out mysticism or yoga for the purpose of obtaining various external advantages, but only for a higher purpose, by which the attainment of perfection in the sense of victory over destiny in general, is understood.

For the guru to be able to safely monitor the development of that quality, which serves for self-initiation, into the consciousness of their disciple, they must preserve an entirely pure sight. The experience has already proven that the students of yoga do not recognise that quality long after it has developed in them. By this they are exposed to an acute danger that they will abuse it and by that they will lose every possibility of the accomplishment of the state of self-initiation. However, the knowledge, which is related to the attainment of the third Buddhist jhana, is also dangerous. The ability to bring about and retain experiential states which are related to the attainment of the third Buddhist jhana without the necessity to observe the moral commandments of yoga, has already brought several people to a spiritual fall. As an example of this I could mention, in the first place, the gentlemen Hejhal and Drtikol, who, based on this fact, understood the relativity of virtues and therefore they ceased to follow them. However, because they, at the same time, forgot about the dangers of the desirous beingness which was not subordinated by means of the developed virtues, and they were again giving in to it, they have forgotten about the relativity of vices. This was the reason why they have, after their first take-off towards transcendence, fallen into ordinariness with broken wings on the body of the transcendence. Thus they have returned full circle to ordinary humanness.

In order for this not to happen, the guru must retain their discerning ability, as well as the ability to monitor this quality, as it develops into the consciousness of his or her obedient disciple. As a rule, they must themselves bring their disciple to the knowledge of this quality after it has sufficiently developed in the disciple. Then the guru must proceed to the initiation of the disciple by teaching him, or her, how to tame this quality and further then how to operate with it in a way so that it serves the further mystical development of the disciple. Only when this has taken place, does the role of the guru end. However, the guru must feel released from their duty only when they are certain that their disciple will not abuse this quality, not only as a thing leading to a spiritual fall, an example of which I have mentioned above, but also not even for the most innocent obtaining of the external advantages. For, by that it would be proven that the guru themselves indirectly abuses the powers obtained by initiation for worldly things and that he or she must expect a karmic punishment for it in the form of a spiritual fall and a forced descent to a worldly path, and gradually even to a hellish path. In this way, the spiritual qualities are beneficial as well as misleading and destructive. It must not be forgotten that any kind of a trace of an effort of the guru to show off in front of their disciples by trying to prematurely acquaint them with that superworldly quality, arising in the third Buddhist jhana, is a manifestation of the guru's worldliness which will destroy him or her in the later sequence of things.

When the guru has successfully acquainted the disciple with that quality, which is in Buddhism classified as an experiential base and quality of the third jhana, and, objectively, as a source of all-surpassing feelings of happiness, or, more precisely, a very effective optimism, the disciple enters the path of self-initiation. The use of this quality for a moral "washing-out" of their entire being in the first stage and for its gradual spiritualisation in the second stage, is considered to be a precondition of the self-initiation. During this process, the already initiated disciple must themselves recognise that a light of a superworldly origin develops in them. Something, that promises the overcoming of every suffering by spiritualisation – by a transformation which is related to his or her passage from one level of beings to another with a prospect of "blowing out"; that in fact means the loss of form to which all usual sufferings known to us are linked.

While the "one being self-initiated" in this way, and from their own will, spiritually develops themselves, they are taking part in the glory of divine living and existence. Only experience, which teaches them about the impermanence of everything, gives them the prospects of full liberation which they will find only in unifying themselves with the absolute. Before they arrive at it, they will obtain the knowledge that is it possible to end everything by attainment of the state of the "living Buddhas", in a form, which is no longer subject to the laws of destruction of all natural formations.

The path to self-initiation thus winds through the states of a perfect registering: Whether these are states of ecstasy or beholding the light in one's own being and actualising the light in it, the person is always aware of themselves as well as of the fact that no "wind of the spirit which blows from wherever it itself wants and wherever it itself wants" operates here, but it is an appropriate use of qualities, which were developed by correct actions during the process of initiation and which become known, as a rule, only with the help of the guru.

Therefore, let us not assume that initiation is related to secretiveness, or, to a mysterious and extraordinary power. Let us know that initiation means obtaining the knowledge of the quality which is entering consciousness by the attainment of the third Buddhist jhana, which is properly embedded in the order of the psychological qualities of the life being experienced, even though, admittedly, this quality is initially not as pronounced as the quiver of the body, brought about by the sensory perceptions and impressions. It only becomes pronounced when the person, within the emotional experience of the different inner states, provides for it the needed space. Therefore, this quality is not divine in the usual sense, but only transcendental in the framework of the physical qualities represented in the being.

Thus, we have in ourselves both slavery and freedom, and it only depends which we provide the space for in our consciousness. If we desire only for the sensory experiences, we are giving space only to slavery and sufferings originating from it. When we renounce the sensory experiences, we will find the principles of freedom. Developing these principles means reaching bliss and happiness, which we were looking for, now in money, now in something else, but we have never found it in anything. Also, that recognition of the relative character of virtues is here a bad thing; this knowledge is always abused when, as a consequence of animality which was not eradicated, a person forgets about the relative value of vices.

Nevertheless, I will attempt to describe a state which serves the mystical disciples for their self-initiation. It is not easy, however, it is well enough possible to describe the conditions of its accentuation; for, it is not possible to create it. It is in the being in a potential state and it is constantly drowned out by the sensory living, by excitements, which set the entire emotional life into a 'pounding of waves', which ends up the same way as intoxication by alcohol, or by various opiates, or, narcotics – actually literally by a hangover. Therefore an opposite effort must be taken up – an effort to suppress the cravings for sensory excitements. In this way, one will arrive at an inner calming down which, because it is not potentially disturbed, gains a character of an absence of craving.

The absence of craving is a condition to the arising of the state of 'the happy little innocent ones', which is, in highly developed intellectuals, modified into feelings of happiness of a certain kind, which break their way through to awareness. This "happiness" modifies itself into a subjective optimism, into an optimism of the mind, which, as a consequence of this, ceases to be active in reflexes and begins to be active in conscious thinking.

The conscious thinking, which no longer hatches plans to obtain things which are pleasing for the senses and emotionally arousing a person, transforms this 'happy state of the little innocent ones' into an ability of intellectual penetration which leads to the knowledge of the impermanence of everything that can be achieved in the sensory world. By this, the tendencies of awareness to pay attention to the external phenomena and things, are suppressed and, conversely, feelings of happiness, arising in solitude or from solitude, develop.

Solitude is something that one certainly has to get used to. However, the knowledge of the impermanence of everything facilitates it; when a person realises that it is best not to seek any happiness in the external world, their mind will calm down in such a way that it can be considered, in another sense, to be a rapidly developing third Buddhist jhana.

From the psychological point of view, in particular, the qualities of experiencing, and, after all, also the mental, qualities, which arise during the attainment and development of the third Buddhist jhana, are non-worldly. Precisely that submersion of the consciousness in itself, from which every relationship to the external world is excluded, helps a person to transfer to a sphere of commonly absolutely unknown experiences, which can be classified as now paradisiacal, now heavenly, now divine and now, in turn, as transcendental. If the principle of transcendence dominates in them, the consciousness is a totally suitable tool for the attainment of self-initiation. As, both the consciousness and the mind are supposed to be like this, if they are to be a suitable tool for a washing-out of the being, which means eradication of humanness by washing-out.

However, when the transcendental principle is well developed in the mind and the mind continues, by means of conscious thinking of the body and of the entire being, with concentration, the process never stops only at this "washing-out", because the transcendence purifies not only the body and the feelings, but also thinking and awareness and that, in the final phase, manifests itself as a development of an ecstatic state in the mind.

Until this level, nothing is required which would cause the feelings to become ecstatic. The yogis have a duty to be constantly aware of their body and by that, to stabilise their mind on the earth, in the matter. By this very thing the awareness gradually transforms. A constant observation, or awareness of the body, leads to a spontaneous transformation of awareness, in a sense that the body ceases to be for the consciousness the usual material and heavy form, and becomes only a symbol of matter. When one arrives all the way to this point, the awareness preserves its character of a concrete awareness, however, in the concrete concepts, without destroying the development of the ecstatic thinking, which is the only one in which a possibility of arising of the feelings of an absolute liberation exists.

Precisely with regard to these work procedures, there is not a single moment in the sphere of the psychological phenomena, in which the mental and other processes can escape registering, because, the process in question is a sublimation process of thinking – a process, during which one evidently transfers from reflexive perception, awareness and reflexive thinking to perception, awareness and thinking which are fully conscious. This is considered to be a victory of the person over themselves, and resolving of all the problems of suffering, which can occur due only to the fact that the inner processes escape from the consciousness of a person, or they take place under the threshold of the conscious perceptions.

The role of the guru is, above all, to bring his or her disciple to the development of that state of the "happy little innocent ones". Afterwards they are supposed to teach their disciple how to operate with this state in a way which makes the purification of the entire psyche take place. The disciple is then supposed to be led already to independence, because a systematic purification of the being all the way to the emergence and development of the ecstatic states of mind and consciousness is an extremely subtle matter which is, in the sphere of the inner states, imbued with countless nuances of the inner impulses. A total purification of these impulses requires a continuous control and one's own inner efforts; no one else can relieve a person of this task – or carry it out instead of them.

A good preparation of the disciple by an experienced guru leads to an absolutely certain success in this work. When someone, under the lead of the guru, attains a thorough knowledge of themselves, they then will independently detect every variation from the inner balance. When such a disciple learns to feel responsibility towards himself or herself, achieving this inner balance is not a problem for them. Precisely by a constant maintaining of this balance, which is not at the cost of attenuation of the clarity of the daily consciousness, everybody, who strives in this way, will attain the highest level of self-initiation. This means that they will obtain the possibility of a free choice to continue the path through lives as the so-called living Buddha – a being who will disappear into Nature, or alternatively, they may realise the state of liberation – salvation, by unifying of the personal consciousness with the absolute.

However, before this goal is achieved, a person will obtain the experience and knowledge that, precisely in the course of the states which are accompanying the third Buddhist jhana, one is attaining the understanding of the meaning and purpose of the spiritual or mystical efforts. This understanding is, though, of a high quality only if the one being initiated destroys their selfishness. If they do not destroy it, the states of this jhana, during its experiencing, will appear to them as insufficient to be able to replace that sensory cravings which people gratify either by the relevant contacts between men and women, or by a constantly droning radio receiver, or by being captivated by the television, or also by social pastimes which are now of a seemingly flawless kind, now of a flawed kind. He or she can rate them like the man who has also attained the third Buddhist jhana, but when I managed to describe it to him and by that to bring him to the knowledge that he has attained it, he stated that what use is this success to him, when he has no woman!

This very case bears testimony, for all other cases, to the fact that before the striving one reaches the third Buddhist jhana, they must, from their own will, eradicate sensory desires. Only then will they realise that that terrifying emptiness, which they see in their own personal solitude and in the life without sensory enjoyments, is, in the third Buddhist jhana, substituted by the superworldly inner and feeling states, whose continuous development convinces one that it is a path from the sensory world to the transcendence, thus, a path from the sorrowful to the sorrow-free world. However, still it is necessary to add this: the states brought about by the third Buddhist jhana are not a bad or insufficient substitute for women and pastimes, but they are a new feeling of a general refreshment which is reflected in the consciousness as its development into the limitlessness and even into the absolute.

It is necessary to know that if those who have entered the path of a gradual transcendence neglect the necessary eradication of the sensory desires, no guru has the power to change, in the ones who seek, the worldly tendencies for the superworldly ones. It is only a matter of attachment of the ones being initiated who have to, themselves, put up resistance to their inclinations, and overpower them, and by that, to actually leave that mythical river Styx, in which they are drowning. The path is only theirs, the results are theirs and the mystical goal is theirs. The gurus can only teach them not to commit mistakes and thus, not to exchange worldliness of a certain kind for worldliness of another kind. Those, who believe that the guru can himself or herself remove their moral flaws, are wrong and a guru who would support such a conviction, is a mere trickster.

This whole question is solved in a way in which Dr. Kovář has spoken about this effort – he said that the reason why he has achieved an evident certainty about the good result of his mystical effort, was that he has based his whole mystical striving on the struggle for quality. He has struggled for the clarity of his consciousness, for a perfect vigilance, for the best inner and feeling state, for the annihilation of the undesirable, negative, inclinations, states and qualities and by that also for the development of the positive and desirable states. He quotes from Buddhism, and he often adds that only when he has overcome the five hindrances on the path to perfection, namely the worldly cravings, hatred, torpor, restless speculation and doubt, has he reached a state of joyful feelings by which he was made happy. By this happiness his body has calmed down, and by that he has attained contentment.

In line with his personal experience, I will quote from Buddhism to make it clear how everything develops further. – When a feeling of contentment will arise in one, the spirit will unite, so that then the striving one, who is far away from cravings and from unfortunate things reaches the first Buddhist jhana, which is connected with impressions and thinking, and which has arisen from solitude and is filled with joyfulness and happiness. – By calming down of the impressions and thinking, one attains an inner peace and unity of spirit, and that means attainment of the second Buddhist jhana, which is devoid of impressions and thinking; this jhana has arisen from concentration and is filled with joyfulness and happiness. – When the striving one frees themselves from the craving for joyfulness and dwells equanimous, fully conscious of oneself and clear, he or she feels that happiness, about which noble monks say that equanimous and insightful monk is abiding happy, then they are dwelling in the third Buddhist jhana. – However, when they reject both feelings of happiness, and of suffering, and they also let the earlier satisfaction and worries cease, they are abiding in the fourth Buddhist jhana, which is suffering-free, pleasure-free and made clear by indifference and turning inwards.

All this is a result of concentration whose quality is improved by elimination, or overcoming, of the five hindrances. – By the further works, the striving one attains wisdom which brings the knowledge of their own earlier incarnations and also the knowledge of the cause of arising and ceasing of all creatures in general. By termination of the delusion – by the extinguishment of the thirst for life, they will then get to know the redemption of mind – the redemption by wisdom, already during the current life. By that they will arrive at an evident certainty that their re-creation and reincarnation has stopped, their asceticism is accomplished and the work is finished, by which for them, any kind of world ceases to exist. Thus, this is the result of wisdom, which, together with the previous concentration, brings the striving one into a state in which there is nothing more for him or her to carry out.

It is possible to add to this quote, that, the more the mind gets rid of the relationships to the world by overcoming of the worldly cravings and desires and wandering which originates in them, the more it is able to let itself be engaged by the object of concentration; in this case by one's own psyche as an external object for observation. In this way, the concentration is purified and rid of all potential relationships to the external world. This is a precondition of a deeper and deeper delving of the conscious thinking into the being, however, initially only as into a lifeless emptiness. However, the interruption of the relationships of the mind to the world are also related to feelings, whose tendencies are being modified; this, as a result, manifests itself as the Buddhist jhanas. The third of them is dependent upon such deadening of the person towards the world that his or her surface receptive ability, which delivers the emotional perceptions, is paralysed.

When the striving one arrives at this, in their consciousness a sphere of variously modified transcendence begins to arise; predominantly the sensory world. – However, the depth of immersion of the mind into the psyche can further increase. By that, the feeling of happiness, which is connected with the third Buddhist jhana, fades away and by this the state of concentration turns into the fourth Buddhist jhana, in which a person becomes indifferent to the entire external world as well as to its products reflected in every individual and to the bliss which was accompanying the third

Buddhist jhana and now is fading away. Only an inner tranquillity will be left, permeated by the clarity of the vigilant consciousness. This will cause the conscious thinking to break through the last layers of the psyche all the way to its very centre which, in the first phase, appears to be a sphere of personal atavisms.

In this sphere, the inner life of all beings becomes one; later it is perceived as a mass which is transforming, from its own preconditions, into individualities. This happens by means of potential kindlings of cravings. Thus, the impulses of desire are recognised as the true cause of the forming of individuals which, however, have their roots in this mass at all times. This is noticeable when this process is tracked back, along a retrograde line. Along the retrograde line, in an inverse sequence, the striving one can detect by observation that they are still stuck, with their spiritual legs, in this mass as a mud which is not perceived. When this mud sucks the striving one into itself, they observe this as disappearance of their own individuality. Only his or her persistent desire *to be* causes his or her individuality to emerge again and again, in a precise relationship to its own preconditions.

In this stage of the mystical development, one can already see the function of that continuous submersion in this mass, which is in fact that Buddhist samsara, and if those preconditions of the arising of oneself as well as the others are thoroughly observed, they point the way to how one can escape all this by a correct inner attitude, i.e. by non-attachment to any of the states during their arising. The ability, to see all the way to the level of atavisms in their effective action enables one, at the same time, to observe the line of impulses, which, in the face of the preserved vigilance in the forth Buddhist jhana, creates an ability to remember both the line of the ever renewing own existences in the reincarnation conception, as well as the ability to observe the arising and end of other creatures together with the cause of this. By means of knowledge of the effects of the real non-attachment, one is extricated from the cruel jaws of palingenesis, which means a halt in the process of reincarnation.

This can really be considered to be an attainment of an absolute freedom, which is equal to salvation.

When we return to ourselves again, we may know that only that equanimity and insight make a person able to know those inner states which are always hidden behind the sphere of the experiential categories, of the sensations linked to sensuality, and then, by means of the third Buddhist jhana, to develop them as dominant states. A characteristic of these states is, that a person ceases to belong to people living a sensory life, but they will belong to those who live the states of transcendental consciousness with all the implications of this: this actually means initiation. In the course of the further development of this equanimity and insight, the striving one attains also a physical detachment from the sensory world, if they fully share these transcendental states with the body by means of making the body present in their consciousness while they are aware of these states.

In this way, the striving one attains self-initiation and will develop either an ability to disappear into Nature like the Biblical Henoch or Elias, or, they can realise the state of absolute in their consciousness, which, in turn, signifies the extinguishment of their differentiated personality without any trace, and this happens in the state of awareness and experiencing of the state of the absolute. Other states of awareness, thinking and feelings do not prove to be desirable; in each one of them, the mind of the yogi, who is perfectly discerning everything, finds a precondition for a future end, and by that also of suffering. The foolish people try to escape the end and suffering by an exactly opposite method, i.e. by multiplication and intensification of the sensory impulses. On this opposite path, the suffering is closer to a person and it is usually also more urgent. The knowledge, which is provided by the attainment of the third Buddhist jhana, is able to identify these paths. The accomplishment of the self-initiation, by means of "washing-out" of oneself and burning out, then puts an end to the path through sufferings by the states of this jhana, which gradually deepens and becomes the fourth jhana.

On the higher Buddhist jhanas

The followers of Buddhism, whether those for whom Buddhism is a subject of their abstract study, or those who follow its moral and other commandments, are understandably interested in the highest aspects of Buddhism, namely in the so-called 'jhanas'. However, if these people do not have a direct experience from the Buddhist meditation efforts, they are always in danger of forming a false idea about the jhanas, of finding themselves on a wrong track and, as a consequence, of not getting to know the core of the Buddhist teaching as a spiritual teaching. Only a practitioner who does not adhere only to the way of living prescribed by Buddhism, but also adheres to the mental effort as a tool with the help of which it is possible to penetrate into the entire complex of the Buddhist practices, can arrive at a clarification of this whole matter.

This is because the right way of living serves only to attain a change in the tendencies of the being, to reorient from the worldly interests to the liberating spiritual ones. By this the right way of living liberates a person de facto. The mental effort then serves to obtain the knowledge of the mechanics of the inner processes and tensions and it is supposed to peak in the pulling down of all the walls created by constant differentiation in the sphere of awareness, thinking, judgement, opinions and consciousness.

With regard to this, it is possible to consider jhanas to be a psychological and parapsychological issues, which can be solved by the meditation practice. This practice itself, however, requires a completely different inner orientation than the moral effort which serves the attainment of perfection in the active life. Nevertheless, many followers of Buddhism sink into a fundamental misconception that the realisation of the moral commandments of the Buddhist teaching will itself fully enlighten them and, therefore, that it grants them a right to make fundamental judgements about the jhanas, although these strivers are always only worldly followers of Buddhism.

The sphere of Buddhist teaching, where the Buddhist jhanas have their respective strong significance is related to the so-called 'meditation practice'. Here a person is, in turn, influenced by the specific character of each meditation; only the meditations enriched by an ability to precisely analyse the subtle inner processes will lead everyone to the understanding of the meaning of the Buddhist jhanas. The attempts to classify the Buddhist jhanas which are not based on a direct experience from the Buddhist meditations are quite worthless, because this classification is always based on speculations which perhaps may have a logical structure, like every theoretical conclusion reached by a person who studies something.

A reader of works on Buddhism can learn all kinds of things about the Buddhist jhanas. However, if it is not an experienced person who talks about the Buddhist jhanas in these works, their reader always learns only such thoughts which will not help them in the meditation effort. In particular in the classification of the Buddhist jhanas, a lot of things are unclear. One commentator claims that only the first four jhanas are authentic and that the latter ones were added to them only by later interpreters of Buddhism. Another commentator claims that all eight, or, more precisely, nine jhanas develop continuously from the first one up to the highest one. As a rule, a reliable argument is lacking in both cases and that points to the fact that the explanation constitutes sheer speculation.

Speaking for myself, I am not a Buddhist, if this is, to a certain extent, excluded by my personal life course and the problems related to it. These problems can perhaps be, to a large extent, but certainly not as a whole, solved in a Buddhist way, at least as far as the questions of mystical outcomes of the entire moral and spiritual efforts of the person are concerned. However, I have experience from the concentration and meditation practice which I have identified as a key to open the doors of knowledge. But only after my concentration and meditation effort had become a tool for continuous analysis of all inner processes, I realised that the jhanas serve the purpose of obtaining knowledge and solving of the whole structure of being on the psychological level which is behaving in a mechanical way. I have learned that the first group of jhanas solves the problems of non-redemptive living on the emotional or animal sphere; in other words, the problems of living which is, for people, factual, while the second group solves the problems of inner forces as factors which in principle determine the base – the emotional living.

According to the experience, on which I am basing this conclusion, the emotional beingness would not be able to create conditions for reincarnation of the existence of a being, because it is lacking the unifying power of will. The unifying power of will is manifesting itself in the idea of 'I' as a variously behaving intellectual factor. Therefore, the solution of the factual state of things of the reincarnational existence must be supplemented by an intellectual solution, whose core is in the mechanical mental activity.

By that, the question of solving the 'life suffering' – how living is called by the Buddhists – is becoming indeed broader and my experience points to the fact that no uniform, or straightforward spiritual effort can be sufficient to solve it. It is necessary to penetrate into the secrets of the true technique of enlightening concentration. Then a person will realise that the individual levels of concentration, whether described by the yogic or Buddhist teaching, are in essence not different between these two teachings, although yoga speaks of Dharana, Dhyana, Samadhi, Nirvikalpasamadhi and Sahajanirvikalpasamadhi, while Buddhism speaks of the jhanas. In accordance with that, the true enlightening concentration must have all signs of a universally valid spiritual effort. Only an unsuccessful mental effort to carry out the true mystical concentration points to the fact that the differences between the levels of yogic concentration and the Buddhist jhanas exist.

In the case of the jhanas themselves, experience proves that they really develop continuously from the first one up to the ninth. However, they can be divided into two groups. The first group, referring to the first through to the fourth jhana, is supposed to make the life process irreversible. The second group of jhanas, from the fifth through to the ninth, is supposed to lead to the development of the mystical knowledge and thus to support the irreversibility of the life process by the relevant knowledge. This implies that in a fully developed fourth jhana, such a deep indifference to the life process develops, that the anchorage points cease to exist for the ever-recurring forming of the idea of 'I'; 'I' 'leaping out' in a successive line – that means in a line unfolding towards the future. The future becomes a perfectly accurate image of the activity which a person commits at present. However, the indifference arising from the fourth jhana, if it is constantly illuminated by the mystical practice of a constant self-observation, is the basis for successful progresses by means of the further jhanas which lead to the needed enlightenment and to a perfect halt of the always rotating wheel of reincarnations.

Thus, if someone reaches the state of indifference, which can be considered as a result of a developed fourth Buddhist jhana, but they are not exactly a Buddhist monk who has the possibility to adequately personally isolate himself, they will surely clearly understand that they are bound to awareness and thinking in concrete concepts, or, in other words, awareness and thinking differentiated in form. This is a consequence of the habitual activity of mind, even though this activity is considerably silenced in this jhana. A well functioning knowledge indicates that to be bound to a form, even if it is accompanied by a fully developed indifference towards the world, is an insufficiency at the inner level. Out of this, the owner of this knowledge will infer that the complex of problems caused by the function of psyche needs to be solved, too.

A high quality knowledge will bring a person to an understanding that it is necessary to break the limitation of one's own consciousness, which is solid and permanent due to the fact that the mind works in concrete concepts. For as long as a person belongs to the common people, even though these might be indifferent like those who have attained the fourth Buddhist jhana, they always snatch the individual concepts out of reality and then process them, as does a predator its hunted prey. This is a cage for their consciousness and awareness – a cage, which is still firm enough to raise in them a certainty that everything is all right here.

However, a yogi must know that they are firmly closed in this cage and that it is necessary to break free. Therefore, they must start an operation of freeing themselves from this cage. This is done by an effort not to let any concept or perception form itself, or, more precisely, by a volitional effort to destroy the forming ideas, initially by refusing to deal with them. In such a way, they will overcome their imaginary limitation. Then their mind will get to know the world without limitations, that infinity of space, which corresponds to the inner states characterising the fifth jhana.

The knowledge of the states that are dependent upon the attainment of the "infinity of space" leads to experiencing and developing of the feelings of limitlessness. For awareness or perception, feelings are developing, which are feelings of – as the yogi recognises – the beings of those times when they have appeared in the world and started to experience the "children's bliss" of those just born who are discovering the world in which they have not clashed yet – neither due to their ambivalent inner states, nor on the outside – i.e. between each other. However, because the yogis attain this state only after obtaining their own life experience in the state of the common people, the states related to the attainment of the "infinity of space" do not carry the feature of a carefree entangling into the pitfalls of karma which would be created by their attachment to the external world, as it is seen from the perspective of inexperienced beings. The yogis carry a tendency towards the higher level on the path of return to their very origin, to the beginning of the genesis of phenomena in the universe.

This tendency usually makes the yogi suddenly realise that also their consciousness dwells in differentiation and in limitation, which in practice manifests itself by an inclination to adopt everything that they are aware of, or, in other words, by an inclination to a differentiated awareness, to the creation of the subjective world; in a psychological adaptation it manifests itself as a functioning of the consciousness in a narrow area of permanent prejudices. This way the yogi realises that the "infinity of space" is a deficient state, because the differentiation of consciousness automatically binds them by the existence of their own subjective world.

A yogi who thoroughly observes everything, infers from this state that it is necessary to eradicate this tendency of consciousness, which is seemingly a matter of course and only obvious after a deeper analysis of the processes of one's own inner nature. This eradication is dealt with by exerting a constant influence on the differentiating awareness not to behave in this way. In this way a yogi arrives at the developing of an opposite tendency in awareness – a tendency towards its non-differentiation. When they supplement it by a constant elimination of the almost automatic differentiation of consciousness, they will arrive at the reaching of a state called "infinite consciousness".

The experiencing of the state of "infinity of consciousness" is characterised by the non-arising of 'I', or, more precisely, by the arising of an 'I' which is qualitatively different from the one before. This in practice, means that an awareness occurs which is no longer limited to one's own being; an awareness of oneself in infinite or even in limitless dimensions. By this, those who have attained the state of the "infinity of consciousness" already identify themselves as a limitless existence, or, as someone who evidently discovers that the universe is contained in them and it is not they who are contained in the universe. In this state, the bliss of those who "were just called out to life from the bosom of nothingness" no longer arises in them; on the contrary, what does arise in them, is knowledge that they have crossed the border of the origination of these beings, towards the non-manifest Nature – towards the very origin of everything in the first moment of creation, i.e. towards the phenomenon of the origin of tensions and forces of a physical character, which means at the beginning of formation of the inanimate Nature. From this moment, it becomes obvious to the yogi that there is no difference between the animate and inanimate Nature, but that there exists only one creative process, that unified field of forces, which was not understood prior to modern physics.

However, the state of the "infinity of consciousness" is, in the hazy cosmic creation, recognisable only as the beginning of genesis of the differentiated existences. Thus, an idea arises in the yogi that they are occurring in the world of convoluting creative substances, phenomena, which are still unformed in this state, though. This prompts them to keep excluding the differentiation of ideas – of all imaginary delimitations. When they achieve a good success in this activity, the phenomena will disappear from their horizon of perception and they will identify this as reaching the sphere called "the land of entirely nothing".

Yes! Beyond the universe of phenomena, whose origin is determined by a seemingly natural differentiation of the phenomenon known as consciousness and, by that already, also awareness, or, more precisely, above this universe, there exists a bottomless or, limitless emptiness. However, the yogi does not identify it as nothingness, but as emptiness which is able to give rise to phenomena. From this they then infer that they are still remaining in the creative world which extends from nothingness to the sphere filled with phenomena. Therefore, as a rule, they do not stay here. They already sense that from here downwards, there exists the creative process which is, due to its samsaric character, seizing phenomena and this forces him or her to turn "upwards", away from the creative process, back to the beginning. By this they obtain the possibility to realise that the only solution of the question of personal slavery is to continuously destroy the differentiating moments in awareness; this way they will arrive at the "borderline of possible perception". This state means, as its name suggests, the ability to either differentiate the awareness by means of demarcation of one's own personal consciousness, or let everything constantly dissolve. By this they truly dwell on the "borderline of possible perception".

However, as a rule, one remains in this state only until they have fully tried out the function of consciousness differentiating or non-differentiating itself. When a yogi realises that, by this, they would in fact remain on the borderline of the creative and non-creative nature, the last possibility in the field of the mystical development will dawn on them: the suppression or elimination of perception. Only by that they will, by trial – empirically, obtain the power to bring themselves to end in the state of paranirvana. It will depend on their wisdom, whether they use this power or not, because here the situation does not appear quite as simple to the enlightened sage. Existence proves to be a set of tendencies, out of which neither those, leading to the end of oneself in the paranirvanic state, nor those, leading to the creative process, might appear good. However, the yogis who are dwelling here are able, in this state, to solve the present problem. Usually, an unwritten law is observed that everyone must decide for themselves what they should do. Therefore, the last decision must remain in the hands of the individual who has climbed all the way up to this state.

The state of "elimination of perception and feeling" in Buddhism is equivalent to the state of "enlightening Samadhi" in yoga. However, in Buddhism this state is reached by an exact sequence of steps in the process of overcoming barriers identified in the inner activity, while in yoga the enlightening Samadhi is often reached in a tangle of inner tensions, representing the inner activity. Only the impulses of desire for the spiritual liberation form a unifying factor, which, in the crisis of the desiring one, causes an over-all-prevailing inner tension which will result in this Samadhi. Therefore it is possible to say that the sensory desires, together with the desires for the spiritual liberation, where the latter ones can be classified as the potential tendencies towards the state of salvation, will decide the whole matter of the enlightening Samadhi, however, only as a more or less accidental result.

Nothing like this is supposed to occur in those who strive according to the aphorisms of the original Buddhism. From the overcoming of the five hindrances all the way to the first and then further up to the fourth Buddhist jhana, the being is supposed to be brought to accomplishment of the renunciation of the world. This renunciation is then obvious by a complete indifference to this, in fact, sensory world. This is an accomplishment in the creating of a good quality base for a successful passing through the further five, the so-called 'higher', Buddhist jhanas.

Only this indifference creates conditions for an objective evaluation of the inner processes and states, which do not cease by attaining the fourth Buddhist jhana, they perhaps only cease, in a person with this attainment, in the moment of death. These prospects create a reason for the achiever of the fourth Buddhist jhana why they must continue in the effort, if they have not physically died; the result of this effort is supposed to be the attainment of the higher Buddhist jhanas.

During an advancement through these jhanas, when the consciousness is thoroughly abstracted by the attainment of the fourth Buddhist jhana, it is possible to identify, with an absolute precision, the states of the "infinity of space", as well as the states of the "infinity of consciousness" and the "land of entirely nothing" and states of the "borderline of possible perception". As soon as these states are correctly identified, one arrives at a correct registration of the state of "elimination of perception and feeling", i.e. in fact at the attainment of a state of a complete purification from all ideas as waste products of a constant automatic 'rippling' of psyche.

However, the esoteric "superbuddhist" teaching still contains one more aphorism – an aphorism about the possibility of the attainment of a state called the "destruction of consciousness". This, in the empirical mysticism, manifests itself as a state of a permanent stiffness, known in the lower, non-mystical form as catalepsy accompanied by the inhibition of daily consciousness to the extent of becoming undetectable; in the higher, mystical form, it is known as the phenomenon of non-decaying dead bodies of some saints, some of them Catholic.

In yoga those have finished their life in this way, who have, by the depth of their concentration, completely inhibited the inner life while preserving the centripetal tendency of the most subtle energies of the being, which are manifesting themselves as the inner life perceived in the form of impulses. In such a case, the body stiffens and the metabolism, which is leaving behind waste products poisoning the body, ceases. This usually causes the body not to decompose after the person dies, or when they are alive and they are in a permanent state of Samadhi. The esoteric part of the mystical teaching contains a lesson that, in this state, it is possible to last for aeons and, only by the effect of the latent tendencies, such beings then reawaken as spirits belonging to some of the celestial realms (spheres) or, however, less often, as the same people who have once fallen into this Samadhi.

It is possible to infer that this reawakening to life is the true ideal of the advanced yogis, the ideal which arises in them during their mystical development. However, the point of view of the sober Buddhist teaching is that it is correct for the empirical destruction of consciousness to be accompanied by such an abstraction of the whole apparatus which takes part in the mystical work, that no tendencies are retained in the sphere of the inner life. In such a case the mystic disappears without a trace from the sphere of the visible – and this happens on their current psycho-mystical spot. This is classified as a state symbolising the "extinguishment of oneself on the spot", which can be considered the best 'way out' of all. This is because it is judged that the tendencies always mean that a person occurs 'on the pathways', which can prove to be, due to a simple fact that it represents motion, a never-ending wandering; and that is a sign of the Samsara. Only those who have fully extinguished themselves do not suffer from the phenomena which are accompanying movement.

The state of "destruction of consciousness" points, with regard to the end of a person by death, to the fact that the problem of a sorrowful death, preceded by diseases, is solved, without doubt and in its full extent. By contrast, the stiffness caused by a centripetal flow of the mental energies is in fact a blissful state. It is not accompanied by the decomposition of the body, because such decomposition is only possible if the mental energies have a centrifugal tendency. However, this tendency is only eliminated once a person has embraced their whole body by their awareness, while letting the external world slip from their consciousness.

It is possible to assume that all those mystics or Christian saints who are not decaying in the grave have arrived at this state and so did the yogis who understood that this state is an ideal solution of the problem of suffering. However, the yogis, especially those who are simple and intellectually undeveloped, often fall into this state so to be able to avoid the sufferings of life, which are caused by the unfulfilled desires. Then the stiffness, the state of Samadhi, is an escape from the problems of the life lived; and exactly due to that this Samadhi qualitatively becomes only a winter sleep of animals.

We will not find anything similar, neither in those Christian saints who do not decompose in the grave, nor in mystics or yogis who have, in a mystically correct way, solved the problems of the life lived. Nor will we find anything like this in Buddhists, who are correctly adhering to the Buddhist teaching. For, all these people have proceeded in such a way that they were penetrating the greatest depths of their being, until the necessity dawned on them to completely suppress the mechanics of the inner life inside of them, i.e. the emotional and other oscillation of forces. By this, also the life drive ceased in them. The presence of this drive can bother only those who have not fully suppressed those mechanics.

Only this fact changes the real stiffness, which bears a tendency towards an absolute extinguishment of oneself in the feelings of the respective kinds of bliss, into that winter sleep of animals which leaves everyone in their previous inner state – in ignorance, as it is understood in mysticism and Buddhism.

When the life mechanics of the psyche in inner 'heavy waves', is suppressed, that stiffness becomes either an enlightening Samadhi, or an omniscience which will fully absorb the life process. The Buddhists, as well as the mystics, benefit from this redemption during life, which peaks in a total 'blowing out' in that state of disappearance of persons in the Nature, in redemption – there is even a story about it in the Bible, mentioning the departure of Elias and Henoch from this world.

Thus, this is what it looks like from the point of view of the so-called 'higher Buddhist jhanas'. It can be judged that if a person is supposed to reach the state of nirvana, i.e. "redemption during life", they have no other choice than to go through all eight jhanas. For, the completion of the spiritual development by reaching the fourth Buddhist jhana, i.e. by the attainment of paranirvana requires that a person only cares about the finishing or completion of the life process which appears as sorrowful and therefore undesirable, and also as absolutely significant, if we consider it to be a "process on its own". However, those who want to arrive all the way at the irreversibility of the life process in the broadest sense of this word, must achieve that the mental activity takes part in the solving of the "suffering of life", too. Therefore, as a rule, it is necessary to complement the "path of spiritual development" with the higher Buddhist jhanas that make it possible to reach the "redemption during life", the state of nirvana.

However, from the European mentality it can be deduced that people of the white race will never be content with a simple and unexplained destruction of the life process, because some big "WHY" always haunts them in their heads – it is such a "why" that never serves anything good. Perhaps only the Asians are able to believe in their gurus and not to complicate their own life by seemingly important knowledge which is achieved only by an experimental destruction of the entire activity. The result of this experimental destruction is a direct knowledge of the pre-creative state.

When someone reaches all the way to the ninth Buddhist jhana, they will realise that the only thing that has always been important was to uproot the life drive, the desire for life, and this is provided by a fully known fourth Buddhist jhana. However, when we meet a guru knowledgeable about all problems of suffering and their solution by means of the spiritual efforts, we are always standing in front of a person who has reached all the way to that ninth Buddhist jhana; a person, who has certainly come to know that the fifth up to the ninth jhanas are not additional to the original four, but they are logically developing from the first one. However, this is important for the researchers of the technique of the mystical development, but not at all for the simple attainers of paranirvana, salvation.

According to that, the spiritual development from the simple and inborn state all the way to an evident knowledge of the pre-creative state of the universe, which can be experienced by beings only as salvation, nirvana, can be divided into two phases. In the first phase, those will succeed who are already sated by the life experiences and therefore not interested in knowledge, but in a concrete solution. These people will finish their spiritual development by the fourth Buddhist jhana, whose effect initially paralyses and later completely halts the thirst for life. Then the life impulses in the form of sensory cravings and lusts for life, which set in motion the creative and, from the perspective of a being, reincarnation process, no longer arise.

However, those who are not sated by the life experiences, or those who want to attain the spiritual perfection which is peaking in an evidently experienced state of salvation, in nirvana, must proceed through the path of experiment which is relevant only from the fifth Buddhist jhana. If these people remain on this path till the end, if they will be able, by elimination of the "concrete perceptions, concepts, awareness and consciousness", to arrive at a perfect eradication of the conditions of personification, they will surely get to know the state of absence of any kind of contents in the consciousness: only this is related to a perfect freeing and thus also broadening of consciousness all the way beyond the borders of even an imaginary universe. – Only this is considered to be a state of salvation, or, liberation during life. As, only the absence of any kind of contents in the consciousness, makes the consciousness able to make the universe a content of one's own consciousness, and void consciousness of the suggestive influence arising from the conviction that the external universe, as well as the world, exists. The consciousness expanded in this way, and exceeding all that exists, by itself persuades the person that they have reached the final state, an evident state of salvation.

Speculation and reality

It finally became clear to me. From the fact that it took so long, no one should infer that my slow thinking is at fault. When yoga became my spiritual effort, my understanding of it was that it is a mystical school that instructs us not to speculate, but with a diligent mind to delve into one's own being in order to become able to register all its contents, states of feeling, moods, the state of vigilance and, all in all, everything that belongs to the mechanical functions of the psyche. Precisely, thanks to thorough observation even of the subtlest inner changes, the perfection of this self-observation deepened, and thus I have discovered milestones in the process leading towards the culmination of this effort to entirely stop the inner activity. Halting of the inner activity doesn't, though, resemble inner motionlessness and dullness; it is a perfect overview of the "moments of inner tranquillity", for, halting of the inner activity doesn't mean an inability to start or allow the inner activity, either. It is about reaching an inner or mental borderline, on which the inner activity is fully mastered, but also potentially able to develop into the mechanical activity. From the point of view of yoga, this mechanical inner activity means an impulsive moment in a completely certain presage of a particular outcome of this activity; it is thus a consciously loosed off arrow hitting the sought target with certainty.

I have never, even for a moment, thought that people seeking on the path of Spirit could be led by other motives from their mind and from within than precisely those that I have mentioned, because, a victory over the insurmountable forces, as are those which form their destiny, can be sensed only on the path leading to a halt of the activity of psyche. However, I had to fully acknowledge the fact that even though people do seek on the deepest path of Spirit, yet they do not give up the elementary human inclinations to emotionally experience. Perhaps not the feelings of drunkenness as an alcoholic nor – like another sensuous person – excitement from that which they can see while travelling round the world, through the human society or in various idealistic thoughts, but surely at least those sensations which are mentioned in the mystical books, with the exception of instances when they are talking about perfection, or about a gradual realisation of the state buddho. If it was otherwise, how could they, when someone dies, ask me where they are going, what is with them right now, etc.?

These questions are in fact inappropriate and therefore they have always caused aversion in me. However, as a spiritual person who was so thoroughly setting up the milestones of a progressive turning inwards, I have always approached these questions as queries concerning solely these stages. However, when the questions of this type didn't have this relation, I gave evasive replies or didn't reply at all. I then always quickly forgot these questions; therefore it took me so long to realise that it is the worldliness and animality of the questioner which is enquiring, because, how can anyone benefit from learning that their wife, mother, father, brother, friend, etc. have, due to their deeds, got on a wrong track, into the hellish worlds, or on a good track, into the heavenly worlds? After all, these questioners are not able to imagine hells or heavens. They are thus only led by curiosity, i.e. they are only wandering the paths of inner superficialisation towards worldliness of another kind than that of a true atheist, who is only interested whether their salary is high enough for them to be able to cater for their sensory inclinations.

In recent days I was asked again what has happened with a certain person after his death. In connection with this, it has now quite clearly dawned on me to what extent have those, who should strive for attaining the highest degree of mystical initiation, diverted themselves from the true path of the spiritual development. At the same time I have recalled Buddha's reproaching of the foolish ones who were asking themselves a question whether they already existed before their birth and whether they will exist after their death, what they were before their birth and what they will be after their death, etc. By that, they suggest that they are never interested in knowing how to solve the problem of their unfortunate inner state. Therefore I said: "You fear hell and long for heaven. Does it make any sense at all? When you are imagining the path to perfection, you are thinking of a path interrupted by incarnations in some heaven, but you cannot imagine heavenly life otherwise than as your current life, with the difference that you won't have bellyache there, your wife will not contradict you and everything else in your life will work without obstacles and resistance, too."

If someone cannot, by the mystical training, by means of an analysing mind, break the being down to components and elements and only wants to investigate their future incarnations, they always get entangled in images in which they, as the current, and in the current way formed, creature, will come to a place according to their karmic merits and that there they will experience a life of a person having an abundance of experiences which they now long for. That already means going astray, and from a point of view of a mystic it is being away from the path, nursing and strengthening of a delusion, closing oneself to enlightening knowledge.

When I once, a long time ago, entered the mystical path, I understood that all our knowledge is useless. We only know that which was implanted in us by our parents and by the human society, and then perhaps also that which is produced by our atavisms as the psychological qualities inherited from our ancestors – that which in fact means only a subjective conviction about reality, foolish ideas about the world. Therefore, back then, I did not want to acknowledge anything that I had already "known" and, instead of that, I adhered to the commandments of the spiritual part of the teaching: I was delving into myself with a vigilant mind, with an attentive mind, not to perhaps slide into wandering thinking, with a strained mind to discern and to be able to follow the mechanism of changes in the mind, feelings, inner states and in the whole being in general.

As I was, in this way, descending deeper and deeper into the depths of my own being, I understood that certain potentials constituting the nature and characteristics of a person are, at the same time, the heredity of their ancestry and possibly even of the human species. Thus I have remembered my previous lives and the most recent of them were really connected only with the ancestry from which I came. However, when I later descended into the centro-encefalon, into the depths of the cell structure of the brain – cell structure which contains links to the whole history of humankind, I identified that there are still other possibilities in it. Due to the fact that a human being is not composed only of the cells of their own ancestry, but that they are also composed of the cells of the entire humankind, from every "ganglion" in this psychological area, a memory thread can unwind – a memory thread of the previous incarnations, which were outside of the sphere of one's own ancestry. A further result can be the knowledge that there is nothing existing in the universe which a person would not have been as well in one of their previous existences.

When I discovered that this knowledge, and this experience in general, result only from a gradually deepening delving into oneself by means of conscious thinking, I could never ask a question whether I was existing in the past and whether I will exist in the future, nor a question of what I was in the past and what I will be in the future – as everything is so uncertain, because it is possible to rely on different "starting moments" of the psychological beingness as a basis. Besides that, this curiosity does not allow one to continue on the path of a gradually deepening turning inwards, which ends all the way in the centre of everything, in a point, from which everything evolved by a gradual forming; on the contrary, it ends in a sphere of misleading ideas which are cementing ignorance.

The journey to the centre of origination of everything is so appealing to those who desire development of that knowledge which averts further continuation of sorrowful personal existence that their inappropriate curiosity completely ceases. This is surely not just a simple act lacking a substantial background of emotional experience. A person must sense that they must have the courage to cross the boundary separating life and death, the boundary, which an atheist tries to bridge by faith in destruction of existence, while a spiritual, but internally inexperienced, person, by faith in eternal life. Outside of the sphere of these two extremes, there is understanding of the meaning of descent into one's own being, into its centre, into the starting point of the origination of everything. This descent later requires that a person would put into practice that old and classical saying: "Abandon hope all ye who enter here". If they do not give up the hope, they will, by the activity of their mind and imagination, create their future life through their image of it.

From the spiritual point of view, it is exactly the image of a future body, the image about existence, about the place and conditions of a certain abode, which constitutes the creation of conditions for its coming into existence, because the creative forces of existence need only a small impulse to shape in some form, which on the whole corresponds to the images about the future existence. Karma plays a role here. It determines the nature of images about this matter; besides that, the future existence is also formed by the tendencies towards emotional experiences of a certain nature. For a person full of animality, only the way to the world of animals is open. If such a person is, by coincidence, instructed about a path to the mystical goal, and they do not use that descent into themselves, but they only think whether they were existing in the past and will exist in the future, what they were in the past and what they will be in the future, then the driving forces of their existence and their animal inclinations will decide the question of their reincarnation, regardless of their speculations and desires. As a rule, they will descend from the level of humanity, to the level of animals.

"Abandon hope all ye who enter here!" This surely demands that a person looks into the face of death without fear of what will be then. After all, when we think for a while that hopes and images can hardly capture and influence the nature of future things, then reason, the mere reason will suffice for a person to abandon their hopes. By that they give their own meritorious as well as non-meritorious karma the possibility for the process or formation, set into motion by the approaching death, to have an entirely free field of action. Thus, the worst thing in incarnation is removed – the entangling into images about reality, which is then inherited as a flawed characteristic in the new existence. Thus, if a person is lead in their life by images about reality, it is as if they were suffering from cutting the connection between body and mind, as a consequence of which one is not able to learn anything either about themselves, nor about the world, any longer.

See, how proud are those who only know the reality according to their own images! However, this pride prevents them from gaining knowledge. In their imagination they are always perfect and enthroned on the highest level of knowledge, even when their character changes from day to day and they have to correct their knowledge according to the influence of the reality which affects them.

When a mystic realises that they will not learn anything about their future matters, except for their own images about reality applied to their current state, they will, successfully, also cross that layer of their being which is separating the personal life from the higher, impersonal one. It is a layer which is so significant in the process of turning inwards that it is, in fact, a beginning of a successful journey towards the descent, all the way to the centre of the being. This centre is no longer a base of the subject, but it is a base of the entire world of forms, of the whole universe. Then, their finding that they have attained the end of all developmental paths, becomes evident, unshakeable, and removing all suffering.

Those of you who ask, what is going on with your relatives after death, what you were and what you will be and whether you were existing and whether you will exist, will not arrive at any good result, because you do not fulfil the condition of knowledge – i.e. a continuous analysis of all components and states of the being. On the contrary, you are only occupying your mind with fantastic images about reality – with building the basis for the forming of the next existence, because, where a thought is targeted there are the aggressive creative forces of human spirit developing – the forces of physical qualities which do not enable knowledge, because they have been set into the creative process by the wishes to learn "what will I be in the future?".

Knowledge can originate only in a destructive process of the spirit of inquiry which has a function of analysis in the process of mystical development. Only through observation of the mechanical processes in the "psyche" and through the analytical power of mind penetrating them, their laws can be discovered. The yogi can attain the absolute knowledge, whose purpose is liberation, or salvation, because the happening in the psychological beingness is identical with the happening governed by laws of the creative processes in the universe. This must be our aim. The knowledge containing a process from a presage to its materialisation, that ordinary knowledge, which can be obtained in schools, does not have a liberating influence. It is only such externally usable knowledge which can be employed in realisation of the human wishes. However, to realise wishes means to get entangled into the traps of karma, into the irresistible urges, which exclude the liberating knowledge; on the contrary, they strengthen the bonds of our ignorance.

Those who do not search within their own being, but search for reproduced knowledge, frequently become fanatic followers or enemies of some teaching. However, this will not lead them to knowledge. Not to have knowledge conquered by your own effort will really not help you on the journey of life. You might be able to kill for your conviction: you perhaps think that you're obtaining merits by that. But in fact you will always be preaching something or persecuting someone just because you are yielding to delusions.

Thus, ask neither whether you existed in the past and will exist in the future, nor where are you going or will have arrived through your death. Only get used to the idea that you are supposed to abandon all hope face to face with the jaws of death. If you have faith, you are, by it, giving God – if he exists – the possibility to decide where to bring you for your own good. However, if you have a good knowledge, then this accepted hopelessness can mean for you "no return after death", as it is understood by the classical Buddhism. After all, by this behaviour you will stop interfering in the operation of the so-called "self-acting karma" about which you can infer that it always leads to ascent. On the contrary, the karma, originating from deeds of which you yourself want to be the actor, will make you, in the reincarnation sequence, move chaotically now through the hellish worlds, and now through the angel worlds, but never through those in which a possibility to attain the liberating knowledge exists.

Glossary of terms

Beingness – generally entity, existence, essence; from our perspective a structure equipped by vitality and consciousness. We are able to understand it as a process, even though it induces a semblance, that it is a solid material, creating the body, as well as ties, pertaining to psychological (inner) equipment (Minařík, 1992).

Complex of beingness – A set of physical and psychological (inner) elements, which a person as a rule mistakenly thinks of as a being, but about which they know, that it is an ephemeral state. In the expression "complex of beingness", the psychological and physical elements are considered to be autonomous, as some physical agglomeration, in which the higher elements symbolise the inner beingness, while the lower elements the physiological beingness. Thus, by this expression, a type understood from the perspective of natural science is always meant (Minařík, 1992).

Drive – an innate, biologically determined urge (Concise Oxford English Dictionary, 2004).

Mystical – relating to mystics or mysticism (Concise Oxford English Dictionary, 2004).

Mysticism – teaching about unifying of a person with God. A person is understood here as a self-aware being; God as a transcendental factor (Minařík, 1992).

Delusory mysticism – delusions based on an unsubstantiated belief in mysterious powers and forces, superstition or religious preoccupation of a pathological character. Delusory mysticism is a domain of people who are not intellectually developed (Minařík, 1992).

References

Catherine Soanes, Angus Stevenson (editors). Concise Oxford English Dictionary 11th Edition [CD], Oxford University Press, 2004.

Cambridge Advanced Learner's Dictionary 3rd Edition, Cambridge University Press, Cambridge, UK, 2008.

Květoslav Minařík. Malý mystický slovník naučný [A Small mystical encyclopaedia]. Canopus, Prague, 1992.*

---

* A Small mystical encyclopaedia, which was originally meant to be a glossary for his own books about mysticism, grew in the hands of Květoslav Minařík until it became a book of popular science, accessible to every person interested in the spiritual teachings. It explains the basic terms of the spiritual teachings and their relationships to other scientific fields.